The Psychology of

Consumer
Behavior

Rom J. Markin

Associate Professor

Business Administration

Washington State University

PRENTICE-HALL, INC., ENGLEWOOD CLIFFS, N.J.

Printed in the United States of America
Library of Congress Catalog No.: 69-14532

Current printing (last digit):
10 9 8 7 6 5 4 3 2

Prentice-Hall International, Inc., *London*
Prentice-Hall of Australia, Pty. Ltd., *Sydney*
Prentice-Hall of Canada, Ltd., *Toronto*
Prentice-Hall of India Private Ltd., *New Delhi*
Prentice-Hall of Japan, Inc., *Tokyo*

This book is dedicated to
Marcia—a loving and beloved wife

PREFACE

There are many ways of looking at consumer behavior. Characteristically, consumer behavior is viewed from the economic, sociological, psychological, and anthropological point of view. Valuable insights have been obtained from each of these perspectives and by combining some of these approaches, i.e., the social-psychological ones. The point of view of this treatment is mainly social-psychological. This approach regards consumer behavior as a function of many factors. However, the central focus of consumer behavior, viewed in this context, is the concept of *motivation*, but in a social milieu. That is, motivation is a function of the individual's drives or needs and these drives or needs are affected by social and environmental factors as well as by the individual's predispositions arising from hereditary forces.

The central underlying theme of the book is that all consumer behavior is caused or affected by learning and communication.

WHY "THE PSYCHOLOGY OF CONSUMER BEHAVIOR"?

Psychology is the study of behavior. However, behavior is a function of the total field of forces operative at any given time, a field

v

being the sum total of coexisting factors which are conceived of as mutually interdependent. The view here, then, is largely that of *social psychology*, that branch of general psychology which deals with behavior as it relates to other persons. This text is concerned with such phenomena as perception, motivation, cognition, learning, attitudes, expectations, etc.—all concepts which have deep-rooted origins in the field of psychology. However, all the above phenomena are affected or conditioned by a social milieu. Man is a group creature, a gregarious animal whose behavior is almost always a function of his role in group environment. Consequently, such social phenomena as role, status, group norms, life style, and social class, plus culture, will greatly affect consumer behavior.

PURPOSE

The central task of this book is to describe and analyze in some detail the learning process and the fundamental concepts or ideas involved in communication in order that marketers may have better insight and understanding of these processes. Learning and communication are therefore both analyzed and structured within the context of the marketing management framework. An important proposition involved in this treatment is that consumer behavior is fundamentally problem-solving behavior; problem solving of any type involves a search for significant structure or insight, and this, in short, is *learning*. Marketing activity is largely directed toward structuring or altering consumer behavior (affecting learning) via the firm's communication process. From the standpoint of the firm, learning (favorable adaptive behavior) is viewed as an *end* while communication is viewed as a *means* of structuring a learning situation.

SCOPE AND TREATMENT

The scope of this text is general rather than specific. It deals more with principles and generalizations than with specific techniques or methodology. The manuscript is prepared to meet the needs of a managerially oriented audience.

The treatment subsumes only a limited acquaintance with the fields of marketing, sociology, economics, or psychology. In order that certain ideas might be treated adequately, it was necessary to use some of the vocabulary of psychology. In almost all instances definitions are included as a part of the descriptive text material.

Most of this book is concerned with generalizations pertaining to certain behavioral science concepts as they affect the behavior of consumers and their decision processes. The reader should understand that the generalizations set forth throughout this text and summarized at the end of Chapter 10 are viewed as *operational theorems* and that in the aggregate these operational theorems do constitute an important *theory of consumer behavior;* a theory which appears to fit well the matrix of observed behavior, as opposed to one where observed behavior is fitted to a theory. The true benefit of the former is that more progress can be made toward understanding the elusive questions pertaining to the "whys" of customer behavior. If and when these "whys" of customer behavior can be better understood, marketing strategies can be predicated upon more precise predictions of consumer behavior, and the natural result will be better marketing decisions and, ultimately, more scientific marketing.

Rom J. Markin

ACKNOWLEDGMENTS

One does not author much of anything without incurring a great ledger of indebtedness. So it is with this effort. Many of my friends and students have made contributions. So, too, have my colleagues in the College of Economics and Business at Washington State University.

I am very grateful to a former graduate student, Mr. John E. Maxwell, who assisted me in the early stages of the effort, especially in regard to the materials contained in Part III.

Professor Richard Evans, a former colleague now at the University of Calgary, criticized an earlier version of the manuscript and contributed numerous suggestions for its improvement. Professor James Stafford of the University of Houston was a valuable critic. His contributions strengthened the manuscript in many respects, in terms of both content and organization.

I am indebted to all the authors and publishers whose material I have been given permission to use. In the final analysis, however, the responsibility for the effort is mine and no disclaimer of this responsibility is sought or implied.

CONTENTS

PART ONE

INTRODUCTION

ONE

Marketing Management
and Consumer Behavior:
an Overview

Developments in business are often apocryphal and the marketing concept is certainly no exception. Business history may never know with assurance who or what was responsible for developing this potent and revolutionary concept. However, the task of the businessman is seldom to search history for the roots or origins of concepts. Instead, he is much like Kipling's Homer.

> When 'Omer smote 'is bloomin' lyre,
>   He'd 'eard men sing by land an' sea;
> An' what he thought 'e might require,
>   'E went an' took—the same as me!

The businessman is one of nature's foremost eclectics. The very nature of his problems, which are often characterized as dynamic, nonlinear, interdependent, probabilistic, stochastic, and ill-structured, has forced the businessman into this frame of mind. In other words, he is incessantly searching for practical solutions to his problems.

The marketing concept, or what is sometimes called the marketing management concept, fits in well with the businessman's need for practical approaches to problem solving. As a matter of fact, the value of the marketing concept can be judged

largely on the basis of its widespread acceptance. For in business management as in ecology there is validity in the idea that what is fit survives,
what works well is utilized, and, conversely, what does not is discarded.
Apparently the marketing concept works. Should this approach, however, fail to solve the problem or offer the framework needed for marshal-
ing and distributing the firm's resources to the society which it serves,
business will be ready for the next innovation, the next idea or concept
needed to cope with new problems or new complexities. It is important
to remember that the firm's development is largely *teleological,* i.e., development is caused by the purposes which things serve. As the purpose
or role of the organization changes, the organization changes in both
structure and function. The marketing concept represents just such a
change in business organizations resulting from the changes in environmental forces.

During the early 1950's the U.S. economy began to witness a profound and fundamental alteration. Suddenly business firms began to
realize that we were moving into an era of widespread affluence. Consumers, too, began to realize that "no matter how little money [they]
might have, [they] are 'millionaires' compared to most people in the
world." [1] Marketing's task, in the face of this new consumer affluence
which meant in turn greater discernment and greater freedom of choice,
was suddenly focused on the need to produce markets. Firms whose
previous orientation had been toward production of goods or selling
began—some, unfortunately, not quickly enough—to realize that to survive in this new competitive environment they must alter drastically their
business or management philosophy.

The exploding technology of this new era, largely stimulated by
the accelerated pace of spending for military and defense purposes in
World War II and the Korean conflict, began to spill over into business
developments and consumer applications. The technological eggs hatched
by rapidly expanding military and space research began to be converted
into peacetime omelets. As real income continued to increase accompanied by widespread changes in the demographic structure of the
nation, firms poured forth a virtual flood of new products and services.
To survive in this competitive environment, however, many firms realized
that they must pay more than lip service to such by-words as "competition" and "consumer sovereignty." So, born of necessity and ingenuity,
and nurtured by practitioners and by economic reality, the marketing
concept began to be widely adopted and implemented.

---

[1] Steuart Henderson Britt, *The Spenders: Where and Why Your Money Goes*
(New York: McGraw-Hill Book Company, 1960), p. 49.

A NEW BUSINESS PHILOSOPHY

A philosophy is an organized system of thought. Or, more simply, it is the way a man or a firm views tasks and responsibilities. Some philosophies—whether of business firms or of individuals—are considerably more unified than others. Too often, the firm's philosophy has been a crazy-quilt pattern of generalizations, policies, executive opinions, and *ad hoc* solutions to day-to-day company problems—lacking in unity and cohesiveness. Moreover, the philosophy of one functional area, department or division may differ markedly from that of other areas, resulting in the management conflict or phenomenon known as suboptimization.

The marketing concept is a way of rethinking the company's problems which has resulted in a more unified and cohesive approach to the company's tasks, resources, and objectives. Its basic premise is that the firm lacks autonomy: it is not an entity unto itself; it does not have, in a philosophic sense, *free choice*, but instead is inextricably linked to the market place. As Alderson and Green put it, "The firm takes its marching orders from the market." [2] And who is the market? The total of ultimate and industrial users of a firm's output of goods and services.

The firm and its management are now charged with a new and expanded set of responsibilities. "Business is a process which converts a resource, distinct knowledge, into a contribution of economic value in the market place. The (new) purpose of business is to create a customer." [3] Consequently, the focus and orientation of the firm become that of marketing. The firm is linked to its environment through its marketing processes and activities. And the market and its customers become analogous to a gigantic servo-mechanism or feedback loop, modifying and adjusting the behavior and the activities of the firm. However, marketing management views the firm as innovative as well as adaptive. The firm can, through astute management activity, influence and alter behavior in the market place. The consumer is viewed as the key or central concept around which a marketing strategy or program is built. The consumer is to be served, not manipulated. His wishes and cravings are to be discovered and sounded out, not structured and artificially altered to meet the needs of the company. In short, the consumer and the market are viewed as an end rather than a means.

The manager's task is to develop, formulate, and implement

---

[2] Wroe Alderson and Paul Green, *Planning and Problem Solving in Marketing* (Homewood, Ill.: Richard D. Irwin, Inc., 1964), p. 5.

[3] Peter F. Drucker, *Managing for Result* (New York: Harper & Row, Publishers, 1964), p. 91.

Figure 1: Central Elements of Marketing Management.

Source: John Howard, *Marketing Management: Analysis and Planning,* rev. ed. (Homewood, Ill.: Richard D. Irwin, Inc., 1963).

strategy. Strategy, given the linkage between firm and market, is the movement and countermovement in pursuit of goals and objectives: every decision made in the firm is analyzed and evaluated in terms of its eventual effect on consumer reaction or behavior. Strategy is not viewed as a ruse or deception for fooling or tricking an enemy. Instead, it is a means whereby the firm adapts and reacts to the competitive conditions of the market place.

Broadly conceived, strategy formation begins with an analysis of consumer needs or wants. Therefore, the basic and primary point of view in the marketing concept is consumer orientation. A marketing strategy is a comprehensive plan of action. It involves the adjustment and accommodation of the never-changing elements of a firm's marketing mix, i.e., price, promotion, product, and place, to the ever-changing elements of a firm's environment.

In Fig. 1, Howard depicts what he considers to be the central elements of marketing management. Conceptually, what is desired is that the marketing manager bring about the best possible (optimum) adjustment or "fit" of his firm by his decisions regarding price, products, promotion, and place to the environmental conditions in which he must operate, such as law, costs, structure, competition, and demand.

The marketing manager, like others charged with managerial responsibilities, must plan, organize, and control the elements for which he is assigned responsibility. By planning he decides in advance what needs to be done; he anticipates market and consumer behavior and acts accordingly. By organizing he marshals resources and establishes proper relationships and priorities; he sequences behavior. By controlling he sets standards, compares planned performances with actual performance, and takes corrective action.

He recognizes that there are elements which affect his management and strategy considerations over which he has little or no control. But he recognizes at the outset that the success or failure of his marketing strategy rests ultimately with the consumer or market for which his strategy has been designed. Consequently, most strategy formulations are based on the assumption that consumer behavior can be either (1) analyzed and understood, or (2) analyzed, understood and modified. Both assumptions strongly dictate that the marketing manager know and understand what affects consumer behavior, i.e., how consumers learn, how consumer impressions, opinions, and images can be modified, and how firms can successfully communicate their marketing programs to the consumer.

THE PROBLEM OF CONSUMER BEHAVIOR

Given the emphasis on consumer behavior dictated by the marketing concept, this behavior can certainly be cast within the framework of a problem area—a problem both to the firm and to society as a whole. If consumers alter their behavior significantly, thus causing firms to miss or fall short of marketing targets or to miss marketing opportunities, then the firm has failed to discharge its service obligations, and economic opportunities are foregone. In the aggregate, the failure of firms to correctly know or interpret consumer behavior means the wholesale misallocation of national economic resources.

The American marketer has traditionally been "Socratic" in his pursuit of knowledge and understanding regarding consumers. He has taken as his fundamental task "to know." Often, however, the marketer's inquiries and quests for information have been misguided, based upon inadequate and faulty premises, so that his inferred generalizations have been operationally inadequate. However, slowly and painfully, marketers have groped their way toward the acquisition of a set of generalizations or, more correctly, a mass of data pertaining to consumer activities. This knowledge has been largely descriptive rather than analytical and has usually not shed light or provided insight into the relevant questions regarding consumer behavior. The research departments and analysts' files of large marketing firms are treasure troves of miscellaneous information—much like a boy's pockets containing nails, bits of colored string, a magnet, three rusty washers, and two dog-eared pictures of last season's television hero. The in-use value of such material is highly suspect and questionable. For decision-making purposes regarding certain parameters of consumer behavior, relevant information is simply not extant. Today's marketer, like the small boy, has a penchant for collecting, especially market data. Marketers have overwhelming masses of data and information regarding the quantitative significance of certain markets. The population has been stratified and cross-stratified. The number of people in a given geographical region and their buying characteristics are known with considerable certainty, and this information can be obtained at a nominal price from any number of computer-run data banks throughout the country. And while much of it fills important gaps in the marketer's information structure, his marketing strategy continues to suffer from lack of information pertaining to the mystical marketing question, "why?" Behavior regarding "why" has perplexed mankind since its origin and has been the concern of marketers for an almost equally long period.

Our marketing programs and strategies continue to be built upon the seeming certainty of analysis pertaining to aspects of consumer behavior such as: what they buy, when and how often, from what kinds of resellers, and how much they spend. But information pertaining to what amounts to the crux of the question, i.e., *why* consumers buy certain products and *why* they buy from particular resellers, remains an elusive dimension of consumer behavior.

Nor is the difficulty surrounding this phase of the study of consumer behavior at all researcher-oriented. That is, it is not simply a question of the researcher not being clever enough to structure his analysis in a productive or fruitful manner, though this may be a part of the problem. Instead, the major problem may lie with time. That is, marketers may not as yet have allocated sufficient time to exploring this problem. Another difficulty lies with the dynamics of the investigation. Consumer behavior is seldom ever static in any sense. And the problem with studying consumer behavior is that the subject of our investigation, i.e., the consumer, is in a constant state of change. Just when a researcher is ready to deduce what he considers an important generalization about consumer behavior, the subject, being part of an open system, has perhaps modified and changed his behavior to a significant degree. Until marketers begin considering consumer behavior in a more dynamic context, research in this area will continue to be hampered.

Consumer motivation. A complete discussion of the relevant literature on consumer behavior is beyond the scope of this study. The intention here is to survey briefly only the most relevant generalizations in this area and especially those which seem to hold promise for significant new insights.

It is no longer fashionable to say, "man does not live by bread alone." Even the slow learners fully understand the meaning of this statement. Yet some critics of marketing utilize this dictum when criticizing marketing from the standpoint of its demand-influencing functions. Man's basic physiological need for food could have been satisfied in 1950 with an annual expenditure of about $95. Allowing for the rise in the general price level, he could probably satisfy these needs in the late 1960's for approximately $125.[4] Man, however, is a wanting creature. And allowing for such ideas as the concept of individual differences and man's widened imagination, it is fruitless and even nonsensical to talk about man's basic needs. One of the great contributions of the behavioral sciences has been the concept of a hierarchy of needs. A need may be defined as any requirement of an organism, innate or acquired, which prompts to action and is experienced as a desire. When not satisfied, the need is said to lead to a drive. It matters very little how needs develop, that is whether they are innate or learned; the important point is that individuals, and consequently consumers, want their needs satisfied. The urge to satisfy these needs is called a drive or motive, and the action which stems from these motives or drives is called consumer behavior.

Man is both an animal and a social being. Along with the higher subhuman forms of life, he is possessed with other needs, as well as the classic needs of hunger, thirst, and sex. Maslow has supplied the following list of needs.[5]

1. Physiological needs
2. Safety needs
3. Social needs
4. Esteem needs
5. Self-actualization needs

For marketers, the important insight stemming from a knowledge and understanding of man's needs hierarchy ought to be *that marketing contributes to man's ability to help satisfy this range of needs.* That is, marketing is a *means* to the ends or goals sought by man as consumer. Another important point revealed by current research is that a satisfied

---

[4] George J. Stigler, *The Theory of Price,* rev. ed. (New York: The Macmillan Company, 1952), p. 2.

[5] See A. H. Maslow, "A Theory of Human Motivation," *Psychological Review,* Vol. 50 (1943), pp. 370-396.

need is no longer an important source of consumer motivation. In today's affluent society basic physiological needs have been met. Therefore, marketers ought increasingly to focus their strategies on the upper ranges of the needs hierarchy, and especially to discern with greater understanding the self-actualizing personality—a label which might well describe a whole range of consumer personality types.

The self-actualizing person tends to be problem-centered rather than ego-centered. His work and his consumer behavior are more than a way of earning a living or simply spending money for mundane needs; both are viewed as satisfying activities. The self-actualizer has a mission in life, problems to solve, tasks to be carried out to completion. He views his mission or role in life not as something he would choose or prefer for himself, but rather as something he "must do." Self-actualizing people often tend to be far more creative than the run-of-the-mill type. And they tend to manifest their creativeness in the ways and means in which they consume goods. Given the increased education, awareness, discernment, and income of the "average" American consumer, a considerable but varying degree of self-actualizing behavior may well have infected the mood and mode of consumer purchasing activity.

Consumer behavior viewed as problem solving. It is somewhat paradoxical that the problem of consumer behavior is now being viewed within the context of behavior as problem-solving activity. That is, individuals in the role of consumers are largely concerned with the problem of how they can best fulfill the dictates of a needs hierarchy. In other words, each day the consumer is faced with myriad questions concerning needs, from the simplest to the most complex, and marketers should now realize that to successfully fulfill their role, they ought to act so as to promote the power of consumers to act. In other words, the marketer, if he is to avoid the "extinction mode," must serve customers by helping them to satisfactorily solve problems.[6]

Needless to say, the mechanics of consumer behavior remain somewhat mysterious, but important theories to explain aspects of this phenomenon have been advanced. One general theory of consumer behavior which appears valid, perhaps because of its generality, holds that *needs* lead to *drives*. The drive condition or state is one of tension. That is, as needs arise and as drives to satisfy these needs are intensified, the individual tends toward a state of disequilibrium: he becomes less and less content to remain in the unsatisfied state. If and when the drive is reduced or lessened as a result of the need being satisfied or sublimated,

---

[6] The so-called "power-principle" and the concept of "extinction mode" are ideas of Wroe Alderson. See Alderson and Green, *op. cit.*, Chap. 1.

the individual returns again to a state of mental or physical equilibrium.

This general theory of consumer behavior can be expanded in light of other postulates regarding behavior. Thus, consumer behavior can be viewed as the consumer's rational efforts toward problem solving. Note the term "consumer's rational efforts." This is a step toward removing or eliminating the older dichotomous approach to the study and classification of consumer buying motives in terms of rational as opposed to emotional buying motives—a needless and confusing division. The consumer's efforts are said to be rational as long as they "fit" or conform to the *consumer's own axioms pertaining to rational behavior.* Inasmuch as his behavior is goal-oriented, regardless of what that goal may be, inasmuch as a part of the consumer's behavior is search activity, inasmuch as the consumer is a sensory and data-gathering organism, despite the fact that he wants his information embellished with some fanciful entertainment, he ought to be viewed as rational.[7] On these premises, a set of general conclusions would be that consumer behavior is a rational effort toward problem solving; behavior is therefore caused or determined; further behavior (satisfaction of needs) tends to remove the original causes for behavior and, finally, behavior is affected by learning and learning is often a function of communication.

As marketers tend to become less myopic and more willing to expand their frame of reference pertaining to consumer behavior, other concepts tend to shed light and help to integrate ideas regarding the understanding of consumers. An important concept in this connection is that of life style. It can be argued that consumer life style both influences and shapes marketing and other economic activity. Life style has been defined in the following manner.

> It refers to the distinctive or characteristic mode of living, in its aggregative and broadest sense, of a whole society or segment thereof. It is concerned with those unique ingredients or qualities which describe the style of life of some culture or group, and distinguish it from others. It embodies the patterns that develop and emerge from the dynamics of living in a society.
>
> Life style, therefore, is the result of such forces as culture, values, resources, license, and sanction. From one perspective, the aggregate of consumer purchases and the manner in which they are consumed, reflect a society's life style.[8]

---

[7] For a complete and sophisticated treatment of the meaning of rational behavior, see C. West Churchman, *Prediction and Optimal Decision* (Englewood Cliffs, N.J.: Prentice-Hall, Inc., 1961), Chap. 8.

[8] William Lazer, "Life Style Concepts and Marketing," in *Toward Scientific Marketing,* ed. Stephen A. Greyser, Proceedings of the Winter Conference of the American Marketing Association (Chicago, Ill.: American Marketing Association, 1964), p. 130.

If marketers are to successfully discharge their responsibilities, they must know and understand the meaning and influence of life style concepts on consumer behavior. This also suggests, perhaps, a different approach to the study of consumer behavior, namely, that consumer behavior is a function of a whole host of contextual considerations. The micro-approach, in which we observe individual consumers and then attempt to sum up individual behavior in an aggregate theory, may be inadequate and may lead to spurious generalizations. Instead, what may be needed is a more macroscopic point of view whereby we focus not only on the individual but on the individual in his total environment. We need a fuller understanding of the life style or cognitive map structure of consumers. Marketers must realize that the consumer and his behavior are a function of what he is; what he has been; what others around him are doing, thinking and talking about; what he has witnessed, experienced and felt; his expectations about today and tomorrow; and for that matter, nearly everything else constituting his environment. The consumer is defined by his choices.[9] His choices are subtle and complex. The riddle of consumer behavior, in turn, is both subtle and complex.

THE SOCIAL SCIENCES AND CONSUMER BEHAVIOR

"Business is a system of interlocking human activities." [10] This simple but accurate description is often overlooked by well-trained students and experienced businessmen. Instead of approaching marketing problems from the interdisciplinary angle, many of these problems are simply divided up and allotted to the realm of pure economics or some other "functional" area of business. Recently, however, many marketing men as well as other businessmen are coming more and more to realize that "business," because it embraces such a wide area of human activity, calls for many different approaches to what may be similar problems and that to successfully use these approaches, they must call on the help of those trained in the disciplines of the social sciences.

For many years marketing men have relied on the methods of the economists to guide them in gaining insight into such worthwhile areas as demand theory, consumer choice, national income accounting techniques, and other techniques which aid or give insight to marketers in many important areas of decision making. More recently, the psycholo-

---

[9] This is the dilemma of modern or existential man, i.e., man chooses what he wishes to become. The idea of the existential consumer is developed fully in Chapter 2.

[10] Paul F. Lazarsfeld, "Reflections on Business," *American Journal of Sociology,* Vol. LXV (July, 1959), p. 2. © by The University of Chicago Press.

gists have assumed a significant role, inasmuch as many of their con-tributions in motivation, learning theory, communication theory, and concepts such as identification, projection techniques, etc., are playing a valuable part in the marketing areas of consumer motivation, advertis-ing, and training and compensation of marketing personnel. The sociolo-gists are beginning to feel the impact of this new interdisciplinary ap-proach and are responding with important contributions in population studies, consumer motivation, human ecology, group dynamics, collec-tive behavior, measurement and scaling, and other areas.[11]

This belief in the value of the interdisciplinary approach has not all been on the part of business, though present trends lead one to con-clude that businessmen may be more willing to take on the investigation of social science phenomena than would social scientists to employ the business arena as a valuable area for research and investigation. Lazars-feld states that a majority of the social scientists have an ideological bias against business. "Aiding the doctor, promoting justice, or supporting the agencies of the law—all these are in accord with accepted norms; help-ing the businessman make money is not." [12] For many years the pre-vailing attitude among many of the social scientists has been that the business of business is low, dirty stuff.

Fortunately this attitude is being gradually dispelled, and the so-cial sciences are coming to recognize more and more that the business environment offers a fertile field for inquiry, that it lends itself readily to sociological, anthropological, and psychological investigation, and that the rewards of such investigation are in many instances illuminating and challenging.

The interdisciplinary approach seems to make sense primarily from two important points of view: (1) the pedagogical, and (2) as an ana-lytical framework for decision making by marketing managers in what might be inaptly called the "real world." Actually this framework would conform to what Bartels describes as those whose business is the practice of marketing.[13] From the standpoint of the "practice" of marketing, today's marketing manager must look at many approaches to problem solving and decision making. The day of the experienced "old hand" who makes intuitive decisions off the top of his head or from the seat of his pants is rapidly passing. Decision making is coming more and more to rely on the group approach. An approach favored by many well-

---

[11] Christen T. Jonassen, "Contributions of Sociology to Marketing," *Journal of Marketing*, Vol. 24, No. 2 (October, 1959), p. 29.

[12] Lazarsfeld, *op. cit.*, p. 1.

[13] Robert Bartels, "Sociologists and Marketologists," *Journal of Marketing*, Vol. 24, No. 2 (October, 1959), p. 37.

informed executives is that of operations research, in which the "whole" of the situation is investigated rather than merely one or two of the various parts. And the employment of this overall investigation implies at least a familiarity with the areas of psychology, economics, and sociology, as well as some understanding of mathematics. Therefore, because of the complexity and sweeping scope of many of today's problems, business leadership is calling for an ever-increasing knowledge of the social sciences. This is not to imply that tomorrow's successful business leaders must have engaged in graduate study in all areas of the social sciences; it means simply that tomorrow's leaders must have open minds and, after careful scrutiny, must accept as working tools those methodologies and techniques of the social sciences which have validity and offer insight into the solution of business and marketing problems.

ALTERNATE THEORIES OF CONSUMER CHOICE

One of the areas which has presented itself for solution by marketers has been the area of consumer choice, i.e., what products do consumers buy, in what quantities, for what prices, when do they buy, and most important, why do they buy? This is an area which has received a great deal of attention from many of the social sciences, and this section will be devoted to surveying briefly some of the contributions to the solution of these problems by various disciplines of the social sciences. In no instances are these solutions complete. But many of them offer models which are partial explanations of consumer behavior in regard to choosing products for consumption. Because they are only partial solutions, it is wise to reiterate the need for interdisciplinary action in order to gain total insight into the problem. It should be remembered that two heads are better than one, especially if the heads belong to a marketer and an economist, or, say, a psychologist or sociologist. This is perhaps the true meaning and usefulness of operations research.

Any comprehensive theory of consumer choice must rely upon the concepts developed in the various fields of the social sciences—economics, psychology and sociology—and for this reason an attempt is made here to relate an example of the type of thinking and the approach to problems which has been undertaken by some of these various disciplines.

Economics. The economists have provided us with a rather widely adopted theory of consumer behavior based upon the concept of indifference curves which represent different combinations of two goods, to which the consumer is indifferent. The consumer attempts to move to the highest indifference curve, limited by qualifying factors such as income and the product price. The consumer is visualized as substituting one good for another until the highest level of equilibrium is achieved. Having reached this equilibrium point, he is spending his income in such a way that the last dollar spent on each kind of good results in the same additional satisfaction or marginal utility.[14] Most of us are well aware of the shortcomings of this approach. It rules out the impact of motivations and social status on the consumers in question. Furthermore, it assumes that tastes are autonomous and that changes in taste do not occur, except of an autonomous nature.

The main fact which emerges from a survey of the economic literature is the contrast between the detailed theory of the influence on demand of income and prices in a static situation and the almost complete lack of concern with the way in which tastes and habits, as dictated by social status, affect consumers' behavior.

Psychology. The psychologists have approached the problem of consumer choice and consumer behavior on the basis of observations and data usually subsumed under the categories of needs, desires, and motives. Such terms refer to something which apparently lies behind the observed behavior of people.

A noteworthy application of this type of approach is the Shepherd-Bayton study for the U.S. Department of Agriculture.[15] The study began by using six values which were culled from the literature: comfort, orderliness, economy, pleasure, social approval, and recognition. From interviews, the investigators found that these values were closely associated with four attributes of men's suits which served as means of attaining these goals: color, style, material, and fit. When possible, value-means relationships were coded as a unit. The number of value statements were converted into a score. This score was a percentage based on the total number of each type, that is, the value or means made by a person. For example, if a person made forty value statements and ten of these indicated a desire for social approval, his score for social approval would be twenty-five. Median scores were then computed for both values and means. An attempt was made to find the relationship between income groups, i.e., lower, middle, and upper, and median scores for value and means. This process was repeated. The relation between income and means for obtaining comfort was established, and the same

14 For a more detailed description and analysis, see Ruby T. Norris, *The Theory of Consumers' Demand* (New Haven, Conn.: Yale University Press, 1952), pp. 11-58.
15 Jane A. Shepherd and James A. Bayton, *Men's Preferences Among Wool Suits, Coats and Jackets,* Agricultural Information Bulletin No. 64 (Washington, D.C.: U.S. Department of Agriculture, 1951).

procedure was followed for occupation and age as well as for other values and means.

The study of values or motives has a rather long and, in many instances, fruitful history, but there remain many shortcomings to this approach as a sole predictor of consumer behavior. It would appear to have the following limitations: (1) Semantics, the meaning and interpretation of words—this becomes largely a personal matter for the individual who is responsible for interpretation. (2) The data have not been quantified nor do they seem to be quantifiable, given the present state of psychological measurement devices. (3) Finally, this means that there is a positive validation of conclusions about the number of values and their individual tendencies.

While both the economic and psychological approaches make important contributions, the major limitation in each case has been the tendency to treat each as a separate, independent explanation and to ignore other factors which affect consumer behavior. Most certainly, any theory of consumer behavior must recognize the importance of social forces as they shape consumer behavior.

Sociology. The sociologists have made many noteworthy contributions in terms of insights into consumer behavior and product choice. Many of these studies have been in connection with social stratification and reference groups as they influence buying and product decisions. The importance of reference groups in buying behavior has been reviewed by a whole symposium of marketing students.[16]

Special attention should be called to one study which takes into account varying kinds of personal attitude: the popularity of a beverage among one's friends can override a person's desire to stay slim and his moral objections to the beverage; but if he dislikes its taste, he is not likely to drink it, even if his friends do.[17]

Buying habits can also be used to characterize social position and conceptions of role. Thus, Stone has shown that isolated city dwellers prefer to buy in small stores because this provides them with personal contacts.[18]

A number of activities are considered the sign of a good housewife

---

[16] Francis S. Bourne, "Group Influences in Marketing and Public Relations," in Rensis Likert and Samuel P. Hayes, Jr., eds., *Some Applications of Behavioural Research* (Paris, France: UNESCO, 1961), pp. 205-207.

[17] *Ibid.*, p. 223.

[18] Gregory Stone, "City Shoppers and Urban Identification," *American Journal of Sociology*, Vol. LX (July, 1954), pp. 36-45.

by some women and old-fashioned by others: home sewing,[19] doing one's own laundering,[20] and shunning instant coffee.[21]

The difficulty of predicting human behavior is often lamented. But it is almost as hard to evaluate the effect of past efforts. Amid all today's turmoil of propaganda and advertising, one can rarely tell whether a specific "campaign" has reached its goal. One of the devices which has been tried is to interview people who have performed a desired act. Is it possible to trace in retrospect the influence we are interested in? Lazarsfeld has attempted to assess the comparative role of personal advice and of advertising.[22] He concludes that the former is stronger and suggests that his statistical results could be developed in many directions. In what situations and with what kinds of people is personal influence especially strong or weak? Who are the influential ones?

A final illustration of the sociological approach, one which emphasizes the importance of social class or social status, is that of Barber and Lobel.[23] This study attempted to correlate women's fashion magazine advertising copy with Warner's social class concept. Social class differences in the meanings of the word "fashion" were found to exist, by virtue of the various copy approaches examined. Social status is based largely on occupational position. This holds true for all classes except those at the top, among whom family lineage is an additional factor. This is Warner's Upper-Upper category. According to this study, women in this class do not need to compete for status through consumption; thus their quality clothes may remain roughly the same for several years. It is in the Lower-Upper class that most of the "high fashion" is found. Clothes, as symbols, are related to wealth rather than to family connection. Fashion has a different meaning for the upper middle class. These women have a distaste for high style, or that which is daring or unusual. Their clothes must be conservative and respectable.

While this approach makes an important contribution to the study of consumer behavior in terms of class orientation, it has, along with many of the sociological studies, several important shortcomings. In

---

[19] Joseph Newman, *Motivation Research and Marketing Management* (Boston: Harvard Graduate School of Business Administration, Division of Research, 1957), p. 313.

[20] American Marketing Association, *The Technique of Market Research* (New York: McGraw-Hill Book Company, 1936), p. 275.

[21] Mason Haire, "Projective Techniques in Market Research," *Journal of Marketing*, Vol. XIV (April, 1960), pp. 649-656.

[22] Elihu Katz and P. F. Lazarsfeld, *Personal Influence* (Glencoe, Ill.: Free Press, 1955).

[23] Bernard Barber and Lyle S. Lobel, "Fashion in Women's Clothes and the American Social System," *Social Forces*, No. 31 (December, 1952), pp. 124-131.

many instances, the methodology has inherent deficiencies. Terminology is often "forced" and without standards and little if any mention is made of the importance of the learning process as conditioned by personality and income over a period of time.

Implications. This brief review of the contributions of the various social science areas attempted to show that no one discipline has yet been able to formulate a completely valid theory of consumer behavior. The consumer still remains a bio-psychosociological being and is affected by many diverse and unexplainable stimuli. His behavior remains to be explained in terms of prenatal influences and psychological and sociological environmental factors, as well as biological and physiological phenomena.

LEARNING AND COMMUNICATION

Buyer behavior is thus primarily problem-solving behavior. The nature and kinds of problems which the consumer attempts to solve are affected by economic, psychological, and sociological forces. The consumer's expectations are affected by his present and past roles, and these collective roles condition and shape his life style. From his life style the consumer typically conceptualizes himself in terms of a self-image. The self-image is the total sum of impressions which the consumer forms of himself. Therefore, the consumer's behavior is one which manifests or projects his self-image. His problem, therefore, is one of purchasing goods with the thought of enhancing, increasing, or changing his self-image. The self-image is often likely to be a little distorted inasmuch as the consumer rarely sees himself as others see him. However, he is a striver. He purchases goods in order that he may see himself becoming bolder, smarter, richer, more secure, or more socially acceptable.

The consumer-buyer's principal task is often that of securing a product or service whose image matches his own self-image. An image, once again, is a total conceptualization of a person or object. Images are formed via the cognitive processes which consist of perception, memory, impressions, and acquired value systems.

In an overly simplified form, images can be defined as total impressions of opinions about things. Sometimes, consumers discover that they simply like a certain product. In other instances, the consumer may discover that for some "reason" unknown to himself he simply avoids buying either a certain product or a certain category of products or from a certain institution. In short, his image of these conditions is contrary, for some reason, to his existing self-image or total value system.

Increasingly, it is becoming the concern of marketers to learn more of the process by which consumers form impressions or images of sellers and their products in order that strategies or marketing programs may be better designed. Efforts directed toward this end have led to studies and research in the areas of learning theory and communication. Knowledge acquired thus far is not complete and further research is needed. However, much valuable insight has already been acquired.

Learning about learning.   For a long time marketers ignored many facets of human behavior, reasoning simply that such activity or study was beyond their ken. With the increasing complexity of business enterprise and increased competition, marketers have decided that to survive and serve well they simply must expand their horizons and broaden the scope of their inquiry. As a result, many aspects or facets of consumer behavior previously ignored are now being intensively researched and investigated. One of the important areas which is being explored is "how do consumers learn?" Inasmuch as consumer behavior or learning is a subset of a larger universal set of behavior or learning, relevant generalizations ought to be forthcoming from the universal set or population.

It is important to realize that learning is what ought to take place as a process of education. Marketers perform educational, i.e., information-providing, activities through personal selling and sales promotional activities. In general, education is said to perform three functions:

1. It enables one to learn new skills.
2. It enables one to gain a deeper or fuller understanding.
3. It enables one to change basic attitudes.

Marketers' educational activities are generally focused strongly on the latter two. In the first place, a particular firm, in its advertising and selling message, wants the recipient of that message to be informed about a product or service offering, i.e., how that particular class of products or services might enable him to do a better job of problem solving. Secondly, the sender of the message wants the receiver to react favorably to the action phase of the message; that is, he wants the consumer to buy brand X or to stop in at his neighborhood store and see product Z.

As will be demonstrated extensively in Part III of this study, learning is not a simple mechanistic process even though some researchers and marketers have viewed it as such. At its simplest, behavior can be viewed as the product or function of three important variables: *motivation*—which we have already discussed briefly; *cognition*—which has been touched upon; and *learning*.[24] Learning is the organism's behavioral re-action to stimuli. New stimuli may be a product or a message about a product; a package or a suggestion from a neighbor. The behavior re-action may be the inclination to buy the product or simply to think favorably about it.

Consumer behavior may now be analyzed in light of the three fac-tors mentioned above. A consumer witnesses or manifests some felt need. A tensional state thus develops, and there arise motives or reasons which impel the consumer to respond. A whole set of mental reactions and atti-tudinal sets develop which we call cognitive processes. Strong motiva-tions and those which forego prolonged periods of not being satisfied usu-ally generate the most intense cognitive reactions. Products or activities which are incompatible or inconsistent with our life style, self-image, or cognitive map will elicit conflict reactions within ourselves. Cognitions or values will then have to be altered or rationalized. Finally, the consumer will be forced to choose some goal object which he assumes will satisfy his need in light of his cognitive processes, thereby reducing his drive or motivation. But what shall he choose? Several alternatives may be satis-factory and consistent with his cognitive structure. Each alternative may possess a number of differentiating attributes which are called signs or cues. Certainly not all such signs or cues are of equal importance to the consumer. The signs or cues, however, carry with them particular ex-pectancies, and consumers typically choose that alternative which, for them, carries the greatest expectancy or promised satisfaction. If a par-ticular product is chosen and it proves to be exceedingly satisfactory, reinforcement of the choice has taken place. Reinforcement also tends to affect the cognitive processes so that certain facets of behavior may tend to become habitualized. Often one hears that "consumers are creatures of habit." Perhaps in one sense this is true, but it is futile and even nonsensical for marketers to assume such a view. The important point is how habits are developed and how they can be changed. *The process, of course, is that of learning and reinforcement and the means is often that of communication.*

Marketers, in developing programs and strategies, and in attempting to communicate effectively regarding these programs, might do well to be guided by some relevant principles regarding learning theory in general.[25]

---

[24] For a more complete discussion of these general processes, see James A. Bay-ton, "Motivation, Cognition, Learning—Basic Factors in Consumer Behavior," *Journal of Marketing,* January, 1958, pp. 282-289.

[25] Adapted from Jerome T. Bruner, *The Process of Education* (Cambridge, Mass.: Harvard University Press, 1965), pp. 23-26.

1. "Understanding fundamentals makes a total message more comprehensible." Therefore messages which are unduly complex are not likely to lead to learning.

2. "Detail ought to be placed in a structured pattern." Messages which are grossly incompatible with the cognitive structures of a particular market target or segment will not be "received" and consequently learning will be absent, i.e., behavior will not be altered.

3. "Finally, an understanding of fundamental ideas, as noted earlier, appears to be the main road to adequate 'transfer of training.' To understand something as a specific instance of a more general case—which is what understanding a more fundamental principle or structure means— is to have learned not only a specific thing but also a model for understanding other things like it that one may encounter." This general principle, in its converse form, is often what necessitates a marketer selling first an idea and secondly a product.

Consumer behavior has been cast in terms of problem-solving behavior. A problem exists for the consumer when there is a need or want to be fulfilled (goal) and uncertainty as to how the goal might be best achieved. The consumer then is further cast as a sensory and data-gathering organism. His goals are variable and changing. His alternatives are generally numerous. The existence of innumerable problems forces the consumer to become a decision maker. He must make choices concerning goals, and once a goal is decided upon, he must develop and analyze alternatives. This means that the consumer will receive messages via communication media and will probably alter his behavior or change his attitudes during the course of the decision-making process. The consumer, like other decision makers, should "compute" the relative payoffs from each of the alternatives generated as tentative solutions to his problem and choose that payoff which affords him the highest expectancy of satisfaction.

Figure 2 presents graphically some of the major determinants of consumer behavior which have been discussed and attempts to show what ought to be somewhat obvious; namely, that consumer behavior is only a subset of a larger and more universal set of behavior, human behavior. Consumer behavior is a bounded concept; that is, particular consumer behavior is largely contextual or culturally induced. As will be further elaborated in the text, consumer behavior begins with dimly envisaged needs, wants and strivings; these elicit a kind of trial and error or heuristic problem solving, which has as its major interest a search for significant structure. The search for significant structure is mainly one of seeking insight into problems (needs or wants). Insight means seeing into a subject or acquiring a grasp or understanding of fundamental relationships. Interestingly enough, insight can be cultivated or trained; this implies that the fundamental concepts of learning theory are oper-

Figure 2: Schematic Model of Consumer Behavior: Its Context and Determinants.

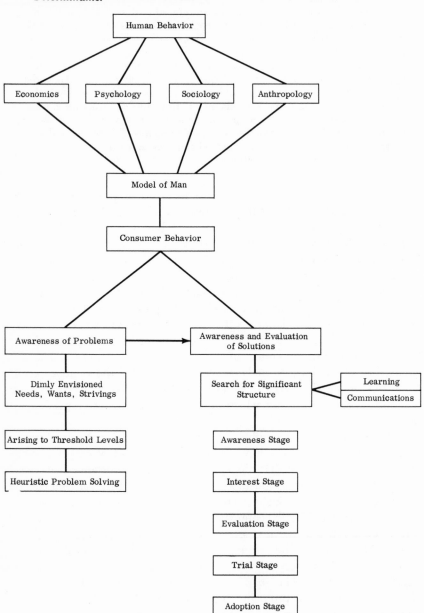

able and that communication such as advertising and personal selling can be used to teach the consumer to look for the right things. The search for significant structure in consumer problem solving, in turn, moves through a series of sequential stages from awareness of alternative solutions in the form of product or service offerings to the final adoption of a specific product or service to meet specific consumer problems or needs.

Consumers make two contrasting types of decisions—programmed and nonprogrammed.[26]

> Decisions are programmed to the extent that they are repetitive and routine, to the extent that a definite procedure has been worked out for handling them so that they don't have to be treated *de nova* each time they occur. The obvious reason why programmed decisions tend to be repetitive, and vice versa, is that if a particular problem recurs often enough, a routine procedure will usually be worked out for solving it.
>
> Decisions are *non*-programmed to the extent that they are novel, unstructured, and consequential. There is no cut and dried method for handling the problem because it hasn't arisen before, or because its precise nature and structure are elusive or complex, or because it is so important that it deserves a custom-tailored treatment.

Consumer problem solving or decision making appears to fit this framework rather well, and learning theory and communication both may be used to the marketer's best advantage if behavior is analyzed within this context. Programmed decisions have, by definition, become routinized. Consumers have been, to a large extent, *programmed* by some force or process to react in some largely predetermined way in solving a particular problem. Once the consumer is programmed as a result of outside stimuli (advertising or sales promotion) or by dint of his own will, i.e., the inner-directed man with a rich and active cognitive process, the ability to rewrite or change his attitude or behavior concerning a given class of products may be very slight. This may be the case for a whole range of convenience products or products such as headache remedies, soaps and detergents, or cigarettes.

Nonprogrammed decisions of consumers are likely to bring forth a heightened amount of cognitive processes. This is because the consumer is largely open-minded about the decision problem. He hasn't made similar decisions of this type before; that is why it is a nonprogrammed decision. At this juncture, the consumer is receptive to information; he is groping and searching and learning. He is testing and feeling himself out regarding product or service attributes. And he is matching these

---

[26] These categories and the definitions stemming therefrom have been adopted from Herbert A. Simon, *The New Science of Management Decision* (New York: Harper & Row, Publishers, 1960).

attributes or images with his own self-images and his life style. For non-programmed decisions, the consumer is looking for detailed and complete information about products or services, and he is likely to respond favorably to the firm which provides such information.

Communication. Communication is concerned with the imparting or interchange of thoughts, opinions, or information by speech, writing, or signs. The important concept or idea involved in this definition is probably that of "interchange," which implies strongly that communication is not only concerned with the transmission of ideas but also with the consequent receiving of the information. The central theme of communication is that there is both action and reaction.

Figure 3 presents a schematic outline of the communication process involving the concepts of both action and reaction.

Figure 3: A Simplified Communications System.

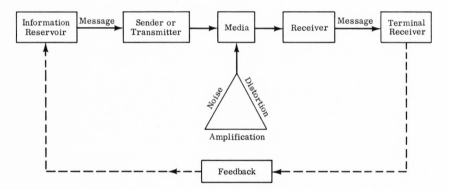

The fundamental dimensions of communications include at least three factors: source, message, and receiver.[27] The source is viewed as the sender, and for marketing purposes the message is composed of information which ought to be designed, structured, and sent for the purpose of modifying or altering the behavior of customers or potential customers, the receivers.

The communications programs of marketers are extensive and complex. The advertising programs of U.S. companies alone run to an aggregate expenditure of about $15 billion per year in the late 1960's. One writer estimates that for each dollar of advertising expenditure, Ameri-

[27] Edgar Crane, *Marketing Communications* (New York: John Wiley & Sons, Inc., 1965), p. 11.

can firms spend three dollars for personal selling activities.[28] This would mean that U.S. firms spend for advertising and personal selling, excluding public relations and publicity, approximately $60 billion a year to communicate their marketing messages. If expenditures for marketing research, a kind of extension of the communication process, are included, the figures would be roughly $80 to $100 billion a year.

Marketing communications systems can be built and analyzed in terms of the three major components of a general communication system diagrammed in Fig. 3. The sender or transmitter of the message is, of course, the marketing firm, sometimes acting through its advertising agency. Messages are constructed on the basis of the reservoir of knowledge which the message designers have relevant to the receiver. This may explain why some messages are so poorly received and interpreted by receivers. That is, the message designers simply lack knowledge or pertinent information regarding receivers. Good message design is predicated on good and adequate information regarding receivers. The media choice for a marketer's message is certainly wide. Two basic media are advertising and personal selling. Advertising messages, because of the nonpersonal basis of the presentation, may be fraught with the greatest difficulties concerning message design. Also, advertising generally elicits feedback over a more prolonged period of time. In the case of personal selling where there is a face-to-face confrontation between sender and receiver, there is the possibility of both minimizing noise and adjusting message as a result of what becomes almost instantaneous feedback.

The message is quite likely to be altered, muted, or amplified between the time it leaves the sender and the time it is received by the receiver. The addition of noise, a concept which means technically an addition to the signal not intended by the sender, may be brought about by competitors sending messages which are in conflict with the message of the original sender. Also, distortion in message can arise as a result of breakdowns or inconsistencies in the communications network. For example, the receiver may experience conflict between a company salesman's zealousness in puffing his wares and the company's advertising message which emphasizes service and the soft sell. Amplification may result from both internal and external considerations. For example, a given firm's advertising and personal selling programs may be in a harmonious balance (internal considerations) and a receiver may receive reinforcement of a firm's message from another customer or user of the product (external considerations).

It was stressed at the outset of this discussion that marketing com-

---

[28] G. David Hughes, "A New Tool for Sales Managers," *Journal of Marketing Research,* May, 1964, p. 32.

Figure 4: Schematic Relationship between Learning and Communication.

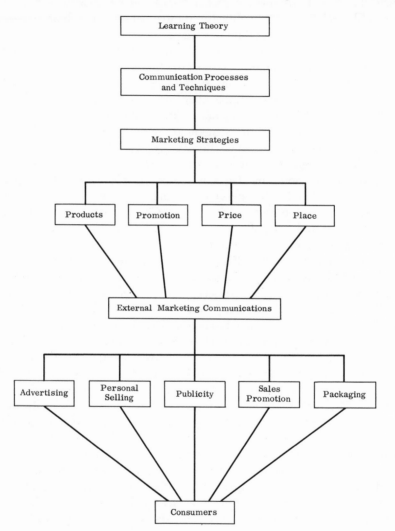

munication is concerned with the interchange of information. Thus, sending and receiving have been stressed. Also to be stressed is the idea that both sender and receiver, if two-way communications are to be established, must play dual or reversed roles. Senders, if our system is to be an open one, must also be receivers and vice versa. This concept is known as feedback. The feedback concept is an effort to recover a part of the output of a system in order to correct, modify, or control the total system. Firms obtain feedback regarding their marketing communications sometimes as a result of the success of their various programs. However, lack of success is also a form of feedback, but often firms have to develop special channels or feedback loops such as market research departments, complaint departments, or even suggestion boxes to learn the reasons why they have failed.

An earlier proposition was that behavior is affected by learning and that learning is often a function of communication. Figure 4 graphically illustrates these relationships in terms of both marketing strategy formulation and the role of marketing communication. Communication, to be effective, must be predicated on sound concepts and understanding of how behavior is affected or modified. *This process is learning.* That is, all communication processes and techniques, inasmuch as they are aimed at bringing about favorable and positive reactions on the part of listeners or viewers, must be based on our understanding of *how* and *why* behavior is modified or adapted over time. Thus, it is necessary to understand the learning process in order that our efforts toward modifying behavior (communication) have some scientific basis. Furthermore, a firm's marketing strategy must be laid upon a foundation of understanding stemming from both the learning theory and the communication theory areas. And while it is certainly true that a firm attempts to "communicate" with its market through product, prices, and channels of distribution, it is through its *promotional* activities in total that the firm most explicitly attempts to develop its external marketing communications program, the purpose of which is to bring about a favorable consumer reaction. Thus, promotion as a part of strategy has as its objective the dissemination of information concerning the firm, its products, its prices, and its locational advantages. It attempts to accomplish these objectives through advertising, personal selling, publicity, sales promotion, and packaging.

The aim of communication in marketing ought to be to influence favorably the behavior of consumers. But as we have seen, consumer behavior is a complex phenomenon and is not generally well understood. How consumers make choices remains obscure. It is the purpose of this study, if not to look widely and perceptively into the contents of that mysterious "black box," to at least partially pry open the lid for some interesting glances at this phenomenon.

PART TWO

EMERGING
MODELS OF MAN

TWO

From Freudian to Existential Consumer: a Framework for a Theory of Consumer Behavior

The study of man's, and thus consumer's, behavior may more properly be the task of the poet than the scientist. Yet, in today's science-minded world, it is science that has received the nod to explore man's inner motivations and instincts and to draw relevant generalizations regarding consumer motivation and behavior. And most of us have a firm and unshaken belief in the efficacy of science. Our general attitude is that given the proper "laboratory" and sufficient funds to sustain research, discovery is inevitable. This may be the case if, by discovery, we mean only additional insight. However, there are those who regard the phenomenon of human behavior and motivation as only a temporary mystery soon to be explained on a more scientific basis. Their argument, which is partially correct, is that it is not sufficient to say that human behavior is too complex to classify and understand. "That same sort of statement used to be made about the stars and planets . . . that they were too complicated to be understood . . . but men like Copernicus and Galileo demonstrated otherwise, and so have today's atomic scientists and astronomers. The Copernicus or Galileo of human motivation will also be found." [1] The secrets of the universe unlocked by Coperni-

---

[1] Steuart Henderson Britt, *The Spenders: Where and Why Your Money Goes* (New York: McGraw-Hill Book Company, 1960), p. 22.

31

cus and Galileo were small indeed compared with the contributions made by those who followed them. But the secrets and mysteries of the universe which *remain* to be discovered would fill a much larger book than the sum total of man's accumulated knowledge about the universe to date. Man, the supreme egotist possessed with the most powerful of tools, reason, believes that there is no limit to his ability to understand, to gain insight, to know. And he is correct in his simpleminded assumption. It is only the infinitude of problems with which he fails to reckon. Over 150 years ago, the philosopher Kant made a valiant effort to prove that there were ineluctable limits to reason, but the singularly positivistic mind of Western man has been willing to concede this only when it shows up in the findings of science. Science, then, in this century, has caught up with Kant.[2]

The physicist Heisenberg has shown that there are essential limits to our ability to know and predict physical states of affairs, and gives us a glimpse of a nature that may at bottom be irrational and chaotic—at any rate, our knowledge of it is limited, so that we cannot know this *not* to be the case. This discovery rather shatters the illusion of physicists who, motivated by a thoroughly rational prejudice, thought that reality must be predictable through and through.

Mathematics has always been regarded as the model of intelligibility and has been the central focus of rational determinism. Yet Godel has shown that mathematics contains insoluble problems and hence can never be formalized in any complete system. What this means, in effect, is that mathematics can never be turned over to a giant computing machine; it will always be unfinished and thus mathematicians—the frail human beings who construct mathematics—will always be in business.

There is no system possible for human existence, said Kierkegaard a century ago. And this has now been emphatically restated by Heisenberg and Godel. There does not exist a rock bottom to human comprehension and understanding. And while marketing or psychology or sociology may yet, in the field of human behavior and motivation, produce its Copernicus or Galileo, they will not reach a rock bottom of understanding regarding this complex and mysterious organism called man. The reason is that man's behavior, as previously stated, is constantly subject to new forces causing him to adapt to his changing environment. This is not to be taken, however, as an excuse or rationalization for giving up in our quest for knowledge or understanding. It simply reinforces the fundamental axiom that man's reach ought always to exceed his grasp.

---

[2] The material here and the examples which follow are taken from William Barrett's *Irrational Man: A Study in Existential Philosophy* (Garden City, N.Y.: Doubleday & Company, Inc., 1958), pp. 36-41.

THE SEARCH FOR HUMAN MAINSPRINGS

The study of marketing from antiquity to the present might very well be characterized by the marketer's attempt to discover what makes his customers "tick." The marketer, as well as others who study human behavior, have approached their subject as if he were possessed by some homunculus, who is the essence of the larger man or personality. Thus, if one could discover this mainspring, this energizing force in all men, he would possess a divining rod of human or customer behavior. And he could then postulate a set of behavior axioms which would enable others to explain, describe, and predict human behavior. All our investigations into human behavior and its resultant implications for business in terms of organizational theory and customer behavior and motivation have been a search for the human essence, the intrinsic nature of man.

There are grave shortcomings to this approach to the study of human behavior and motivation. For one, it assumes the infallibility of man's reason, which we have already found to be fallible. Also, this approach assumes that there exists a rock bottom to human behavior and, thus, understanding. That is, it assumes that man has an essence rather than only an existence—a point which we will attempt to disprove shortly. Finally, the researcher or investigator has been hampered in his study of human motivation and behavior and in his success in drawing meaningful conclusions about man's nature or essence because of his own cognitive or value structure. Whatever the researcher sees as the inner nature or essence of man is most often what he himself puts there —not what actually exists. As a consequence of our studies and generalizations regarding customer motivation and human behavior in the market place, we have, not a single unified theory as to how the mind of the consumer is motivated, but a number of partial theories which in some instances, perhaps, explain consumer behavior phenomena and in others confuse and befuddle the marketer in his attempt to develop meaningful and effective marketing strategies.

Kotler describes five different models of the buyer's "black box" along with brief comments regarding the marketing implications of these models. They are the Marshallian model, stressing economic motivations (see Chapter 1 for a discussion of the model of economic man); the Pavlovian model, learning (discussed extensively in Chapter 4); the Freudian model, psychoanalytic motivations (to be discussed at length in this chapter); the Veblenian model, social-psychological factors; and the Hobbesian model, organizational factors.[3] The Veblenian and

---

[3] Philip Kotler, *Marketing Management: Analysis, Planning, and Control* (Englewood Cliffs, N.J.: Prentice-Hall, Inc., 1967), pp. 82-94.

Hobbesian models can hardly be called models at all. They might more accurately be called threads of a larger and more comprehensive model of man, which will be developed subsequently in this study, i.e., existential man.

CONSUMER BEHAVIOR: A HERITAGE OF
FREUDIAN PSYCHOLOGY

The study of human behavior has characteristically been the domain of psychology. And inasmuch as modern psychology has been so profoundly affected and structured by the research and writing of Sigmund Freud, his ideas have come to dominate the thinking of marketers in regard to consumer behavior. Indeed, it may require another twenty-five or fifty years for marketing to overcome the damage caused by the widespread adoption and misapplication of Freudian theories and ideas. The prevalence of Freudian thinking is so widespread in marketing and its influence in shaping attitudes regarding consumer behavior so extensive that a rather thoroughgoing analysis of basic Freudian ideas is in order.

Sigmund Freud was born in Freiburg, Moravia, in 1856. However, he spent most of his life in Vienna, where he lived for eighty years. Freud came to manhood in the age of energy and dynamics. Men of science during this period were literally changing the world by their discoveries of the secrets of energy. And it was these discoveries with which young Freud became enamored and which furnished him with a new conception of man.

> Darwin conceived of man as an animal. Fechner proved that the mind of man did not stand outside of science, but that it could be brought into the laboratory and accurately measured. The new physics, however, made possible an even more radical view of man. This is the view that man is an energy system and that he obeys the same physical laws which regulate the soap bubble and the movement of the planets.[4]

Freud began his career as a medical doctor, but was less than enthusiastic about practicing medicine. Instead, he was at first considerably more interested in biological research. Frustrated for numerous reasons, however, including some persecution by anti-Semites, Freud was forced to pursue his professional calling by practicing medicine. His interest in energy and physics gradually led him to study and specialize in the area of nervous disorders. He soon began to feel, as a result of some new therapeutic techniques which he himself developed—the "talking out"

---

[4] Calvin S. Hall, *A Primer of Freudian Psychology* (New York: The New American Library, 1955), p. 13.

or free association method—that his patients' disorders had deep underlying causes. His probing revealed what he thought were dynamic forces
at work causing their abnormal symptoms.

Earlier in Freud's career, he had come under the influence of Ernst
Brücke, who was director of the Physiology Laboratory at the University
of Vienna and had the foremost reputation among physiologists of his
day. Brücke had set forth the rather radical view that the living organism
is a dynamic system to which the laws of chemistry and physics apply.
Freud was fascinated at the time by his mentor's theories, and it was
perhaps natural that when he began his investigations into the nervous
disorders of his patients, there began to take shape in his mind the idea
of a dynamic psychology; one that studies the transformations and ex-
changes of energy within the personality. Freud also came to believe
that these energizing forces were largely unconscious.

As he continued his studies and his practice grew, Freud became
better known and his theories and writings began to attract a larger
audience. Psychoanalysis was not only acceptable, it was the rage. Ultimately there was hardly any area of the social sciences that did not
feel the impact of Freudian psychology.

Freud took a seemingly narrow view of psychology. He was ob-
sessed with the idea of psychology as a deterministic science. As a consequence, Freudian psychology has come to be considered as synonymous
with the area of objective, or hard-headed, psychology.

On the basis of the insight and knowledge gained from his many
patients and himself, Freud began to lay the foundation for a theory of
personality. His theories and attitudes regarding personality reflected
his philosophy of life, which was based, as might be expected, on science
rather than on metaphysics or religion. He believed that his scientific
inquiry and research had led him to a true knowledge and understanding
of the human mainspring, or essence, and his so-called discoveries made
him both dourly pessimistic and hypercritical. Holding anything but a
high opinion of mankind, he felt that the irrational forces in man's nature
were so strong that the rational forces had little chance of success against
them. Except for a few exceptional personalities (like his own no doubt)
who might lead a life of reason, the bulk of mankind are prey to their
delusions and superstitions.

The structure and function of personality.   Freud viewed the personality as a total entity, although for purposes of analysis and discussion
he categorized it into three components or subsystems: the *id*, the *ego*,
and the *superego*. However, although these subsystems have different
names, it does not mean, nor did Freud intend it to mean, that they were
separate entities.

This classifying of what Freud considered to be only different processes, functions, and mechanisms has led to some confusion regarding his structural view of the total personality. In the emotionally healthy individual, these three subsystems constitute a unified and harmonious total organization of personality. They work together as a well-structured set of components, and the smooth and harmonious functioning enables the individual to engage in meaningful, efficient, and goal-producing activities. The purpose of the total personality is to enable the individual to attain his basic needs and desires. However, as in any total system, when imbalance exists among the component parts, it is likely to function at something less than complete efficiency and harmony. So it is with Freud's concept of personality.

The id.   The main function of the *id* is to release or discharge quantities of energy or excitation. The id fulfills the primordial or basic principle of life which Freud called *the pleasure principle*. The goal of the pleasure principle is to rid the person of tension or, at least, to reduce the amount of tension to a reasonably low level and to keep it as low as possible. The characteristic factor regarding the id is that it is not controlled by the laws of reason or logic, and it does not possess values, ethics, or morality. The id is compulsively driven by one basic goal or consideration and that is to obtain satisfaction for instinctive needs in accordance with the pleasure principle. The id is constantly confronted with either-or decisions. Either it discharges in action or wish fulfillment, or it succumbs to the influence of the ego and thus becomes bound or locked up.

The id has all the characteristics of a spoiled, pampered, or perhaps even neurotic, child. Even though the id is the foundation on which the adult personality is built, it nevertheless maintains its infantile character throughout life. The id is petulant and impulsive. It cannot tolerate tension and thus seeks immediate gratification. A unique thing about the id is that it is omnipotent because it possesses the somewhat magical power of fulfilling its wishes by imagination, fantasy, hallucinations and dreams.

The id is man's center of Bentham's felicific calculus—the world of subjective reality in which the pursuit of pleasure and the avoidance of pain are the only functions that matter. The id manifests itself most dramatically, argued Freud, whenever a person does something impulsive like throwing a rock through a window for no apparent reason. Conversely, the person who spends his time daydreaming or fantasizing is also under the strong and domineering influence of the id. It is important to remember that the id, like some students, does not think. It only wishes, feels, or acts.

The ego. The id utilizes two major processes in order to discharge tension: impulsive motor activity and image formation. Neither of these processes, however, is sufficient to insure the organism any degree of success in coping with or accommodating to the reality of existence in the real world. Neither impulsive motor activity nor image formation will necessarily enable the hungry man to find food or the sexually motivated person to find a mate, thus assuring the evolutionary goals of survival and reproduction. The organism, in order to cope with reality, needs a mechanism other than the id to more completely harmonize his behavior and personality. This psychological subsystem, Freud called the *ego*. The ego in the well-adjusted personality acts very much like a thermostat or any other servo-mechanism. It enables the personality to maintain some sort of equilibrium between its external environment or the demands of the external environment and the impulsiveness of the id. The ego performs the executive functions of personality and, in the language of the executive, the ego plans, organizes, and controls both the id and the superego and maintains commerce with the external world in the interest of the total personality and its seemingly bizarre and diverse needs.

While the id impulsively pursues the pleasure principle, the ego is governed by *the reality principle*. Reality means that which exists. The goal or objective of the reality principle is to delay the discharge of energy until the actual or true object that will satisfy the need has been discovered and produced. A marketing example might be the buyer who passes an automobile dealer's window or sees his neighbor's new car parked in the driveway. The id, for any number of selfish reasons, might be compelled to go right out to the dealer and buy one like it. The *ego* directs the individual to think it over, to question his ability to purchase the car or his desire in light of other needs. If the id wins these arguments, the ego may still say, "Let's look around and be sure we get the right make, model, color, appointments, etc."

In any event, the postponement of action means that the ego has to be able to tolerate tension until it can be discharged by an appropriate form of behavior. The reality principle does not mean that the pleasure principle of the id is abandoned; normally it is only temporarily suspended in the interest of reality. Freud reasoned that the reality principle was served by what he called a *secondary process*, which developed after the primary process of the id. This secondary process consists of discovering or producing reality by means of a plan of action that has been developed through thought and reason. Consequently, the secondary process is nothing more or less than what is ordinarily called problem solving or thinking. When the thinking or cognitive process results in some general plan of action and when the plan is put into effect to see if it really works, the person is said to be engaged in reality testing.

The ego, it should be remembered, is basically a product of an interaction with the environment. However, its lines of development are laid down by heredity and it is guided by natural growth processes. This means that every person has inborn potentialities for thinking and reasoning. It is experience, training, and education which make possible the realization of these potentialities.[5]

The superego. There is yet another facet to Freud's concept of personality. This is the subsystem which he called the *superego*. The superego was viewed by Freud as the moral or judicial branch of personality. The superego represents the ideal rather than the real, and the goal or behavioral manifestation of the superego is that it strives for perfection, rather than for pleasure or reality. The superego becomes the person's moral code, and it develops out of the ego as a result of the child's assimilation of his parents' standards regarding what is good and virtuous and what is bad and sinful. The child thus learns that he must not only obey the reality principle in order to avoid pain and obtain pleasure but also attempt to behave according to the moral pronouncements and dictates of his parents. The extremely long period of childhood and its consequent dependency on parental influence greatly favor the formation of the superego.

The basic components of the superego consist of the *ego ideal* and the *conscience*. The ego ideal is analogous to the child's conceptions of what his parents consider to be morally good. Conscience, on the other hand, is analogous to the child's conceptions of what his parents feel is morally bad, and these notions are established through experiences with punishments.

The superego, in effect, becomes an emotional manifestation of the parent. However, like a parent, the superego must have some way of controlling the behavior of the child, i.e., some way of enforcing its moral rules. Again, like the parent, the superego enforces its moral rules by rewards and punishments. And these rewards and punishments are inflicted upon the ego. Remember, too, that we are dealing with emotional phenomena and therefore a thought is the same as a deed in the eyes of the superego. In this respect, the superego resembles the id, which also makes no distinction between subjective and objective phenomena. The superego punishes the ego for thinking bad or evil thoughts, even though the thoughts may never be translated into action. The psychological re-

---

[5] For a profound yet comprehensible treatment of the topic of heredity and the attainment of potentialities, see Theodosius Dobzhansky, *The Biological Basis of Human Freedom* (New York: Columbia University Press, 1956), especially Chap. 3.

wards and punishments employed by the superego are feelings of pride and feelings of guilt or inferiority. When the ego behaves well, it is rewarded by virtuous feelings. Conversely, misbehavior on the part of the ego brings thoughts of shame, embarrassment, or self-contempt. To return to our earlier marketing example, if the executive function or ego of personality placates the id by permitting purchase of the automobile, the superego may reprimand or scold the ego severely, especially if one's puritanical conscience is angered by the high price of the automobile or if the purchaser commits himself to thirty-six easy payments. As a result, therefore, the subject may be ridden with guilt feelings or anxiety for having violated the "rules" of the superego. More broadly conceived, the purpose of the superego is that of controlling and regulating those impulses whose uncontrolled expression would endanger the stability of society, or of a well-established social order. Essentially, as viewed by Freud, those impulses are sex and aggression. Therefore, the superego, by placing these moral restraints upon lawlessness and anarchy, enables a person to become a law-abiding member of society. Thus, if the id is the product of evolution and the psychological representative of one's biological endowment, and the ego is the result of one's interaction with objective reality and the result of thinking and cognitive processes, then the superego can be viewed as the product of socialization and the vehicle of cultural tradition.

The dynamics of personality. The structure and function of the personality of the individual having been discussed in terms of Freud's trichotomy of psyche, i.e., *id, ego,* and *superego,* we need now to turn our interest to some other dimensions of Freud's dynamic psychology. The personality functions as a result of what Freud called psychic energy. He believed that the energy which ran the personality was no different from other forms of energy operating in the universe. Psychic energy performs psychological work—thinking, perceiving, and remembering. The source of this psychic energy, Freud believed, was the instinct. As a matter of fact, Freudian psychology is often referred to as instinct or drive psychology. An instinct, defined as an inborn condition which imparts direction to psychological processes, has a *source,* an *aim,* an *object,* and an *impetus.* The principal sources of instinctual energy are the bodily processes, needs, or impulses. The aim of an instinct is the removal of a bodily need. Put another way, the aim of an instinct is to eliminate the source of that instinct. Freud called the final goal of an instinct its internal aim and the subordinate goals of an instinct its external aims. He believed that psychic energy was subject to the same physical laws as other forms of energy and, therefore, that an instinct was *conservative* because its goal is to return a person to the quiescent state which existed prior to disturbance by an excitatory state. In other words, an instinct always tries to bring about a *regression* to an earlier condition. And this tendency of an instinct to repeat over and over again the cycle from excitation to repose is called the *repetition compulsion*. The individual's desire for cigarette smoking may be in part explained in Freudian terms as the desire to satisfy the repetition compulsion.

Finally, the object of the instinct is the object or means by which the aim is accomplished. And the object or means is the most variable feature of an instinct, since many different objects or activities can take the place of one another. The seat of the instincts is the id. Because the instincts constitute the total amount of psychic energy, the id is said to be the original reservoir of psychic energy. In order to form the ego and superego, energy is withdrawn from this pool. As energy is converted from the id to the ego, logical thinking takes the place of wish fulfillment, and the beginning of the cognitive processes marks the initial step in the development of the ego. This redistribution of energy from the id to the ego is a major dynamical event in the development of personality. As was previously mentioned, the energy of the ego is used to effect a synthesis or integration of the three subsystems of personality. It should be borne in mind that there is only so much available energy and no more. This means that if the ego gains energy, the id or the superego—or both—have to lose energy. The energizing of one system of personality means the de-energizing of other systems. If the bulk of the energy is controlled by the superego, the resultant conduct will probably be moralistic. If it is controlled by the ego, the behavior will be realistic. And if it is retained by the id, which is the source of all psychic energy, the actions will be impulsive.

The reader will recall from our introductory statements that Freud had a rather low and pessimistic opinion regarding man: At best, man was vulgar, if not somewhat bestial. The primary reason for this belief was his view regarding the id. Freud thought the id was virtually all-powerful, and he saw man's lot as that of a rather prolonged but unsuccessful struggle of the ego and superego with the id. He was also somewhat narrow-minded about man's basic impulses which motivated the id: Freud was a pan-sexualist who thought that man's life centered around his compulsive desire for sexual satisfaction and he reasoned that society's taboos on free and unlimited sexual gratification as they affected the superego and the superego's punishment of the ego for curbing these urges resulted in most of man's frustrations and anxieties. Freud further believed that the ego, functioning in its attempt to control the id and mollify the superego, underwent a process of development by which the personality tried to resolve its frustrations, conflicts, and anxieties which are essentially sexually caused. These methods of development are identification, displacement, sublimation, and defense mechanisms.

Identification is the incorporation of the qualities of an external object, usually those of another person, into one's own personality. This results in the tendency to copy and imitate other people; it can be accomplished by vicariously identifying with other people through purchase behavior or the use of certain products known to be used by others.

Displacement is the process whereby energy is rechanneled from one object to another. There are major reasons why displacements follow a particular course. First, society, acting through its principal agents, the parents, influences the direction of displacement by sanctioning certain object-choices and prohibiting others. In children, thumb sucking is ordinarily condemned while licking a lollipop is condoned. Adults who lick lollipops are apt to be ridiculed, but society permits, and may even encourage them, to suck on a cigarette, a cigar, or a pipe.

When the substitute object is one that represents a higher cultural goal, this type of displacement is called sublimation. Freud argued that the direct expression of sexual aggression instincts is transformed into apparently nonsexual and nonaggressive forms of behavior. He believed that a person is always looking for his first love in the substitute object. Failing to find a completely satisfactory substitute, he either continues his search or reconciles himself to something that is second best. When a person accepts a substitute, he is said to be compensating for the original goal object.

Thus, the Freudian takes sex as the foremost and dominant derivative of the human behavior equation. Marketers have almost overwhelmingly adopted these Freudian ideas and assumptions and incorporated them into programs and strategies for consumers.

FREUD AND MARKETING: THE ID AND THE IDIOTS

It is no accident that Freud chose to call that impulsive facet of personality the id. The id in man, according to Freud, presumably causes him to resort to infantile or idiot levels of behavior. Furthermore, it is unfortunate that far too many marketers have allowed themselves to be affected by the Freudian point of view, the basic and fundamental assumption of which is that consumers are not very smart, that their behavior is guided far more by irrational forces and motives stemming from the id or unbalanced superego than by rational or cognitive processes. Marketers who have adopted this point of view look upon the majority of their customers as an undifferentiated mass of humanity subject to endless manipulation by careful and Freudianly structured motives and appeals. As a matter of fact, a large and important segment of marketing activity is now engaged in an attempt to discover the most effective means of exploiting the hidden or inner impulses of consumers so that more effective appeals may be utilized in order to trigger their id-dominated behavior. This activity is generally referred to as *motivation research*. It is based almost exclusively upon the premises and assumptions of Freudian psychology. In fact, motivation research utilizes many of the "scientific" techniques of psychology—depth interviews, projective training techniques such as the Rorschach test and thematic apperception tests, and various other word and image association tests—in order to discover what it is that motivates or triggers customer behavior. The results of these findings are often used in an effort to channel customer attitudes and behavior.

The fundamenal assumption of the motivation researcher, like that of the Freudian psychologists, is that most customer behavior is triggered by subconscious motivations heavily laden with sexual overtones. While one would hardly question the importance of sex as a motivator of certain kinds or levels of behavior, it is indeed questionable whether sex is of paramount importance in the motivation of all kinds of human and customer behavior. Yet the Freudian-oriented market researcher most frequently views the American consumer as "bundles of daydreams, misty hidden yearnings, guilt complexes, irrational emotional blockages. We are image lovers given to impulsive and convulsive acts." [6] Furthermore many motivation researchers believe the typical consumer does not have the slightest notion about what he really needs or wants to satisfy these inner compulsive impulses. The last thing the motivation researcher would do would be to ask the consumer. For, it is argued, the consumer is the least reliable index the marketer can have on what he ought to do to win customers. The explanation for this is twofold. First, the customer does not know the meaning or ramifications of his motives; therefore how can he possibly know what products or services are required

---

[6] Vance Packard, *The Hidden Persuaders* (New York: David McKay Co., Inc., 1957). Copyright © 1957 by Vance Packard. Reprinted with permission of David McKay Co., Inc. This book was an explosive and revealing treatment of the use of motivation research to manipulate consumer behavior. The marketing profession has since tried to refute and deny many of Packard's arguments. Packard himself acknowledged that there were many reputable motivation research organizations and that the entire marketing industry was not to be indicted for the shady practices of some of its members. This is largely the view of this writer. However, casual observation of much marketing and advertising behavior suggests that the Freudian model of man is the one which still guides their basic analysis and the resultant structuring of marketing programs. The examples in this section have been taken largely from Packard.

to satisfy them. Secondly, the consumer is not at all likely to admit his motives, even if he himself knows them, because they might not appear to be socially acceptable. Hence the consumer may say that he bought a commodity for a socially acceptable reason, i.e., warmth, durability, economy or dependability, whereas the true motive, whether known or unknown to him, was that the product held out the possibility of satisfying some yearning of the id, perhaps even with sexual overtones.

Man's most humanitarian and noble motivations are not free from the taint of Freudian implications. One researcher turned up the fact that many of the more successful greeting cards were loaded with sexual symbolism: artistic moons, candles, ovals, and circles. The greeting card company, armed with these discoveries, instructed their artists to design cards with a heavier emphasis on these unconscious symbols.[7] And so many marketers, whose programs and strategies are predicated on the findings of Freudian-oriented motivation researchers, view their subjects as idiots, full of sound and fury, signifying nothing; nothing, that is, except the anxiety and frustrations of internal psychic conflict—the conflict of the impulsive rampaging id in pursuit of the pleasure principle doing battle with a weakened and underdeveloped ego whose energy is at least partially drained by the self-ideal and conscience of the superego. The task of the marketer thus viewed is not so much that of selling products as of giving moral permission to have fun without guilt. Dr. Ernest Dichter, one of the high priests of the occult "science" of motivation research, has stated: "Every time you sell a self-indulgent product . . . you have to assuage his (the buyer's) guilt feelings . . . offer absolution."[8]

A most effective strategy adopted by many firms was based upon the theme of rewarding oneself. Inasmuch as the superego rewards the ego when it does noble deeds or thinks noble thoughts, this idea, it was thought, might be more fully exploited by merchandisers if they led the subject to believe that their products would satisfy this yearning for rewards. Consequently, candy, cigarette, and alcoholic beverage manufacturers all began utilizing this theme. The subtle, and not so subtle, implications of their messages were: reward yourself; you deserve the satisfaction or gratification which this product will bring; there is no need to feel guilty, all your friends are doing it; this is a socially acceptable practice.

A large part of the energy of the id is said to be directed toward certain love objects, and was therefore called by Freud *libidinous*. The motivation researchers were quick to point out to marketers that suc-

---

[7] *Ibid.*, p. 60.
[8] *Ibid.*, p. 48.

cessful merchandising campaigns for certain products could be built around libidinous themes. The promotion of women's undergarments, especially brassieres and girdles, became bolder in their appeals, with strong implications of masochism and body exhibitionism. An example of this, which even the uninitiated reader will recall, was the "I dreamed I went shopping in my Maidenform Bra" campaign.

Even the promotion of sporting events was not immune from the Freudian-oriented motivation researchers. A Neilson analysis of fans watching wrestling matches revealed that women outnumbered men two to one. The promoters of the matches surmised that something more than the interest in a half-nelson or a flying mare was involved, and concluded with the aid of motivation research that these women derived a high degree of erotic satisfaction from watching the matches. Consequently, the emphasis on sadism (men writhing in torture), male symbolism (chest beating and muscle flexing), and fashion interest (more elegant costumes for the performers), was stepped up.[9]

A highly touted theme of the motivation research frequently sold to marketers and included in their merchandising programs has centered around other aspects of Freudian psychology such as regression or infantile cravings for oral stimulation and satisfaction, and the Oedipus complex. Cigarette, cigar and pipe smoking, as previously mentioned, is a displacement device or substitute for the infantile cravings of the subject to return to the warmth, comfort, and security of the mother's breast. The inoffensive habit of gum chewing is also considered to be in this category.

The Freudian concept of the Oedipus complex, the unresolved desire of a child for sexual gratification through the parent of the opposite sex, is presumed to be an important motivator of certain consumer behavior regarding automobiles, houses, clothing, and food. Products merchandised and promoted as "like those mother used to make" may fall in this category. Soup is allegedly a product with heavy Oedipus implications. It takes us back to our earliest sensations of warmth, protection, and feeding. Its deepest roots may be in prenatal sensations of being surrounded by the amniotic fluid of the mother's womb. Seemingly there is no limit to the insight that may be gained regarding consumer behavior on the basis of Freudian analysis. It has been suggested, for example, that: [10]

> Many a businessman does not fly because of a fear of posthumous guilt—if he crashed his wife would think of him as stupid for not taking a train.

---

[9] *Ibid.*, p. 73.
[10] Philip Kotler, *Marketing Management: Analysis, Planning, and Control* (Englewood Cliffs, N.J.: Prentice-Hall, Inc., 1967), p. 88.

Men want their cigars to be odoriferous in order to prove that they (the men) are masculine.

A man buys a convertible as a substitute mistress.

A woman is very serious when she bakes a cake because unconsciously she is going through the symbolic act of giving birth.

Consumers prefer vegetable shortenings because animal fats stimulate a sense of sin.

Men who wear suspenders are reacting to an unresolved castration complex.

But what of the predictive powers of these associations? Do these attitudes underlie the behavior of all consumers in regard to these products? The answer is probably an emphatic *no!* Even Freud did not believe his psychology to be a predictive science; he considered it a *postdictive* science in the sense that, given a result, it could look back and perhaps unearth the causes.

> So long as we trace the development from its final stage backwards, the connection appears continuous, and we feel we have gained an insight which is completely satisfactory or even exhaustive. But if we proceed the reverse way, if we start from the premises inferred from the analysis and try to follow these up to the final result, then we no longer get the impression of an inevitable sequence of events which could otherwise not be determined. We notice at once that there might have been another result, and that we might have been just as well able to understand and explain the latter. The synthesis is thus not so satisfactory as the analysis; in other words from a knowledge of the premises we could not have foretold the nature of the result.[11]

How fortunate for motivation researchers and marketers *if they had read and understood* this important qualification. Not to mention the embarrassment and insult that countless consumers would have been spared by not being subjected to the blatant and often tasteless appeals of these merchandisers. In short, it is doubtful that we can generalize at all about overall consumer behavior on the basis of the premises and findings of Freudian analysis and investigation and, furthermore, many of its basic premises are open to question.

FROM ESSENCE TO EXISTENCE

The Freudian psychologist and the motivation researcher utilizing these techniques are guided in their inquiries by what might be called an *essence philosophy*. Both of these words have been defined previously,

---

[11] Sigmund Freud, "The Psychoanalysis of a Case of Homosexuality in a Woman," in *Collected Papers*, II (London, 1933), p. 226.

but in order to avoid ambiguity, let us decide that this term means that they take as their unifying force (philosophy) the idea that there is some basic mainspring or fundamental derivative (essence) of human behavior. Furthermore, it must be realized that they use their essence philosophy in a particular way—a way, incidentally, which Freud himself, as we have just seen, disavowed. However, much market research information has been gathered and many inferences regarding consumer behavior have been made as a result of reasoning from an essence toward an existence position. This may require a word or two of explanation. For example:

> Our use of mathematical sampling methods to test our products and our markets is grounded on the assumption that all men have certain natures or essences which can be quantitatively and qualitatively measured. This way of thinking may make certain accurate predictions possible, but because we view other men in this light, it follows that we view ourselves from a similar point of view.[12]

In effect, what we are saying is that we take our notions about a man's essence and generalize about his behavior or existence; this, in light of much current thinking, is erroneous and leads to specious results.

A very important point to consider is that psychology, as the study of human behavior, often springs from the investigator's deeper feelings and understandings about the nature of man. Hence Freud and his followers were guided by certain philosophical considerations, including a belief in essence as well as determinism. Even at the time Freud was making his discoveries there were those who disagreed strongly with the central assumptions of Freudian psychology. More recently, new and, what some consider, fresher philosophical approaches are bringing about a complete rethinking and restudy of many of our assumptions regarding man's essence and especially the idea of determinism.[13]

Much of this new philosophy is to be found in *existentialism*.[14] Ex-

---

[12] John H. Rice, "Existentialism for the Businessman," *Harvard Business Review*, March-April, 1960, p. 138.

[13] The concept of determinism is a philosophical one. The basic idea of determinism is that all events are the inevitable result of antecedent conditions, and that the human being, in acts of apparent choice, is the mechanical expression of his heredity and his past environment. The reader might ponder this statement for a moment, for it really amounts to both the description and the philosophy of Freudian psychology.

[14] There are several good primers on existential philosophy that are certainly not beyond the comprehension of the interested freshman or sophomore. In addition to the *Harvard Business Review* article previously quoted, the interested reader may wish to peruse Barrett's *Irrational Man* (previously cited); Walter Kaufman, *Existentialism from Dostoevsky to Sartre* (New York: Meridian Books, 1956); and Marjorie Green, *Introduction to Existentialism* (Chicago: Phoenix Books, University of Chicago Press, 1948).

istentialism is not a unified philosophy in the strict academic sense. What it really amounts to is a combination of several widely different revolts against traditional philosophy. However, the central theme of much of what is labeled existential philosophy is the insistence on the insufficiency of the abstract intelligence to grasp the richness of experience, on the urgent and irreducible reality of time, and for our purposes—perhaps in the long run the most significant insight of all—on the inner depth of the psychic life *which cannot be measured by the quantitative methods of the physical sciences.*

Probably the foremost argument of existentialism is its fundamental premise that existence precedes essence. Jean Paul Sartre, in his work *L'Etre et Le Neant,* has made a careful and analogous argument regarding this idea. Sartre says simply that a man's existence comes before his essence. A man can be nothing but what he is. You will recall the earlier statement that a man is his choices. Sartre reaffirms this statement by arguing that a man is nothing *except* what he is. He cannot be a concept nor an idea; he is his existence, nothing more nor less. He thus argues by analogy:

> The artisan, before he fashions the knife, visualizes it in his mind. He knows what it is to be used for, he knows its qualities, he is familiar with the techniques required to produce it. These and other concepts held by the artisan concerning the knife are its essence. They exist in the artisan's mind before the knife itself exists. The knife's essence precedes its existence.[15]

This really means, according to the existential interpretation, that man has no essential qualities. Human nature is a misnomer for man because man makes his own nature out of his existence. And it is this argument which frees man from the determinist forces on which both science and theology have relied to explain man's actions and behavior.

Many of the concepts and ideas of existentialism are turgid and fuzzy. However, there are several pivotal concepts or ideas around which the philosophy centers. We shall examine these briefly and then proceed to explore how the ideas and concepts of existential philosophy are affecting the formation of what might be called an existential psychology and, in turn, how our attitudes regarding existential psychology would affect and shape our attitudes regarding consumer behavior in the market place.

One of the key concepts of existentialism is "ontological." The word has its derivation from the Greek *onta,* meaning things which exist. Man *is.* Therefore this is the singular and foremost fact regarding man. Existential philosophy makes no effort to prove or disprove any such thought

---

15 Jean Paul Sartre, *Being and Nothingness* (New York: Basic Books, Inc., 1956).

as the divine origin of mankind. "It does not measure man and his actions to discover universal characteristics against which he may be measured: it does not presume immutable natural laws that he can disobey at his own peril." [16] In short, the existentialist refutes what might be called the universal concept of man. Several other ideas central to the concept of existentialism will be discussed in turn.

BEING AND BECOMING

The idea of being has important and special implications for existential philosophy. The ordinary dictionary definition does not suffice. In existential terminology, being does not refer to a person or thing which simply is or exists. Instead it has meaning only for those persons or things who by living or existing are in the process of "becoming": being refers to potentiality. Therefore being is a process of growth and development. Man, thus, is not a function, but only a point on a function. He is not what someone might define him to be but rather he is what he is *becoming.*

DASEIN

Man is in the state of becoming, but he is not alone. He becomes, and in turn exists, in an interdependent state with his environment. *Dasein,* in German, means "being there." Man exists in the world and he is part of his world. Removing a man from his world or the world from man destroys the concept of *Dasein.* Reality for man consists only of his own personal experiences. Therefore, man's personal experiences cannot be abstracted because the process of abstracting would sterilize the reality and immediacy of the experience. To understand a man, he must be considered in his world. The marketing concept which appears closely analogous to *Dasein* is that of *life style.*

EITHER/OR DECISIONS

Man, in his effort to become, effects the process by what Kierkegaard called his "either/or decisions." The central idea here is that of freedom of choice. Man becomes by exercising his freedom of choosing. These either/or decisions become the critical turning points in man's life, the

---

[16] Rice, *op. cit.,* p. 137.

forks in the highways of man's travels. And existentialism is like a road map in this respect. It tells one neither where to go nor the best route to take to get there; only that there are alternative routes to travel. Man's growth and development are strongly affected, then, by these either/or decisions.

FREE CHOICE

The ideal of free choice stems from the fact that man can choose. He can or he can not. He can exercise choice as a result of his own cognitive processes (which would include his value system as affected by his *Dasein*). The events of his life are not the inevitable result of antecedent conditions, and his behavior in acts of choice is not the mechanical expression of his heredity and his past environment alone. This is what really makes man so *responsible* for his behavior. When a man exists he is completely free and what he does or does not do is the result of his choice.

NONBEING

If being is concerned with becoming, nonbeing then is a situation whereby one ceases to become. This can occur other than by reverting to the inorganic state, i.e., death. It can result from simply refusing to exercise one's choices or will. One who fails to use his ability to reason or his cognitive power is guilty of nonbeing. Furthermore, a failure to wrestle with the problems of becoming, taking the easy way out or withdrawing from conflicts or decision-making situations, is one form of nonbeing.

ANXIETY AND GUILT

Anxiety results from man's awareness of eventual nonbeing, the ultimate form of which is death. The existentialist argues that man must be anxious if he is to fulfill his potentialities. The fact that he has freedom of choice and could conceivably, as a result of wrong decisions, impair his possibility for becoming makes him anxious. Some individuals, argue the existentialists, have denied their possibilities for becoming or the fulfillment of their potentialities and therefore their *anxiety* has been replaced by *guilt*. Notice that this view differs markedly from the Freudian conception of guilt which regards all guilt feeling as resulting from traumatic and repressed childhood incidents.

KNOW THYSELF

"Know thyself" was a command issued by Socrates to mankind. And while Socrates was certainly not an existentialist, this command has been made the central tenet of existential philosophy. If man is responsible to himself alone, that is, if he is free to *become* via the exercise of his *either/or decisions;* if he is to be only *anxious* and not *guilty*, there is then a highly important predicate on which this argument rests and that is that man know himself. It means that there are few prescribed rules of conduct, that one must know and understand his own value system and must develop his own sense of personality and self, and he must do this within the context of his total *Dasein.*

Thus, in the reality of today's existence, the ideas of existentialism are having a profound effect on man's thinking about man. Existential philosophy is now permeating much of man's thinking about religion, existence, literature and, notably, psychology. While it is psychology which is responsible for formulating conceptualizations and ideas about man's behavior, it is philosophy which constitutes the framework and the context out of which a psychology of behavior emerges. Thus, from existential philosophic thinking is emerging a body of thought, a discipline, concerned with the causes and ramifications of man's behavior and the need for determining better means of exploring and describing this phenomenon.

EXISTENTIAL PSYCHOLOGY

Existential psychology is the study and investigation of behavior phenomena based upon certain existential concepts. We saw earlier how Freudian psychology envisages human beings and their resultant behavior in terms of drives, forces, and conditioned reflexes. This approach is an approach via essences. The distinguishing characteristic of existential psychology is its abandonment of the essence approach and its focus on the existence and behavior phenomena surrounding the subject. *Phenomenology,* which is the endeavor to clear one's mind of the presuppositions that so often cause us to see, in the subject of our investigation, only our own theories or the dogmas of our own systems—the effort to experience instead the phenomenon in its full reality as it presents itself—is a central tenet of existential psychology.

Existential psychology has its roots and antecedents, of course, in the area of existential philosophy. James and Dewey were philosophers, but they were psychologists as well. As a matter of fact, the confluence of these two disciplines indicates another aspect of the existential approach: it deals with psychological categories such as "experience," "anxiety," "motivation." The existential implication, however, is that these things be dealt with at a deeper level which one writer calls *ontological reality*.[17]

The existential approach is not billed, or in the language of marketing, *merchandised* as a movement back to the armchair of speculation but is instead "an endeavor to understand man's behavior and experience in terms of the presuppositions that underlie our science and image of man. It is the endeavor to understand the nature of the man who *does* the experiencing and to *whom* the experience happened."[18]

The existential psychologist, like his philosophic counterpart, the existential philosopher, holds that existence precedes essence. Man can have no essence until he exists. That is, his essence stems from and is an outgrowth of his existence. This means, of course, that you cannot adequately describe or understand a human being on an essentialist basis. Truth or reality only exists for the human being inasmuch as he participates in it, is conscious and aware of it, and has some interrelationship with it. Existential psychology does not attempt to completely rule out the essentialist approach to behavior, oriented around such concepts as conditioning, drives, and inner mechanisms; it holds only that one can never explain or understand any living human being on that basis.

"The distinction (between objective or Freudian psychology and existential psychology) is whether the person has meaning in terms of the mechanism or the mechanism has meaning in terms of the person. The existential emphasis is firmly on the latter."[19] For this reason, then, from the standpoint of existentialism every mechanism or dynamism, every force or drive, presupposes an underlying structure that is infinitely greater than the mechanism, drive, or force itself. In short, it is the underlying structure from which they derive their meaning. The existentialists largely agree that this underlying structure is the pattern of potentiality of the living individual.

It is well to remember that in philosophy and psychology *existentialism* indicates an attitude as much as a school. It is an attitude or an approach to human beings. It is not necessarily a new set of techniques but a concern with the understanding of the structure of the human being and his experience that must underlie all techniques. The existentialist does not see man as the passive plaything of unconscious forces which determine what he is to be. Most existentialists refute the existence

---

[17] Paul Tillich, *Love, Power, and Justice* (New York: Oxford University Press, 1954), Chap. 11, p. 19.

[18] Rollo May, ed. and contributor, *Existential Psychology* (New York: Random House, Inc., 1961), p. 14.

[19] *Ibid.*, p. 18.

of an unconscious mind completely. If the mind manifests itself, they argue, it is consciously.

> A human personality or human life is not to be understood in terms of some hypothetical unconscious mechanism at work behind the scenes and pulling all the wires that manipulate the puppet of consciousness. A man *is* his life; which means that he is nothing more nor less than the totality of acts that make up that life.[20]

Existential psychology is not, figuratively speaking, of whole cloth. It is woven and pieced into a meaningful and unified concept from several different brands of psychological methods or attitudes. *Personalistic psychology* or the science of a person having experience; *Gestalt psychology* or psychology which emphasizes the whole rather than the elements; *Field theory,* a special aspect of Gestalt psychology; *Understanding psychology* which aims at understanding the psychological process; all these are today looked upon as being *existential* in orientation.

Existential concepts of motivation and behavior. In spite of the peripatetic and far-ranging nature of our inquiry, a complete analysis and synthesis of the various "schools" of existential psychology are beyond the scope of this treatment. Our investigation will necessarily be focused only on the salient concepts of existential psychology, especially insofar as they are relevant to better insight regarding consumer motivation and behavior.

The important consideration at this juncture is that Freud gives us one set of assumptions and concepts regarding personality and the manner in which its structure and functioning affects human behavior, and the existentialist school, the forerunner of which was Alfred Adler, gives us another. These two schools of thought can be contrasted categorically as the objective versus the subjective approaches to behavior and motivation. Freud reduced all motives to basic drives whereas the existentialists believe in the functional autonomy of drives. Some contrasts between these two opposing schools are listed below.[21]

Objective Psychology	*Subjective Psychology*
Minimizing consciousness	Full appreciation of consciousness
The depleted self	Self as central
Atomism	Holism
Emphasis on learning	Emphasis on perception
Stimulus-response	Cognitive theories
Determinism	Immanent teleology

---

[20] Barrett, *op. cit.,* p. 255.
[21] Taken from Heinz and Rowena Ansbacher, *The Individual Psychology of Alfred Adler* (New York: Harper & Row, Publishers, 1956), pp. 4-5.

This list, it has been recognized, bears an obvious resemblance to William James' memorable distinction between the tough-minded and the tender-minded temperaments.[22] The objective psychology is likely to be "hard-nosed" or tough-minded, while existentialism falls in the tender-minded category. These terms are further contrasted by the following list of descriptive qualifiers.[23]

Tough-minded	*Tender-minded*
Empiricist (going by fact)	Rationalist (going by principle)
Sensationalistic	Intellectualistic
Pessimistic	Optimistic
Pluralistic (from parts to whole)	Monistic (from whole to parts)
Irreligious	Religious
Fatalistic	Dogmatic

As we have just seen, there are several schools of existential psychology and many psychologists who are willing and anxious to wrap themselves in the mantle of existentialism. However, as in most disciplines, there is one whose contributions stand out above all others and whose work appears to integrate and unify the thinking of existentialists generally. This is Alfred Adler. Interestingly, Adler was at one time a contemporary of Freud and a member of the Freudian school. However, he soon found his views to be more and more alien to those of Freud and thus began his own school of individual or existential psychology. Adler's views, which we shall now summarize, are the basic tenets of existential psychology.[24]

The basic energizing force of human behavior, motivation, and thus personality development, is a single unifying force. This force is a striving for superiority, a striving from a felt minus situation toward a plus situation, from a feeling of inferiority toward superiority, perfection, totality. Adler argued that we all wish to overcome difficulties. We all strive to reach a goal the attainment of which will make us feel strong, superior, and complete. Adler argued that there is always present in human beings this compelling line of activity—this struggle to rise from an inferior to a superior position, from defeat to victory, from below to above.

The striving for perfection is innate, but not in a concrete way as if there were a drive which would in later life be capable of bringing everything to completion and which only needed to develop itself. The striving for perfection is innate in the sense that it is a part of life, an

---

[22] Ansbacher and Ansbacher, *op. cit.*, pp. 4-5.

[23] William James, *Pragmatism: A New Game for Some Old Ways of Thinking* (New York: Longmans, Green & Co., Inc., 1907), pp. 12-13.

[24] This summary and analysis of Adler's ideas, though essentially the author's, leans heavily on the Ansbacher and Ansbacher treatment cited previously.

urge without which life would be unthinkable. In short, it is part of every man's existence. Furthermore, it is not necessary that every man become a Nietzschean superman, only that each man be granted his ontological freedom, i.e., his freedom and ability to *become.*

Let us be sure that we in turn are "existential" in our analysis of existentialism. The parts divorced from the whole have little or no meaning; it is necessary to view each tenet in relationship to the aggregate.

In relation to the ceaseless striving onward, or becoming, another important aspect of existential psychology is that the striving receives its specific direction from an individually unique goal or self-idea, which, though influenced by biological and environmental factors, is ultimately the creation of the individual. This concept is closely related to the idea of self-image. Our self-image, built by us through our own cognitive processes, causes us to strive in our behavior, in order to come closer to attaining this image. Thus, our self-image is affected by our goals and our goal attainment is, to a degree, affected by our self-image. Because both the self-image and the goal are ideals, the goal toward which one strives is a fiction. Moreover, the goal is only dimly perceived. We are not really sure, always, in concrete terms, specifically what it is for which we are striving. We may want a better job, but just which job, or where, we do not know. We want an education, but for what specific purpose we may not be totally sure. Thus, the goal is largely unknown to the subject in specific concrete terms. It can be described to some extent in terms of the attitude and mood, "Oh! I know what I want, I just can't describe it." In truth, it is questionable *if* the subject really does know. Probably not. He has a glimpse of his goal, but the final goal may not yet be crystallized. In any event, the goal behavior of a subject becomes the key to understanding that individual. For the investigator it is a working hypothesis. Consequently, all the psychological processes of the individual form a self-consistent organization from the point of view of the goal. It is much like a play constructed, from the beginning, with the finale in view. This self-consistent personality structure is what Adler called the *style of life.* This style of life is the consistent movement, ontologically speaking, of the individual toward his goal.

Adler believed that what is frequently labeled the ego is nothing more than the *style* of the individual. Life style thus had an important and significant meaning. Adler believed that if psychology could give us a full and complete meaning of life style, it would automatically include all the phenomena now referred to, somewhat vaguely, as a self or ego.[25]

---

[25] See Gordon W. Allport, *Becoming: Basic Considerations for a Psychology of Personality* (New Haven, Conn.: Yale University Press, 1955).

In other words, a wholly adequate psychology of growth would discover all the activities and all the interrelations in life which are now either neglected or relegated to the ego. In effect, what all this means is that we must know more about man's existence. If we know the characteristics of his *life style*—the way he exists, his yearnings and strivings, the goals, accomplishments, or conquests he wishes to achieve—then we may begin to learn something about the nature of man's motivation and behavior.

This is the central theme of existential psychology. However, one or two important factors essential to a full understanding of the concept remain to be discussed. Biological factors and past history as determiners of behavior are important in the sense that they do not function as direct causes but only in a probabilistic sense. The individual uses the objective factors only in accordance with his style of life. The opinions of the individual regarding himself and the world, his "apperceptive schema," his interpretations, all as aspects of his style of life, influence every psychological process. The individual is immersed in his environment; he is a part of his total social situation. He cannot be analyzed in a vacuum as an isolated human being. Therefore, all important life problems, including the whole of *becoming,* are social problems. All values become social values.

Now we are ready to postulate on the basis of our analysis and summary of basic existential concepts a new theory of human behavior and motivation, one which is not an essence theory or, necessarily, deterministic. The reader will recall the Freudian interpretation and analysis of motivation and behavior stated earlier. Freud believed behavior and motivation to be determined by the instincts, as a result of being charged with psychic energy. He further believed that the aim of the instincts was to remove bodily excitations and restore the person to a state of mental and physiological quiescence (freedom from tension). In short, he believed in an equilibrium theory of personality and behavior, a theory which has been shown to be misleading, if not false, and one which offers little insight or explanation or possibility for generalizing about customer behavior. The ideal Freudian subject would be a vegetable—one who was in a constant state of equilibrium. And the quickest way to arrive and remain in this state would be a frontal lobotomy.

Stemming from the existential point of view is a different set of axioms regarding behavior which arise from existence. Man does not avoid tensions, or necessarily wish to reduce them, as long as they remain balanced and consistent with his life style. Instead, he seeks out tensions and excitements via his process of becoming. In his search for fictional goals and problem solving, he looks for means of enhancing his experiences, of adding to life's glamour and excitement. He wishes to strive and to become and those impediments or forces which get between him and his goals cause him ontological anxiety. This anxiety heightens his striving, intensifies his behavior and causes him to increase his search for effective solutions. Motivation, therefore, can be viewed in the light of *growth motives* which call for the maintenance of tension or excitement in the interest of distant and often unattainable goals. Existential man living in a Freudian world would be apt to kick the windows out of this crystal palace or, just for the fun of it, run next door to stick pins in his neighbor.

THE EXISTENTIAL CONSUMER

Are consumers existential? Does existentialism and its concepts from either philosophy or psychology shed any light or offer any insight to help explain, predict, alter, or influence consumer behavior? The answer would seem to be an obvious yes. The existential concept regarding personality development and therefore motivation and behavior certainly appears to be a more logical and more realistic explanation of these phenomena than does the Freudian model. Yet the Freudian model, or salient aspects of it, is still the principal "model" around which customer behavior is analyzed. These models have as their central thesis the idea that consumers are motivated by conscious or unconscious forces toward some sort of behavior or decision whose aim is to reduce tension and thus return the individual to a state of emotional and/or physical equilibrium. Thus, hidden "motives" and semiconscious or unconscious "mechanisms" are central to the Freudian model.[26]

As we have seen thus far, existential psychology is concerned with the "individualizing manner," which places special emphasis on the life-style concept. This really makes existential psychology something of an *idiographic science.* The term idiographic pertains to laws which are particular to the individual case, while nomothetic formulations are laws of general validity. It must be pointed out that existential psychology, like other sciences, developed some important nomothetic principles; the concept of compensation, the striving for superiority or becoming, and the idea of social interest all meet the requirements for nomothetic

---

[26] See, for example, Arthur Kornhauser and Paul Lazarsfeld, *The Techniques of Market Research from the Standpoint of a Psychologist* (New York: American Management Association, 1935). The date of this publication would indicate that perhaps these ideas may at least by now be somewhat dated or that subsequent research would have altered our views and reliance on the Freudian concepts, yet this article appears in a collection entitled "Paradigms of the Consumer" in a recent collection of works published under the general title *Marketing Models: Quantitative and Behavior,* ed. Ralph Day and published by International Publishing Company, Scranton, Pa. (1964), pp. 13-26.

principles. The important point, for our purposes, is to recognize that the emphasis rested, in the final analysis, on the idiographic aspects such as style of life, the opinion of the self, and the individual goal. It must be remembered that whatever generalizations we derive from our knowledge and analysis of existentialism must be based on a study of *existence* and whatever conclusions are drawn about the nature of behavior, i.e., the essence of a given target market or market segment, can only come after the *existence* of the target or segment.

What nomothetic generalizations might then be postulated regarding consumer behavior from the idiographic principles derived from studying existence? It would appear that, first of all, our conventional model of consumer behavior would have to be modified considerably, especially to rid it of many of its voodoo-like characteristics which can be attributed to none other than Freud. Our model would focus upon the intelligence and cognitive aspects of behavior, unlike one which viewed the consumer as some quivering, child-like apparition, taking its direction and momentum from some unseen set of deterministic forces. In short, the model would rest fundamentally on certain existential considerations.

The central focus of the existential model remains much the same as earlier. It begins with a central hypothesis that consumer behavior is problem-solving behavior. The problem solving is inextricably bound up with and a part of the individual's life style or *Dasein. Therefore, the purchasing and acquisition of goods are important means or vehicles in the individual's ontological or becoming process.* People, it now becomes apparent, are purchasing goods and services because the goods and services are a means of attaining what we called earlier their fictional final goal. The purchase of goods and services serves their ontological needs in various degrees. Thus, the needs hierarchy takes on even more meaningful aspects. Customers have minimum needs and these needs, for most Americans in the affluent society, are attained and served by a minimum of ontological striving. However, other higher-level needs, the satisfaction of which may not be readily available to all, call forth a higher level of ontological and cognitive activity. Needs, whether high or low in the level of the hierarchy, are relative to the individual, depending on his goals and his life style.

Therefore, it might be concluded that the motives or forces which are autonomous and arise within the individual, but which impel certain kinds of behavior, take on two characteristics. In some instances, certain behavior may be the result of specific *deficit* motives. This may be strikingly true in the case of certain biological and physiological needs. A man is hungry, for example, and craves food. The craving and excitation resulting from hunger increase certain tensions. However, having eaten, the individual returns to a state of quiescence—the tension is gone.

His behavior might easily therefore be described as goal-oriented and tension-eliminating resulting from deficit motivation. Deficit motivation, as has been stated, may offer an adequate explanation for certain kinds of consumer behavior responses, and for certain individuals or groups. However, this explanation is inadequate and incomplete for other aspects of consumer behavior. Most behavior is manifested for higher needs than biological and physiological satisfaction. For example, in the affluent United States, only a small portion of consumer behavior can be explained as an urge to satisfy basic needs. Man not only needs, he wants. And it is his ontological yearning and seeking which causes him to want. It is this aspect of behavior which Freud and most of his followers have missed, and which has never been adequately incorporated into a meaningful model of consumer behavior. Man is seeking to become. This, as was stated, gives him a certain futuristically oriented momentum. He seeks goods and services which will enable him to express or find himself during and throughout this ontological process. Thus, this existential man discovers that salvation comes to him who ceaselessly bestirs himself in the pursuit of objectives that in the end are not fully attained. The existential man is not necessarily guided in his consumer behavior by an urge to reduce tension. He seeks it. He looks for goods and services which offer him a heightened sense of satisfaction. He wants an "exciting" automobile or an "exciting" house in an "exciting" neighborhood filled with "exciting" people. This idea is most compatible and consistent with our earlier statement about a needs hierarchy and especially pertinent in regard to the self-actualizing personality. The self-actualizer is one who is striving for a greater sense of excitement or enjoyment of life's pleasures. He is existential in the sense that he wishes to have, to know, and to become. An overwhelming amount of consumer motivation and behavior can be characterized as existential or self-actualizing. This behavior is called, in existential terminology, *propriate striving.*[27]

The proprium is in effect the individual's personality, but it is really more because it includes all aspects of personality that make for inward unity. Thus *propriate striving*, from the standpoint of consumer behavior, is that pre-purchase, purchase, and post-purchase behavior on the part of the individual which attempts to unify and integrate the purchase idea, or situation, with his own life style or cognitive map. Allport develops the concept of the proprium and propriate striving as serving as a unifying agent in several dimensions or aspects of behavior, including self-identity, ego-enhancement, ego-extension, and as a rationalizing agent.[28] Consumer behavior as propriate striving behavior fits this scheme

[27] *Propriate striving* and the discussion of the concept of the *Proprium* are taken from Allport, *op. cit.,* pp. 36-68.
[28] *Ibid.,* pp. 42-47.

rather well. Consumers, it would appear, buy goods for reasons of more clearly defining in their mind's eye their identity. Hence, the expression often heard, "That product looks just like you." There is little doubt that consumer behavior is almost totally ego-involved, not at all in the Freudian sense, but rather as ego or self is used in the life-style concept. Finally, much behavior of the consumer is a unifying or goal-directed kind of activity, the principal purpose of which is to, in some sense, synthesize inner needs and outer reality. The true or essential characteristic of *propriate striving* is that its goals are, strictly speaking, unattainable. The unity which propriate striving confers upon personality is never the unity of fulfillment, of repose, or of reduced tension. Our reach, and thus our propriate striving, continues to exceed our grasp.

A critical factor in existential consumer behavior, and one which offers fresh insight for analysis, centers around the concepts of *guilt* and *anxiety*. Anxiety is ontological; that is, it is a part of the ontological process. Anxiety arises because of man's knowledge that he may fail and attain less than that for which he strives. Remember that he has set himself a goal. It is fuzzy and ambiguous and, perhaps, poorly defined. But nonetheless, he "knows" what he wants and for what he is striving in a fictional sense. The consumer with budget or other purchase constraints is a good example. Classical economics has always held that this consumer would attempt to maximize his utility or satisfaction derived from spending this budget. But, in truth, the consumer doesn't know how to do this because he really does not know what specifically it is that he wants. In other words, our consumer is in a situation of decision making or problem solving under conditions of partial ignorance. However, the thought that as a decision maker, he, the consumer, might fail or attain something less than satisfaction causes him to be anxious. He can rid himself of this anxiety by relinquishing some of his freedom. Because his freedom is his choice, he can forego choosing, or pass the buck to some other member of the family. However, relinquishing freedom or one's choices is a form of nonbeing. The existential view is that man must be anxious if he is to fulfill his potentialities. This anxiety will very likely motivate the individual to be more deliberate in his search for effective decision processes as well as effective decisions. *In effect, the more anxious the consumer is about a given purchase situation, the greater the perceived risk surrounding that situation.* In short, in purchase situations that are an important part of the consumer's propriate striving, and that he believes to be vital as manifestations of his becoming, the more anxious the consumer is likely to become and the more deliberate and careful he is likely to be.

Guilt arises on the part of consumers if they believe they may have made a wrong choice, one which sidetracks or impedes them in their ontological process. For example, if a consumer buys a product and later has doubts as to how well, in the light of alternative products or alternative goals, this product serves his concept of self or propriate striving, he is likely to feel guilt. This post-purchase phenomenon has been observed before and discussed to some extent in the literature. Leon Festinger has described certain psychological consequences pertaining to consumer decisions: "dissonance" occurs if, after a decision, a person is faced with doubt that he made the right choice.[29] Festinger was correct in one sense of the word, but he went too far, because at one point he argued that dissonance occurs after all consumer decisions. "Dissonance then will be a result of the simple act of having made a decision. Consequently, one may expect to see manifestations of pressures to reduce dissonance after a choice has been made."[30] This is dubious, especially in light of our existential analysis. True, if the consumer has doubts about his choice and these doubts manifest themselves as ontological guilt resulting from his failure to achieve that which he perceived or thought he should, then dissonance arises and we have now something which we lacked before, an existential explanation for it. But what about the consumer who, after having made a choice, discovers that he is even more satisfied than he imagined he might be. This could hardly be called "dissonance." Instead, what we have here is an example of ontological acceleration.

In summary, consumer behavior might very well be viewed within the framework of heuristic problem solving. The behavior of the consumer is goal-directed and, therefore, purposive. His goal is often non-specific; he is open to recommendation and suggestion; thus, learning and communication can be considered as important means for helping the consumer in his propriate-striving consumer behavior. The consumer cannot be manipulated or controlled in any mechanistic sense; his behavior is largely directed along the lines of search and discovery. Therefore it is *heuristic*. Inasmuch as it is heuristic, he develops certain rules of thumb which he utilizes as guidelines to shape and structure his behavior. He learns what later become habitual modes of reducing tension, and yet he learns also that some of his past satisfactions become as useless as yesterday's newspaper. He looks for some excitement, though at the same time he is still interested in stability and variety. He learns to rely on dependable modes of reducing tensions, but he is constantly sloughing off old habits and taking risks in searching out new means of problem solving and becoming. The existential consumer recognizes that it is only through risk-taking and variation that growth or becoming can occur. But he also recognizes that risk-taking and variation are fraught

---

[29] See Leon Festinger, *A Theory of Cognitive Dissonance* (Evanston, Ill.: Row, Peterson, and Company, 1957).

[30] *Ibid.*, p. 35.

with new and unavoidable tensions, which he views with both anxiety and contempt.

The existential consumer looks for principles or devices that contribute to the reduction in the average search for a solution.[31] The existential consumer is more a *satisficer* than a *maximizer*. He looks for solutions that are satisfactory and consistent with his cognitive structure and life style. Maximization is out of the question, because he "knows" he does not have all the relevant information necessary for maximization. He is a decision maker under conditions of uncertainty. Since he is looking for "satisfactory" solutions, he attempts to unify and bring in balance the various variables of his decision model. The variables are of two types: *inputs* and *outputs*. The inputs may be time, money, energy, or, in an existential sense, commitment. The outputs are as many and diverse as there are decision makers. Essentially however, the existential consumer views the output as a certain satisfaction which carries him up or toward his potential. The existential consumer, in light of these considerations and considering the heuristic nature of his behavior, is likely to be more interested in optimal solution procedures than in optimal solutions.

IMPLICATIONS FOR MARKETERS

The existential consumer's behavior is manifesting itself in today's market place in many important ways. For one thing, consumers' attitudes regarding status are changing markedly. Today's consumer is often buying and searching for goods with which to impress himself rather than the community. For this attitude to develop, it was first necessary for more people simply to have more money. Today's affluent consumer says in the market place much what he says in the classroom or in his recreation room at home, "I am my choices." Recognizing this, the consumer sets about to seek goods that are truly fitted to his needs and desires, not those of the mythical Mrs. Jones.

American consumers are developing some immunity from the blandishments of advertising, and some of this immunity has come from the consumers' reaction to the existential commandment "Know thyself." Consumers today have a greater sense of identity and individuality than ever before, and they are finding the advertisements and appeals of some marketers in such hideously poor taste that they not only refuse to react favorably to these advertisements, but in fact mentally blacklist the manufacturer's entire product line.

---

[31] A. Newell, J. C. Shaw, and H. A. Simon, "The Process of Creative Thinking," *The RAND Corporation Paper,* P-1320, August, 1958.

The consumer's quest for identity is the motive force behind much of what we call fashion merchandising today. But fashion is no longer the privilege of a few New York or Boston ladies in the east or movie stars on the West Coast or rich Dallas ladies in the Southwest. Today's market for fashion merchandise has expanded and includes many persons from all walks of life throughout the entire economic and social spectrum. Fashion merchandisers as well as designers need to think small, not large. They need to think in terms of individuals, not masses. Miniature but lucrative markets are emerging all over the country for which it is worth developing marketing programs.

Many of today's existential consumers feel trapped by the encroachments of civilization and especially the increasing abstraction of reality. People find it hard to see their place in the total reality of things. They are lost in the large office buildings; they find it difficult to grasp the meaning and significance of their lives. They feel an increasing insecurity in regard to their total surroundings. As a result, many are retreating to a safer, more secure, or more familiar reality, the reality of the backyard, the seashore, the mountain retreat, the basement workshop, the art gallery, the museum—where life is somewhat more concrete, more objective, and less abstract. Existential motivations are causing people to bring themselves to a point of commitment and involvement. This yearning for less abstraction is not a form of retreat or nonbeing. The existential consumer wishes to commit himself and become involved with the here and now. He is not running and hiding from a world which he doesn't understand. He simply wishes to take for himself a "slice of life" which is warm, real, and meaningful and to enjoy it. He is buying goods and services that facilitate his propriate striving, his sense of becoming, his yearning for identity and individuality—guitars, fishing and hunting equipment, boats, motorcycles, automobiles, houses, clothing, and even food are means which serve these needs.

Are marketers aware? Are they, to any degree, existential in the sense that they "know themselves"? Do they recognize the vast institutional role played by marketing firms individually, as well as in the aggregate? The answer is in the affirmative, but with qualifications. Most marketers do, but too many, unfortunately, do not or don't care.

We return now almost to the point from which we departed. Our analysis began with the analysis of "The Marketing Concept" and the principles which underlie this managerial philosophy. In the intervening pages we have woven a more general theory or context in which to place our marketing firm and we have given it a more complete and, hopefully, better unified framework within which to analyze consumer behavior.

The marketing concept underlines the importance of consumer behavior. It recognizes the key role that consumers' needs and motives play in the success or failure of any marketing program. If this is true, as it is, *then* marketers must know fully not only customer needs but their own strengths and weaknesses, their own comparative advantage. This knowledge is needed in order to build "marketing strategies," which we defined earlier as the movement and countermovement in pursuit of goals. The difficulty often encountered is that a firm will build a marketing strategy to meet the exigencies of a given time and place. But time, and consumers, march on. The firm remains transfixed, and its effectiveness therefore wanes. What is needed is a faster reaction time resulting from better linkages and hookups between the firm and its market.

The marketing concept underlines the importance of marketing research. And many marketing firms do marketing research. But if research and research methodologies continue to be based on older, outmoded theories of consumer behavior, then the effort is wasted. What may be needed is not more research but research predicated on different attitudes or directed toward different aspects of behavior and motivation. We need better theories—more unified, more explanatory, more descriptive and more predictive—regarding customer motivation and behavior. "The need for a psychological view grows out of the very nature of market research. For that research is aimed predominantly at *knowledge by means of which to forecast and control consumer behavior*." [32] How right and yet how *wrong!* Controlling, in the literal sense of the word, is anathema to the existential consumer. It robs him of his freedom and choice. Control is fine for a production process concerned with quality output, but it is highly questionable whether in a free society control really has any place at all in the firm's relationship with its consumers. The firm can and must control or accommodate its behavior to the needs of the market place, but it cannot, or must not, attempt to accommodate the market place or customers to the will of the firm. Unfortunately the viewpoint of some firms that they can control customer behavior still stems from the archaic notion of deterministic forces. Marketers all too often want to be puppet masters and pull the strings of their subjects willy-nilly.

What marketers really need to do—and some are trying—is to get back to a genuine reality. Consumers are tired of watching white knights, birds turning into soap bottles, washing machines sprouting from the floor. They are tired and a little more than indignant at seeing the skeptical housewife who finds her washing not just white, but luminescent, the round-table discussion about the transforming powers of a hair dye, the harried gentleman for whom life is regularly made beautiful again by a restorative headache elixir. They are tired and indignant be-

[32] Kornhauser and Lazarsfeld, *op. cit.*, p. 14.

cause these are not real people with real problems and the viewers cannot identify—they can only be repulsed. Too much of what we have called psychology in the study of customer behavior has really been the study of tricks we use to avoid the anxiety of absolute novelty or ignorance by making believe the future will be like the past.

Our thinking regarding customer behavior has been conditioned by a belief in essences, i.e., what a man is determines how he behaves. And our conceptualization is an essence configuration. What we need is a new conceptualization regarding behavior—one which emphasizes that the way a man behaves determines what he is. We need to know more about the way man behaves. In short, we need more, much more, study and understanding of what might be called *consumer style*. Style is the stamp of individuality impressed upon our adaptive behavior. In our culture and climate we all wear clothes, but our style of dress is individual and expressive. The same is true regarding all our adaptive acts from hand shaking, or composing a symphony, to strolling down the street.[33] A task for marketing research in the future is to find methods for relating style to its fundaments in personality and, in turn, relating this phenomenon to adaptive behavior in the market place.

Marketers need to realize that a man's culture is one of the sets of circumstances, or a part of the *Dasein*, out of which he develops or draws his style of life. Thus, they need to examine and explore this aspect of personality—this subjective side of culture. That the cultural approach yields valuable facts, we cannot possibly deny, for culture indeed is a major condition in becoming.

What is needed, of course, is a better science of human and thus consumer behavior, a science which would serve as a basis for marketing management. There are several principles on which such a science might be formulated.[34] First, the science must be relevant to the distinguishing characteristics of what we are trying to understand, in this case the human being. It must be relevant, that is, to the distinctive qualities and characteristics that constitute the human being as *human,* that constitute the self as self, characteristics without which this being would not be what he is, namely, a human being.

A second guiding principle is in opposition to the assumption in conventional science that we explain the more complex by the simpler. In the case of consumer behavior, and from the point of view of the marketer, the simpler can be understood and explained only in terms of the more complex. In short, we need to stop thinking of customer behavior from the point of view of a man representing the lowest common denominator of society.

---

[33] Allport, *op. cit.,* p. 78.
[34] Adapted from May, *op. cit.,* pp. 39-40.

The third and final guiding principle which is to underline our "marketing science" is that our fundamental unit of study in consumer behavior is not just man but man with a *problem* existing in a world of reality. And this consumer with his problem is one with which the marketer must react, and interact. Thus, this world and the understanding of it are situations in which both "persons," customer and firm, must participate. This point has far-reaching implications, not only because it bears directly on our research and practice in *marketing*, but because it also suggests the guidelines of an existential approach to the utilization of learning theory and the role of communication in developing better, more effective, marketing strategies.

Having developed a more general theory of consumer behavior based upon existential concepts, we shall turn our attention in the next section to a discussion of learning theory and the learning processes as determinants of adaptive, problem-solving consumer purchase behavior.

PART THREE

THE LEARNING
PROCESS: VEHICLE
FOR ADAPTIVE CHANGE

THREE

Motives and
Motivation Research

Within the past few years, students and practitioners of marketing have become increasingly interested in the application of the behavioral sciences to marketing problems. This interest has centered largely around psychological studies of the needs or motives of consumers and has become known as motivation research.

> Psychological research, or what commonly goes under the name of "motivation research," has received new attention during the last decade when the postwar sellers' market changed into a buyers' market. This economic change stimulated widespread recognition of the need to understand the consumer thoroughly.[1]

By attempting to understand the motives which initiate consumer behavior, the researcher hopes to uncover certain information which will be applicable in the marketing situation. Application of the research findings has the end objective of improving marketing strategies. The basic motives of the con-

---

[1] Herta Herzog, "Behavioral Science Concepts for Analyzing the Consumer," in *Marketing and the Behavioral Sciences*, ed. Perry Bliss (Boston: Allyn & Bacon, Inc., 1963), p. 76.

sumer must be understood in order to increase the efficiency and effectiveness of these strategies.

However, the application of the behavioral sciences to marketing is not a panacea. One writer has expressed this idea as follows:

> The attempts so far have been quite encouraging but they represent only a beginning. Motivation researchers have been busy doing specific studies; we have not yet had enough time to think through what we are doing and what general findings emerge. We have made uneven use of the available behavioral science concepts, and for some of the marketer's problems the behavioral sciences do not yet offer concepts or methods.[2]

Motivation research, as the name implies, concerns itself mainly with the motives or drives of the individual which in turn initiate his behavior. Behavior, defined as the actions or conduct of an individual, is of a dynamic nature, that is, behavior is modified and it changes over time. This modification or change in human behavior is known as learning and plays an important part in the understanding of behavior.

James Bayton has divided human behavior into three classifications:

> . . . motivation, cognition and learning . . . each broad area is pertinent to particular problems of consumer behavior. All three are pertinent to a comprehensive understanding of consumer behavior.[3]

Motivation, according to Bayton and other writers, while important to an understanding of human behavior, is not the only factor involved. Any attempt to understand consumer behavior must therefore expand the study of motives to include cognition and learning as well.

> It is important, therefore, that businessmen understand how people *learn to like,* for this will explain to some extent how they come to adopt objects and ideas.[4]

The objective of this section will be to study the various theories of learning and their possible applications to marketing and consumer behavior. Because the field of human behavior is complex and specialized, the focus here will be on the learning process and its effects upon behavior—specifically, consumer behavior.

---

[2] *Ibid.*

[3] "Motivation, Cognition, Learning—Basic Factors in Consumer Behavior," in *Marketing and the Behavioral Sciences,* ed. Perry Bliss (Boston: Allyn & Bacon, Inc., 1963), p. 45.

[4] Gerald Zaltman, *Marketing: Contributions from the Behavioral Sciences* (New York: Harcourt, Brace & World, 1965), p. 19.

While motives and motivation research will be discussed to some extent, the intent will be only to point out the need for investigation into the other aspects of behavior and to show the difficulty in using motivation research to solve marketing problems. It is, of course, realized that motivation, cognition, and learning are interrelated and therefore the discussion of one factor of behavior will necessarily have at least some reference to the others.

Our intent at this juncture is to point out the effects of the learning process on consumer behavior. Since studies of behavior as applied to marketing are generally based upon motivation studies, which, in turn, are based on some of the methodologies and theories of the social sciences, it would seem profitable to begin with a discussion of motives and motivation research. It is also the intent of this chapter to point out the limitations of motivation research in fully understanding consumer behavior.

MOTIVES: THE IMPETUS TO BEHAVIOR

Motives have been defined as "a conscious experience or subconscious condition which serves as a factor in determining an individual's behavior or social conduct in a given situation." [5] Motives are those wishes, desires, or drives which bring about the sequence of events known as personal or human behavior. These motives or drives (the two terms are often used synonymously) can be either conscious or subconscious in nature.

Consciousness, as the term is used in this text, is any experience that we are aware of in life. As defined by Moore, "consciousness is a generic term that we use to designate the various forms of experience that we are aware of in our mental life." [6] Conscious motives, then, are recognized as such by the individual; e.g., the biogenic or physical drive of thirst is recognized by the individual as a need satisfied by drinking water or some other beverage.

Unconsciousness, as used here, refers to those experiences of the individual of which he is not aware. Therefore, unconscious motives are those which are in the person's subconscious,[7] and of which he is unaware. As will be pointed out later, it is this type of motive which is most important in motivation research. And, since the individual himself is unaware of these motives, they are the most difficult to uncover.

---

[5] Howard C. Warren, ed., *Dictionary of Psychology* (New York: Houghton Mifflin Company, 1934), p. 171.

[6] Thomas Verner Moore, *The Driving Forces of Human Nature* (New York: Grune & Stratton, Inc., 1948), p. 63.

[7] ". . . pertains to processes of which the individual is not aware, but which appear to be otherwise akin to the processes of (conscious) experience." *Dictionary of Psychology*, p. 265.

CLASSIFICATION OF MOTIVES

Motives are generally considered to be of two types: those of a physiological or biogenic nature and those of a psychological or psychogenic type.

The physiological needs are generally agreed upon by social scientists to be those of hunger, thirst, warmth, and sex. However, the psychogenic or psychological needs are harder to define and are, therefore, not universally agreed upon in the literature.

One author has grouped these needs into three broad categories: [8]

1. Affectional needs—the need to form and maintain warm, harmonious and emotionally satisfying relations with others.

2. Ego-bolstering needs—the need to enhance or promote the personality; to gain prestige and recognition; to satisfy the ego through domination of others.

3. Ego-defensive needs—the need to protect the personality; to avoid physical and psychological harm; to avoid ridicule and "loss of face"; to prevent loss of prestige; to avoid or to obtain relief from anxiety.

Thus we see that motives can be many and varied.[9] In other words, while behavior begins when a person is motivated by some need, this does not necessarily mean that there is only one motive. In fact, it has been found that behavior is a response to many needs or drives—some taking one direction and some another.

Motivation arises out of tension systems which create a state of disequilibrium for the individual. This triggers a sequence of psychological events directed toward the selection of a goal which the individual *anticipates* will bring about release from the tensions and the selection of patterns of action which he *anticipates* will bring him to the goal.[10]

This multitude of motives, each exerting its influence on the behavior pattern of the individual and the resulting goal direction of his behavior, indicates a hierarchy of motives. As one writer has expressed it, "we should not be surprised if we find organization of drives by some sort of ruling drive; the consequent shifting of satisfaction and dissatisfaction, approvals and disapprovals; approval or disapproval of the ruling

---

[8] Bayton, *op. cit.*, p. 46.
[9] For an extensive list of motives, see Darrell Blaine Lucas and Steuart Britt, *Advertising Psychology and Research* (New York: McGraw-Hill Book Company, 1958), pp. 96-102.
[10] Bayton, *op. cit.*, p. 45.

drive, with consequent redirection of the central tendency." [11]

Maslow has defined a hierarchy of needs which begins with the lowest needs—those of thirst, hunger, etc.—and ends with the need for self-actualization or self-realization.[12] Accordingly, the needs at the lower end of the hierarchy must be met before the individual can begin to satisfy his higher needs. Maslow, however, does not say that the individual does not have the next need until the first is satisfied but rather that some needs, specifically those on the lower end of the scale, must be met before going on to the next. In other words, one drive takes precedence over the others.

This variety of needs, then, complicates the study of motives and hence the work of motivation research. It means that to be successful one must not only bring to light an individual's motives but he must also distinguish between these motives as to their preference and their strength of influence on that individual's behavior. What may be an important motive to one individual will not necessarily be the ruling motive for another unless, of course, all other sociological, biological, psychological, and environmental factors are the same.

DEFINITION OF MOTIVATION RESEARCH

Motivation research, especially pertaining to the area of marketing, has been defined in many different ways; though to some, it has no meaning at all.

According to an article in the September, 1959, *Management Review*, two studies up to that time revealed that the educated business community was lacking in a complete understanding of motivation research.

> In the summer of 1958, *Tide* magazine asked its panelists (representing many of the country's top advertisers and agencies) what they understood MR to be. Only 5 per cent claimed they "understood MR thoroughly": 76 per cent said they "knew something about it." The remainder admitted very little knowledge (and a few gruffly barked that they "simply couldn't care less").[13]

---

[11] George A. Coe, *The Motives of Men* (New York: Charles Scribner's Sons, 1928), p. 94.

[12] A. H. Maslow, *Motivation and Personality* (New York: Harper & Row, Publishers, 1954).

[13] George Christopoulos, "What Makes People Buy? A Progress Report on Motivation Research Today," *The Management Review*, September, 1959, p. 64.

Another study cited in the same article revealed that "research men stated that top personnel in their own fields had no 'understanding' of the very tools they were expected to employ." [14]

While this lack of understanding has probably been somewhat alleviated in the past five years (at least by those employed in MR), it is still safe to assume that motivation research is a somewhat foggy idea to many people. It has been defined as:

> a special type of marketing research that concentrates on developing new concepts in all phases of business through the use of theories and practices adopted from the behavioral sciences, that are concerned with the nature and development of the human personality and the social forces that act upon it.[15]

Another simpler definition is that presented by L. Edward Scriven, in a speech to the American Marketing Association in 1955:

> Motivational analysis can be defined simply as a set of tools, borrowed from the fields of psychology and sociology, to uncover and evaluate the motives or drives that are back of human behavior in the consumer market.[16]

Many other definitions of the meaning and scope of motivation research could be presented; however, it should be evident that these definitions have basically the same meaning. They all indicate that motivation research uses the same general theories and concepts of the social sciences. Also, it is clear that the purpose of motivation research is to explain or predict the behavior of individuals in a given set of circumstances.

The main difference in motivation research as used and defined by various sources is in the techniques employed and the scope and use of the research findings. The various techniques used in motivation research will be discussed in the latter part of this chapter.

ORIGINS OF MOTIVATION RESEARCH

Motivation research is by no means a new tool of analysis for the marketer. It has been a basis for psychological research for a number of years and, as applied to the analysis of consumer behavior, has been in

---

[14] *Ibid.*

[15] *Ibid.*, p. 64.

[16] Adapted from a talk, "Rationality and Irrationality in Motivational Research," by L. Edward Scriven, given to the Washington, D.C. chapter of the American Marketing Association, June 23, 1955. Reprinted in *Motivation and Market Behavior*, ed. Robert Ferber and Hugh G. Wales (Homewood, Ill.: Richard D. Irwin, Inc., 1958), p. 65.

use since before World War II.[17] In 1935, Paul F. Lazarsfeld, founder of the Bureau of Applied Social Research at Columbia University, wrote a chapter on motivation research for a book published by the American Marketing Association.[18] However, it was not until after World War II that motivation research came into its own.

There was little need for understanding the consumer during the war: with rationing and the scarcity of consumer goods, manufacturers could not even supply the existing demand let alone try to create a larger demand for their products. This seller's market continued for a few years after the war while supplies were still relatively low and consumer spending high. As the seller's market ended, however, marketers were faced with the problem of creating demand for their goods. This involved a change in both thought and strategy. And a part of this new strategy was to utilize all available marketing tools to their best advantage. Advertising had to be effective and products had to appeal to the consumer. It was this attempt to appeal to the consumer's desires that led to increasing use of motivation research. The seller could not appeal to the needs and desires of the consumer until he knew what these desires were. In an attempt to find out, attention turned to the behavioral sciences and specifically to those areas of the behavioral sciences which had developed methods and techniques for the systematic study of behavior.

TECHNIQUES OF MOTIVATION RESEARCH

Basically, techniques used in motivation research are the same as those employed by social scientists in behavioral studies conducted over the past seventy-five years. These methods have been used by psychologists in investigating behavior in a variety of approaches, depending upon the individual doing the research.

The so-called laboratory psychologist, utilizing the oldest approach to motivation study, emphasizes the biological drives or body needs, using as his main technique the study of animals.[19] While the laboratory psychologist confines his study to these biological drives, many of the theories and data are applicable, and have actually been applied, to human motivation.

The clinical psychologist places his main emphasis on the psychological influences on motivational patterns.[20]

---

[17] Christopoulos, *op. cit.*, p. 62.

[18] *Ibid.*

[19] For a discussion of these various techniques, see Charles Cannell, "A Psychologist's View," adapted from a talk, "A Psychologist Looks at Marketing," reprinted in *Motivation and Market Behavior*, pp. 4-11.

[20] *Ibid.*

It is not that he regards the biological factors as unimportant in determining motivation, but because at the psychological level he can best control, influence, and change motivational patterns.[21]

The clinician, according to Cannell, recognizes the conflict between motives and acceptable behavior in society. He sees motives as being repressed in the individual's subconscious because of this conflict between more or less natural drives and social norms. Depending upon the degree of conflict, the motive may or may not be recognized by the individual.

Another important view of motivation is that held by the social psychologist. In this area of study of behavior, perception as well as motivation is emphasized, since man reacts in his social environment. According to the social psychologist, we can understand motivation only to the extent that we also understand the environment in which the individual is reacting.[22] The social psychologist uses theories from the field of Gestalt psychology while the clinical psychologist utilizes principally the tools of psychoanalysis associated with Freud. Psychoanalysis considers behavior as determined by instinctive drives which unconsciously motivate man to seek goals that he may not even recognize. Gestalt psychology, on the other hand, is "concerned with goal-directed behavior and rational use of the resources of the environment to attain conscious ends." [23]

More will be said about these various theories and approaches in other chapters; it is important to note here that most motivation research to date has been involved with the techniques of the clinical psychologist.

Motivation research calls for techniques different from the quantitative methods of traditional market research. Statistical market research has generally used the questionnaire method of gathering information on physical characteristics and the physical composition of markets. Research directed toward understanding the consumer's motives cannot be obtained through these direct techniques of information gathering. Although statistical market research data indicate what people spend their money for and in what proportion this income is distributed among products and services, it is increasingly necessary to find out *why* people spend their incomes on certain items.

Once we understand the determinants of motivation we must realize too, that such knowledge alone contains more information than a ques-

[21] *Ibid.*, p. 5.
[22] *Ibid.*
[23] Wroe Alderson, "Advertising Strategy and Theories of Motivation," *Cost and Profit Outlook,* December, 1956, reprinted in *Motivation and Market Behavior,* p. 13.

tionnaire survey can supply, because it makes us see into the human mind.[24]

Because motives are sometimes hidden even from the individual, it is necessary to probe deeper in order to find these undiscovered or unknown motives.

Leonhard has pictured the human mind (in a very simple form) as consisting of three layers (see Fig. 5). The first two layers, the white

Figure 5: Three Areas of the Mind.

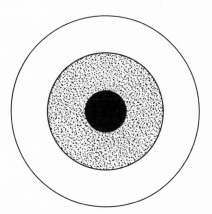

White and Gray: Top of the mind;
  conscious
Black: Unconscious; sub-conscious

White: Rationalizations, beliefs, attitudes, existing in verbal forms
Gray: Concepts, feelings, emotions which can be verbalized
Black: Nonverbal, nonrational emotions

Source: Dietz Leonhard, *Consumer Research with Projective Techniques* (Shenandoah, Iowa: World Publishing Co., 1955), p. 43.

area and the gray area, are conscious layers of the mind. It is with these areas that motivation research deals. The black area, according to Leonhard, is the realm of the psychiatrist and consists of nonverbal, nonrational emotions.[25] However, this "black" area seems to be of the greatest importance in understanding consumer behavior. Leonhard does not deny its importance, but is merely considering in his discussion those methods which are most useful to the nonpsychologist business researcher. He points out that by using certain techniques the first two layers of the conscious mind can be explored to yield some of the answers needed in successfully marketing a product. As implied above, trained psychologists and more refined techniques may be needed to bring to light the subconscious motives of man.

Techniques applied in motivation research have been borrowed from the behavioral sciences, and in some cases modified to enhance their usefulness. The type of technique used depends to a large extent on the particular problem and the training of the researcher.

[24] Dietz Leonhard, *Consumer Research with Projective Techniques* (Shenandoah, Iowa: World Publishing Co., 1955), p. 33.
[25] *Ibid.,* p. 44.

Of the various techniques available in motivation research, one of the more popular, and sometimes highly criticized, is that of depth interviewing. Drawn from the field of clinical psychology, depth interviewing has been modified in most instances by shortening the length and scope of the interviews. Basically, this type of interviewing asks indirect questions which are interpreted along with the subtle reactions of the interviewee. While the questions are not direct, the interviewer tries to give the interviews some central direction toward the product or problem at hand.[26]

Usually, these interviews are limited to from 50 to 200 individuals.[27] The reason given for this small number of interviews is that basic motivations are common to different individuals. Incidentally, this is an assumption which in itself has drawn strong criticism. After the responses to this type of interview are gathered, they are generally interpreted by analysts to determine common responses and other pertinent information. It is the interpretation of results that causes the greatest amount of criticism of this motivation research technique. The fact that there is no generally systematic structure for the interpretation of the results, along with the lack of psychological training of many engaged in this research, has raised serious doubts as to the validity of these interpretations.

> Another difficulty is that no quantifiable data are obtainable in the depth interviewing process. This means that human judgment is involved in summarizing the findings. Different results will be obtained by different people in the same situation. As a result, there is little or no opportunity for verification.[28]

Another, very similar, motivation research technique is that of group interviewing, which also attempts through indirect questioning to uncover motives and attitudes. This is done usually with a small group where free interaction is encouraged to bring about the motives of various members of the group. It is this interaction of ideas and beliefs that differentiates this type of interview from the individual depth interview. Several advantages of this type of interview have been claimed by the users. One of the claims is that this interaction broadens the base of communication—thus ideas are shared and more ideas are brought out to think about and discuss. By recording these interviews oral expressions can be noted along with actual words. This is one means of helping to interpret the actual meanings. Of course, the same objections can be

---

26 Lyndon O. Brown, *Marketing and Distribution Research,* 3rd ed. (New York: The Ronald Press Company, 1955).

27 *Ibid.*

28 *Ibid.*

raised in regard to this technique as are made against the depth interview. That is, the skill of the interviewer and the analysis are all-
important, and the nonquantitativeness of the data makes verification
impossible.

The last and possibly the most useful group of techniques of motivation research are those of the projective type. There are many variations in these projective techniques: for example, free word association,
successive word association, sentence completion, and picture responses.
These tools have as their fundamental principle that of placing a person
in an ambiguous position. Supposedly, his motives will be uncovered as
he projects his unconscious thought to interpret that situation. By placing the individual in this situation, he responds more or less in terms of
other people instead of thinking of himself.

Leonhard expresses the principle of these techniques as follows:

> Instead of interpreting the meaning of survey results on the basis of
> people's yes-no answers, or their notes on the subject, we are going to
> reverse the process by asking people to interpret actions of others which,
> of course, they can only do by projecting their own experience, person-
> ality and outlook. They thus reveal unknowingly their real attitudes or
> motivations which become invaluable to the manufacturer in merchan-
> dising and advertising.[29]

The particular projective technique to be used, of course, depends on
its appropriateness to the situation and the audience to be tested. The
value of projective techniques seems to lie in their ability to get at
hidden motives which cannot be uncovered easily by other techniques.
However, as with the other methods, the success of projective techniques
depends upon the skill and training of those administering the tests and
evaluating the results. In fact, it is the skill and training of researchers
which presents the most common and persistent problem in the application of these projective techniques. Brown suggests that their success
depends upon three things:

> The first requirement is the development and selection of materials
> (stimuli) which are.most successful in obtaining responses that project
> beyond the conscious surface level. The second requirement is that stimuli
> evoke responses which are related to the motivational problem being
> researched. The third requirement is that responses can be interpreted
> into a logical motivational pattern.[30]

In each of these requirements human judgment and evaluation are cru-

---

[29] *Op. cit.,* p. 31.
[30] *Op. cit.*

cial; thus any method used in motivation research to uncover motives may be said to be only as good as the person or persons conducting the research.

LIMITATIONS OF MOTIVATION RESEARCH

In the literature, there seem to be two main criticisms of motivation research—in addition, of course, to the criticism that motivation research has no value at all. These are criticisms of (1) the limitations and errors in the techniques used; and (2) the scope and application of motivation research studies.

Before discussing some of the reasons why motivation research falls short of its goal, we should again define that goal. Earlier in this chapter motivation research was defined as a set of tools, borrowed from the fields of psychology and the other behavioral sciences. These tools are used to uncover and evaluate the motives or desires that underlie human behavior in the consumer market. According to this definition motivation research is synonymous with the techniques it employs. This concept of motivation research alone may be the basis for some of the complaints about its usefulness. According to Steuart Britt, the concept is wrong.

> Certain psychological or clinical techniques should not be given the fancy name of motivation research. Why should the name of a technique be given the name of the objective it is supposed to accomplish? And certainly it is a mistake to think that the psychological techniques are the only tools of learning about people's motives.[31]

Other students of motivation research feel the same way about the narrowness of concept and the use of these psychological techniques.

Many of the attacks on motivation research revolve around the methods used by the researchers and the researchers themselves. It has been stated that "the value of this type of research depends greatly upon the technique employed."[32] Although these methods have been fashioned after those of psychoanalysis, when applied to the business problem they are radically changed, both in content and in the intensity of their application. In psychoanalysis, the trained psychologist works closely with an individual who has come to him for help. The psychologist works for months developing a mass of data covering the entire life of the individual. Out of this information he arrives at certain conclu-

---

[31] "Four Hazards of Motivation Research: How to Avoid Them," *Printers' Ink*, June 17, 1955, p. 40.

[32] Louis Cheskin, *How to Predict What People Will Buy* (New York: Liveright Publishing Corp., 1957), p. 85.

sions about the factors motivating the patient's current behavior.[33] However, as Alfred Politz points out:

> In consumer interviews, the motivational mechanism is the opposite. The interviewee does not look for help. It is the researcher who goes to the consumer for a selfish motive—that is, to get money, or fame. He does not try to help the consumer. An individual who agrees to be interviewed does so for much less powerful motives than pain. Under these motivational circumstances the "depth of the unconscious" cannot be uncovered.[34]

This, then, is one basis for criticism of motivation techniques. They are said, first of all, to be too superficial—that is, they cannot actually reach the hidden motives of consumers in a period of two hours or even longer. Depth interviews are generally attacked on the basis that the interviews cannot reach beyond the defense mechanisms of the consumer and also that depth interviewing is too limited by the skills of the interviewer.[35]

These same limitations also would seem to apply to the projective techniques which have gained great support in motivation research. The success of any of these techniques hinges directly upon the training, experience, and skill of the person conducting the research. And since the results of these techniques cannot be quantified in any meaningful manner, it is up to the researcher to interpret and draw conclusions as to the validity and reliability of the results. This of course leaves room for a great deal of subjectivity and uncertainty about the findings. Doubt about the validity of these methods still persists even in the behavioral sciences themselves, where the same techniques are used in greater depth and in conjunction with other methods.[36]

The closest approach to testing the validity of these techniques seems to be verification through similar interpretations by other analysts. This of course is not a very accurate test of validity since, under the same circumstances, two analysts may agree on the findings but they may both be wrong. According to Brown, "motivation research therefore suffers from the lack of any outside criteria which can be employed to validate its conclusions."[37]

Quantification of data, as was mentioned above, is another problem area of motivation research. Because quantification is generally regarded as a major element in any science, motivation research has been attacked

[33] Brown, *op. cit.*
[34] " 'Motivation Research' from a Research Viewpoint," *Public Opinion Quarterly,* Winter, 1956-1957, p. 669.
[35] Cheskin, *op. cit.*, p. 86.
[36] Politz, *op. cit.*, p. 671.
[37] *Op. cit.*

on the grounds that without this quantification, no reliance can be placed on the results. Along with this criticism goes that of applying techniques which are designed for individuals to small samples and then generalizing the unvalidated findings to a great mass of people. One writer on the subject, Edward Scriven, goes so far as to state that "the attempts to apply the methods of the clinical psychologist to marketing research are irrational and doomed to failure." [38] To determine the importance of any motivation factor in the marketing field we have to know the relative frequency with which that motive occurs in a cross section of the buying public, and this, he says, cannot be done by utilizing the present techniques of motivation research.

The second direction taken by the critics of motivation research seems to be centered around the idea that motivation research findings are relied on too heavily and are applied to specific problems without much thought as to the other environmental factors and principles of marketing. Politz asserts that motivation research has impressed people as overcoming the need for numbers—an erroneous assumption which violates the scientific principle of quantitativeness and does not consider the frequency of motives among consumers. In many writings it is stressed that motivation research is only an aid to traditional market research. Politz also states that "the problem of the researcher is not to find causes, but to find controllable causes on which action must be taken." [39] In other words, motivation research should be used as a means to an end—that of finding useful information for marketing decisions—not as an end in itself.

Motives, as was pointed out in the first section of this chapter, are many and diverse. The motives affecting behavior vary among individuals and are probably not sufficiently homogeneous to be added together. Thus it is difficult if not impossible to attribute any one single motive to a certain behavior pattern, let alone project this motive to the behavior pattern of a mass of individuals.

A final criticism of motivation research is that the findings are often applied to products of the same kind; hence individual products within this group lose all competitive advantage. Theodore Levitt in a *Harvard Business Review* article has said that "uncritical reliance on consumer and motivation research is becoming a threat to sales-building originality in advertising and product policy." [40] He cites as examples three product groups: liquid cleaners, mentholated cigarettes, and compact

---

[38] *Op. cit.*, p. 68.
[39] *Op. cit.*, p. 664.
[40] "M-R Snake Dance," *Harvard Business Review*, November-December, 1960, p. 76.

cars. In each case motivation research was done by the originating companies of the "new products," and in each case others followed suit with the same images, and similar brand names and advertising campaigns. The result was that all of the products took on a "sameness" which, according to Levitt, violated some of the basic rules of marketing. The reason for this, he states, is that management relies too heavily on these research findings and is too eager to climb on the bandwagon. In Levitt's words, "managers failed to manage."

If these limitations and criticisms are true, what then can the concept of motivation research do for marketing? Obviously, there have been some results from this type of research or its use would have diminished long ago.

One of the greatest contributions of this type of consumer research appears to be the *increased awareness of the importance of understanding the consumer*—not only his motives but everything that is involved in his behavior pattern. Motivation research, as outlined in this chapter, however, does not seem to be enough—there are too many unknowns and generalizations in motivation research for this concept to be able to give *the* correct answer to a marketing problem. Certainly more is involved. The question is, what other factors are involved in consumer behavior besides motives and what must the marketer understand about these factors in order to allow him to make sound marketing decisions based on predictions of the individual's behavior.

Psychologists have long recognized that human behavior consists of more than motives. How a person perceives a given situation or action will also influence his behavior regardless of his basic motives. For example, sex is one physiological motive which oftentimes must give way to the mores of society.

Perception is but one of the elements of cognition (the processes involved in knowing).[41] According to Bayton, cognitive processes serve the person in his attempts to achieve satisfaction of his needs.[42] They also largely determine the direction and particular steps taken in his attempts to attain satisfaction of the initiating needs.[43]

Learning is another step in the sequence of human behavior. Through the process of learning, the consumer develops his attitudes toward the product. If the product brings satisfaction to the user, this satisfaction is a reinforcement which *may* induce another purchase. If the product does not bring satisfaction, a negative reinforcement will occur and the probability of further purchases is lessened.

---

[41] *Dictionary of Psychology*, p. 47.
[42] *Op. cit.*, p. 48.
[43] *Ibid.*

This type of behavioral change—increasing likelihood that an act will be repeated is learning: and reinforcement is necessary for learning to take place.[44]

Consumer behavior might be diagrammed as follows (in a simple manner):

Frustration $\longrightarrow$ Need arousal (motive) $\longrightarrow$ Cognitive processes $\longrightarrow$ Goal object $\longrightarrow$ Action $\longrightarrow$ Reinforcement $\longrightarrow$ Learning

Showing behavior in this manner points up the fact that motivation research is only the first step in a full understanding of consumer behavior. Cognition and learning also play a vital role. A more explicit model of consumer behavior related to the behavior determinants of motivation, cognition, communication, and learning is shown in Fig. 6.

Figure 6: A Model of Behavior Response Determinants.

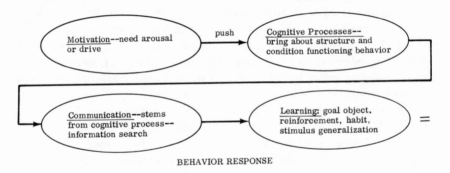

BEHAVIOR RESPONSE

Our model attempts to show that behavior is elicited by some kind of need arousal or drive which we call motivation. The motivational drive exerts a push or impetus on the consumer's cognitive processes. It is the cognitive processes which bring about the unifying aspects of behavior. Cognitions are values, ideas, constructs which individuals use to make "sense" out of perceptions. The cognitive processes work to bring about certain structured relationships to our motivations or drives. For example, our cognitions act to enable us to develop criteria of choice models and to develop attitudes and behavior consistent with our criteria of choice models, e.g., to act "rationally." Motivation and cognition processes create a desire for given responses. The desire may be for an

---

[44] *Ibid.*, p. 54.

immediate goal object as in the case of certain kinds of learned responses or instant insight which we call habit. Where the relationship between motivation-cognition and goal objects to satisfy the former are not yet established or where previous relationships are no longer satisfactory, the response is likely to be a search for more significant information. Communication therefore is important in the learning process, inasmuch as it can be structured in terms of the consumer's cognitive style or set and then used as a series of cues or stimuli for the purpose of structuring new habits or for developing or changing consumers' attitudes. Learning is the process or the act of acquiring new insight. When one learns, at least within a stimulus-response framework, he discovers that certain goal objects can successfully satisfy certain needs arousals.

In the next chapter we will look at the process of learning in some depth in order to ascertain its implications for consumer behavior.

FOUR

The Learning Process
and Models of Learning

To acquire a full and complete understanding of consumer behavior, research into consumer motivation is not enough. Motives are but a part of the total behavior pattern of an individual and therefore, taken alone, will not yield the insight necessary to accomplish the researcher's purpose—to improve the means by which products are marketed. An understanding of this consumer behavior should improve methods of advertising and promoting products and should also give some insight into the types of products which will appeal to the consumer. Whether or not this will be the outcome remains to be seen.

In this chapter we shall discuss another element of consumer behavior—the learning process: what it is, how it takes place, and when it takes place. We shall then take a look at how learning theory ideas have been incorporated into "models of learning."

Learning defined.   As defined in Webster's, learning is the acquisition of knowledge or skill; or the knowledge or skill received by instruction or study.[1] For our purposes this definition

---

[1] *New Collegiate Dictionary,* 2nd ed. (Springfield, Mass.: G. & C. Merriam Co., 1959), p. 479.

is obviously too narrow. Framed more along psychological lines, learning has been defined as:

> The process of acquiring the ability to respond adequately to a situation which may or may not have been previously encountered; the favorable modification of response tendencies consequent upon previous experience, particularly the building up of a new series of complexly coordinated motor responses; the fixation of items in memory so that they can be recalled or recognized; (gestalt) the process of acquiring insight into a situation.[2]

Thus learning has many meanings, and is usually defined in terms of the various theories of learning. It means different things to different people. To find out what learning is, we need to look at some of the various theories of learning and see in what ways they differ.

Behavior changes over time. Often this change is referred to as learning, but as a definitional tool, the idea of learning as synonymous with change does not seem to help. In fact, some authors contend that "it does not necessarily follow that for learning to take place a change in observable behavior must take place at the same time, or that from a change in overt behavior we can always accurately infer the full nature of the insight behind it."[3]

We are, however, interested in these changes in behavior; thus it is important for the purposes of this study to understand how these behavioral changes take place. And, since learning is defined in terms of the various theories of learning, we must look at these theories in order to understand what learning is, how it takes place and when it occurs.

A SHORT HISTORY OF LEARNING THEORIES

Although the study of learning processes has come to prominence as a discipline only within the past seventy-five years or so, the foundation for these theories can be traced back to the early fifteenth century and beyond.[4] Early theorists seemed to have developed as associationists because of their interest in the association of ideas. According to Horace B. English, these men were "philosophers concerned to show not how knowledge takes place, but how it can be valid; not how rational think-

---

[2] Howard C. Warren, ed., *Dictionary of Psychology* (New York: Houghton Mifflin Company, 1934), p. 151.

[3] Morris L. Bigge and Maurice P. Hunt, *Psychological Foundations of Education* (New York: Harper & Row, Publishers, 1962), p. 301.

[4] Horace B. English, *Historical Roots of Learning Theory* (Garden City, N.Y.: Doubleday & Company, Inc., 1954).

ing goes on, but how it can enable men to grasp reality." [5] Among these early philosophers were Hobbes, Hume, Locke, and Berkeley, who agreed that compound images essentially drawn from sensation were thoughts. What they wanted to know was how these images were held together.[6] Locke conceived of mind as a mere spectator of ideas. "Hume argued that mind was itself a compound idea, hence essentially passive. How then could a passive onlooker tie the ideas together?" [7]

Out of these early beginnings of theory came that of association, which originally consisted of four "laws." These were the laws of similarity, of contrast, of coexistence in space, and of succession in time (English traces these laws back to Aristotle). According to these laws of association, one idea "calls up another because it is like another, unlike another (contrast) or close to another idea in time or in space." [8] Subsequently, however, those four laws were reduced to a law of contiguity, according to which "it was the fact that two objects had been thought about (or perceived) simultaneously or in close succession which was said to be the basis for association." [9] Other theorists seized on this law of close succession to build their theories of nervous impulses.[10] According to this theory, bonds of association are the nerve pathways leading nervous impulses from one to another.

In Britain around 1810, Thomas Brown was investigating learning and memory apart from philosophy. He was interested basically in finding out why one idea suggested one thing to one individual and something completely different to another. Brown set up some principles based on the principle of contiguity which stated that the "strength or relative potency of association depended on the frequency of association, on recency, on liveliness, on lack of conflict, on prior habits of mind, on primacy, on emotional congruity." [11] As we shall see later on, some of these "principles" of Brown's are still relevant in learning theory today.

In the early nineteenth century James Mill was credited with introducing the concept of motivation in learning by proposing that learning was motivated by pleasure and pain. During the mid-nineteenth century Bain developed perhaps the first systematic general psychology.[12] By the last quarter of the century, learning theory began to expand and become somewhat systematized. Experimentation was taking place in

---

[5] *Ibid.*, p. 5. Reprinted by permission of Random House, Inc.
[6] *Ibid.*
[7] *Ibid.*, p. 6.
[8] *Ibid.*
[9] *Ibid.*, p. 9.
[10] H. C. Warren, *A History of Association Psychology* (New York: Charles Scribner's Sons, 1921).
[11] English, *op. cit.*, p. 10.
[12] *Ibid.*

psychology and in psychophysics. It was during this period and the early twentieth century that "learning as a unified topic including memory and habit was probably first put forward by E. L. Thorndike." [13] Writing in 1913, Thorndike explained the theory of association which we have symbolized as follows.[14] (The double-lined arrow means a "stronger tendency.")

$$A \longrightarrow R \qquad\qquad A \Longrightarrow R$$

In the above, if a situation A has resulted in the response R, then A is likely to bring the same response again more readily. This was, according to English, a modification of Hamilton's formula which again modified an earlier formula of association. Thus we have the following series of developments in associationist theory:

1. $A + B \left.\begin{array}{c}) \ A \\ ) \ \text{or} \\ ) \ a\end{array}\right\} \rightarrow b$

2. $AB \left.\begin{array}{c}) \ A \\ ) \ \text{or} \\ ) \ a\end{array}\right\} \rightarrow ab$

3. $A \longrightarrow R \qquad\qquad A \Longrightarrow R$

In (1) above, if A and B were in close succession in experience, the image of A would invoke the image of b.[15] This was refined by Hamilton as shown in (2). Here the coexistence of A and B in experience set up a fusion of AB. After time, the presence of A or of a tends to reintroduce the fused whole as an idea. Thorndike then reduced this idea to the form as shown in (3) above, indicating that if A brings the response R, then in the future A is likely to bring the response R more readily.

Building upon Thorndike's formula merely by changing the letters from A to S, we find the standard $S \longrightarrow R$ relationship of the associationist theory. The setting up of a bond between the stimulus and the response is learning according to associationist theory.[16] In Thorndike's words:

The oftener or more emphatically a given response is connected with a

---

[13] *Ibid.*, p. 14.

[14] Edward L. Thorndike, *Educational Psychology: The Original Nature of Man*, Vol. I (New York: Teachers College, Columbia University, 1913).

[15] Capital letters stand for external situations and small letters stand for some kind of representation of the external situation.

[16] English, *op. cit.*, p. 15.

certain situation, the more likely it is to be made to that situation in the future. . . . Other things being equal, exercise strengthens the bond between situation and response.[17]

Based on the stimulus-response formula and the idea of satisfying the response (reinforcement) to strengthen the bond, this theory has been the basis for most theories of learning, and, as we shall see later, it is still used by some as *the* theory of learning.

Around this same time Pavlov was experimenting in Russia with conditioned reflexes of animals. Pavlov, a physiologist, became impressed with the modifiability of certain "digestive reflexes" in animals. He showed one way in which behavior can be modified—by conditioning.[18] Conditioning pertains to the process of achieving a response with a neutral stimulus that has been paired with a stimulus that "reflexly" produces a given response.

> This and this alone Pavlov averred was the basis of behavior flexibility and adaptibility. But, it will be noted, responses which have been thus conditioned were still reflexes, "conditioned reflexes." [19]

This can be shown as follows:

$$S_a \longrightarrow R \longrightarrow S_b \text{---} \atop S_a \longrightarrow R \qquad\qquad S_b \longrightarrow R$$

In the above, some response R can be brought about only by an unconditioned stimulus S_a. However, S_a may be closely associated with some other stimulus S_b. As a result of this association, conjunction, or "temporal contiguity," response R is associatively shifted from S_a to S_b.

The classical view of S-R learning is often referred to as association or connectionist learning and is usually depicted diagrammatically as follows:

$$\text{given together} \left\{ \begin{array}{l} S_1 \text{ given} \\ \\ S_2 \text{ learned} \end{array} \right. \longrightarrow R$$

---

[17] Reprinted with the permission of the publisher from Geraldine M. Joncich, ed., *Psychology and the Science of Education, Selected Writings of Edward L. Thorndike* (New York: Teachers College Press), p. 179. © 1962, Teachers College, Columbia University.

[18] O. Herbert Mowrer, *Learning Theory and Behavior* (New York: John Wiley & Sons, Inc., 1961).

[19] *Ibid.*, p. 14.

where S_1 is an unconditioned stimulus and S_2 is a conditioned stimulus. For example, the relationship between hunger and eating is considered self-evident by anyone with even the slightest degree of maturity, and in this given relationship S_1 is considered as an unconditioned stimulus. Unconditioned stimuli are often considered a part of the organism's innate behavior pattern. On the other hand, placing the subject in an environment of fine foods and aromas is likely to lead to the desire to order a delicious meal and eat. The placement of the individual in the environment which suggests the given response is a conditioned stimulus.

The relationship between the stimulus and the response is referred to as the S-R bond. It would follow that some bonds are likely to be stronger than others and that some may be quite weak and even become extinct over periods of time.

Again, a diagram may offer some help in explaining bond relationships.

$$S_1 \longrightarrow R_a \qquad (\text{strong})$$
$$S_2 \dashrightarrow R_b \qquad (\text{neutral})$$
$$S_3 \dashleftarrow R_c \qquad (\text{weak})$$

Stimulus S_1 is shown eliciting a strong or a positive response. Thus the bond between S_1 and R_a is likely to be forged into some kind of lasting relationship. S_2 could lead to a strong response R_a but the dotted line leading to R_b shows that it might also elicit a relatively weak or neutral response and therefore the bond is not likely to be reinforced and the subject is likely to be indifferent regarding the association S_2-R_b. S_3 is a stimulus which may elicit one of several responses: R_a, a strong response; R_b, a neutral response; or, R_c, a weak response. As a matter of fact, it could be shown that any given stimulus is likely to elicit a hierarchy of responses. Under conditions shown by S_3-R_c, association is not likely to occur, no habit or bonds are likely to be forged, and this response, R_c, will no longer be used to satisfy the drive state elicited by the stimulus S_3. However, as we shall learn subsequently, the S-R bond or simple habit learning is not an intellectually popular idea today.

In 1910, Max Wertheimer, a German, introduced what is known as gestalt psychology by identifying what he called the phi phenomenon.[20] The phi phenomenon pertained to the impression of apparent movement seen when two lines are exposed at the same time at a determined

---

[20] Edna Heidbreder, *Seven Psychologies* (New York: The Century Company, © 1933), p. 329.

optical rate.[21] The attempt to explain this and other optical phenomena was historically the starting point of gestalt psychology.[22]

Two students of Wertheimer introduced the idea of gestalt psychology into the United States in the 1920's when their books *The Growth of the Mind* and *The Mentality of Apes* were translated into English. The authors, Kurt Koffka and Wolfgang Kohler, respectively, are considered, along with Wertheimer, the fathers of gestalt psychology. Heidbreder has noted that "it is largely due to Kohler and Koffka that the present interest in the movement exists in the United States." [23] Although this statement was made in 1933, interest in gestalt psychology and in variations of the theory (which we will lump under "field" theory) is still very strong in the United States today. This is evident from the wide range of books and articles printed on the subject in the last twenty years.[24]

Gestalt and, more broadly, field theories of learning deal with such things as perceptions, cognitions, insights, and "life spaces." They are concerned more with the whole than with the parts or elements of the associationists and place much more emphasis on "intelligent behavior" as opposed to passive, trial-and-error behavior. These differences and concepts will be noted more fully as we proceed in our discussion of the theories of learning.

TWO BASIC THEORIES OF LEARNING

In investigating the learning process, one is immediately impressed by the overwhelming volume of literature dealing with the subject. Upon further investigation, however, it appears that most of the literature dealing with various theories of learning can be divided into two basic groups. Hilgard has classified the theories of learning into two groups labeled *stimulus-response* (connectionism, conditioning, behaviorism) and *cognitive*, consisting of gestalt, organismic and sign-significant theories.[25]

Within each of these two groupings is a wide range of theoretical ideas and experimental results (outside of these groups as well),[26]

---

[21] *Ibid.*, p. 328.
[22] *Ibid.*
[23] *Ibid.*, p. 334.
[24] See Mary Henle, *Documents of Gestalt Psychology* (Berkeley, Calif.: University of California Press, 1961).
[25] Ernest R. Hilgard, *Theories of Learning*, rev. ed. (New York: Appleton-Century-Crofts, © 1955), Chap. I.
[26] *Ibid.*

none of which really seems to have been totally proved or disproved. William Burton claims that "Pure theory, an absolute necessity for full understanding, is not available." [27] John McGeoch seems to agree that "there are, at present, no specific theories of the learning process in general." [28]

The range of these theories is so broad and complex that no effort will be made here to explain or even to mention all of them. However, for the purposes of marketing and gaining an understanding of consumer behavior, the two basic groups of theories should be discussed.

It should be noted that while these theories may, in general, be applied to analysis of consumer behavior, individual differences among consumers affect the applicability of the learning process. Such things as the learning capacity of an individual, learning types, and the "set" of the individual all must be taken into consideration when attempting to apply specific theories to behavior. These three elements imply that there are differences as to the amount and extent of learning an individual is capable of absorbing, the rate at which an individual can learn, and the "set" or the conditions surrounding the learning situation, e.g., whether or not the person has a reason to learn what is being taught.

Whatever the differences between individuals, *the important implication, for the marketer, is that learning makes an individual changeable.*[29]

Stimulus-response learning. In the simplest case, learning involves new patterns of behavior or reaction in a pliable, passive organism.[30] According to Haggard, the stimulus-response theory of learning assumes that the subject is passive and his behavior change can be controlled by manipulating external forces (stimuli).[31] In Tolman's words:

> According to the stimulus-response school, the subject in learning a maze responds helplessly and passively to the succession of external and internal stimuli.[32]

---

[27] "Basic Principles in a Good Teaching-Learning Situation," in *Readings in Learning,* ed. Lester D. Crow and Alice Crow (New York: David McKay Co., Inc., 1963), p. 8.

[28] *The Psychology of Human Learning,* 2nd ed. (New York: David McKay Co., Inc., 1952), p. 39. Reprinted by permission David McKay Co., Inc.

[29] Mowrer, *op. cit.,* p. 10.

[30] Bigge and Hunt, *op. cit.,* p. 292.

[31] Ernest A. Haggard, "Learning: A Process of Change," *Educational Leadership,* December, 1955, pp. 149-156.

[32] E. C. Tolman, "Cognitive Maps in Rats and Men," *Psychological Review,* 1948, p. 189.

While there are those who do not agree that this implication is present in stimulus-response theory,[33] in the simplest cases the passivity of the subject does seem to be an integral part.

The key concepts presented in the S-R theory of learning are, as the name implies, those of the stimulus or situation, the response to that stimulus or situation, and what occurs between them. Stimulus refers to a situation presented to the organism, and response refers to the reaction of the organism when confronted by such a situation. In other words, what behavior does the subject elicit in a given situation? Thorndike states this concept as follows:

> Any fact of intellect, character, or skill means a tendency to respond in a certain way to a certain situation—involves a *situation* or state of affairs influencing a man, a *response* or state of affairs in the man, and a connection or bond whereby the latter is the result of the former.[34]

On these concepts of stimulus and response has been built the theory of stimulus-response learning. These responses to stimuli are said to be learned. This includes "the specificity of likes and dislikes, indeed the whole range of effective and emotional response to stimulation." [35]

Differences of opinion as to the relationships of these variables in the stimulus-response theory of learning are quite apparent in the literature. Much of the discussion of the theorists seems to have been centered upon the sequence between the stimulus and the response.

> Guthrie is convinced that learning occurs when a stimulus and a response happen simultaneously. Hull centered the essence of learning in what occurs between the stimulus and the response; and Skinner places his emphasis upon the stimulus which follows a response.[36]

Using S for stimulus, R for response and O for organism, we can represent the above theories as an S-R; S-O-R, and an R-S theory.[37] Thus one of the areas of disagreement among the stimulus-response theorists is in the timing and relationship of the learning variables of stimulus and response.

According to the S-R theory, learning is the selection of the appropriate response for a given stimulus and the strengthening of the con-

---

[33] "Cognitive Versus Stimulus-Response Theories of Learning," *Behavior Theory and Learning: Selected Papers,* ed. Kenneth W. Spence (Englewood Cliffs, N.J.: Prentice-Hall, Inc., 1960), p. 259.

[34] *Op. cit.,* p. 1.

[35] McGeoch, *op. cit.,* p. 2.

[36] Bigge and Hunt, *op. cit..,* p. 293.

[37] *Ibid.*

nection between the stimulus and the response. This "strengthening" of the connection is said to be the "result of exercise." [38] This so-called exercise or repetition is another integral part of S-R learning theory. In fact, the use of this variable has been so general that it has become known as the "principle of frequency" or repetition.[39] According to Guthrie, "one of the oldest laws of association has been that the strength of an association depends directly on the frequency with which it has occurred." [40] He goes on to say that "it is an undeniable fact that this frequency of connection . . . influences the degree of probability that the response will follow its signal." [41]

While other "laws" of learning have been developed over the years, the only two which seem to have survived the attacks of theorists and are still being used today are the above law of frequency and the "law of effect," [42] which will be discussed later in this chapter. According to Haggard and others, these "laws of learning" developed by the S-R theorists have been disproved many times in careful research and in everyday experience.[43] Why do they persist?

> The reason for this persistence lies partly in their simplicity, and partly in the fact that they fit neatly into a more general stimulus-response theory of behavior and learning.[44]

Guthrie, in general, makes the same criticism of laws of learning. In regard to the law of frequency he states: "Close examination however, makes the law of frequency less certainly true." [45] However, he cushions his criticism by citing the law of "vividness" and the law of "intensity." These two "laws" supposedly cover the exceptions to the law of frequency by explaining that, "other things being equal, of two associations with the same cue, that one made the experience more vivid, or [was used] under circumstances which included greater excitement." [46] Another qualification of the law of frequency, says Guthrie, is the law of "recency" which explains that of two associations which have equal practice, the more recent will prevail.[47] The law of frequency and its qualifications would seem to have many implications for the marketer.

---

[38] English, *op. cit.*, p. 16.
[39] E. R. Guthrie, *The Psychology of Learning*, rev. ed. (Gloucester, Mass.: Peter Smith, 1960). © 1957 Harper & Brothers.
[40] *Ibid.*, p. 78. Reprinted by permission of Harper & Brothers.
[41] *Ibid.*
[42] Haggard, *op. cit.*, p. 151.
[43] *Ibid.*
[44] *Ibid.*
[45] *Op. cit.*, p. 79.
[46] *Ibid.*
[47] *Ibid.*, p. 80.

The other "law" mentioned in the discussion above is that of "effect," which involves another important concept of the S-R theory of learning—that of reinforcement or reward. Tied to the concept of reinforcement is that of drive reduction. Drive or need reduction refers to the process of reducing the drive which initiates the behavior. When this drive sets up the stimulus which leads to behavior or the response, reinforcement or reward of this response then reduces the original drive.

According to the S-R approach:

> As long as an individual is being rewarded for what he is doing, he will learn these particular responses more thoroughly but he may not learn anything new by trial and error. This is partly because strengthening of the dominant response makes the occurrence of any new responses less likely, and partly because its rewards if ample, will keep the drive at a low level.[48]

While not universally held by all S-R theorists, the idea of the law of effect is that learning does not take place without reinforcement. Reward, as will be seen later, is one of the controversial issues in learning theory. While some writers have written off the differences of opinion as problems of definition,[49] there does seem to be evidence of a conflict of theories as to the importance of reward.

Guthrie, for one, although not denying the effect of reinforcement, believes that rewards influence learning in a particular way and that the manner of their operation can be deduced from more elementary concepts.[50] Thorndike and Hull, on the other hand, "regard the principle of reward as irreducible to more elementary concepts. They are not in complete agreement, however, as to the nature of the reinforcing process." [51] In Hull's *Principles of Behavior,* he has divided reinforcement into what he calls primary reinforcement and secondary reinforcement. Under primary reinforcement, the rewarded response has drive reducing properties, while secondary reinforcement may arise through the association of the stimulus with the reinforcement. This consistent association may reinforce stimulus-response connections without drive reduction. Hull's theory suggests, at least, the answer to the important question of how rewards or goals act to increase the future likelihood of the responses which precede them. Hull argues that when these "re-

---

48 N. E. Miller and J. Dollard, "Four Fundamentals of Learning," in *Theories of Motivation in Learning,* ed. Richard C. Teevan and Robert C. Birney (Princeton, N.J.: D. Van Nostrand Company, Inc., 1964), p. 58.

49 For an excellent discussion of theoretical differences, see McGeoch, *op. cit.,* Chap. II.

50 *Op. cit.,* Chap. 8.

51 McGeoch, *op. cit.,* p. 47.

inforcing stimuli" follow *S-R* sequences, they strengthen the connections between the stimuli and the responses involved. These connections between stimuli and responses are called, in the language of learning theory, "bonds." The stimulus of the *S-R* sequence includes both a peripheral and a drive or motivation component. After the occurrence of the peripheral and drive stimulus, a response follows and then a reinforcing stimulus appears. The connection between the preceding peripheral and drive stimulus and the response is thereby strengthened so that later the same composite stimulus will be more likely to bring about the response.

The following diagram may help to clarify these generalizations.

Figure 7: Hull's Learning and Stimulus Response Bonds.

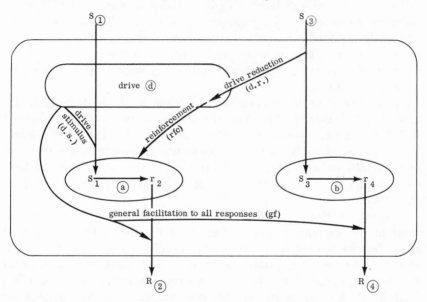

Source: James Olds, *The Growth and Structure of Motives* (Glencoe, Ill.: The Free Press of Glencoe, 1956), p. 91. By permission.

The argument is that *learning* strengthens the *S-R* bond, *a*, between a stimulus S_1 and a response R_2, if the stimulus S_1 precedes the response R_2 and the response is followed by a reinforcing stimulus S_3. The reinforcing stimulus S_3 has a special relationship to the drive, *d*. That is, it is either (1) a reducer of the drive state, or (2) a stimulus which has been regularly associated in the past with a drive reducer. It is important to note that only a reinforcing stimulus will strengthen the

S-R bond, *a.* Only because a reinforcer is presented after the response does any learning occur in this situation. If the presented stimulus is not a reinforcer, the trial would be called an extinction trial and *unlearning,* as opposed to learning, would occur. The motivation or drive behavior can precipitate the learned response on a later occasion as a direct component of the stimulus S_1 which elicits the response R_2.

All this can be summarized pithily by stating that the connection created in learning acts to increase the action of a stimulus S_1 upon a response R_2 which succeeds it. However, the stimulus S_3, which produces the learning, acts upon the *S-R* bond which precedes it. The stimulus S_3 produces this effect only if it is a reinforcer or a secondary reinforcer. The implications of this statement are numerous and far-reaching. The statement is, first of all, an abandonment of the classical *S-R* bond conception of habit. In effect, it says that changes in reaction potential, or more simply performance, are not dependent upon the previously assumed "strength of association" between stimulus and response but upon the presence or absence of a reinforcer, by which is presumably meant a secondary reinforcer or some kind of further incentive or motivator.

Another view of reinforcement is taken by B. F. Skinner in his book *The Behavior of Organisms: An Experimental Analysis,* published in 1938.[52] Skinner's work with partial reinforcement indicated that learning could take place when reinforcement was present in only one out of one hundred and ninety-two of the responses. This would tend to indicate, then, that reinforcement is of less importance than believed by some theorists.

However, the important point to note about the role of reinforcement in the stimulus-response category of theories is that in most of these theories reward is not dismissed entirely and in many cases it is viewed as an essential variable in learning. The effect of reinforcement has been explained also in terms of experimental extinction, a term first used by Pavlov. According to this concept, an unreinforced response will be unlearned or become extinct. That is, if a stimulus produces a response and this response is unrewarded, a new response will be forthcoming. If this new response is rewarded, it will be learned. If not, it too will become extinct and another response will be elicited. This process of search for a rewarded and thus "learned" response indicates some sort of hierarchy of responses and ties in with the phenomena of "random behavior."[53] We may diagram this as follows:

---

[52] New York: Appleton-Century.
[53] Miller and Dollard, *op. cit.,* pp. 49-50.

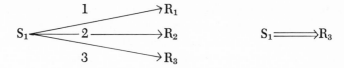

In the first diagram, the stimulus may produce three (or more or fewer) responses. If the first response R_1 is unrewarded, the subject may then move down the hierarchy of responses to elicit the second response R_2. Again, if unrewarded, he continues to elicit responses until a response is rewarded. In the above case, if R_3 is rewarded, the bond or association between the stimulus and response is strengthened and, in the future, if the subject is again confronted with the stimulus S_1, R_3 will probably be the response given.

The word "probably" brings up two more areas of interest to the S-R theorists. These are the implications of the amount of reward and the delay of reward. Again, it should be emphasized that much study has been done in the area of reinforcement and that there is no absolute agreement on the findings of various learning theories.

In discussing the importance of the amount of reward, McGeoch has stated that:

> If reward is influential at all in determining learning, then learning must, of logical necessity, be some function of the amount of reward. When reward is of considerable magnitude, learning occurs. On the other hand, when reward is of zero magnitude, learning ordinarily does not occur and, in the case of already established habits, extinction occurs. Between these two extremes must lie some sort of function.[54]

He goes on to say that the simplest way to look at this is to hold that reward operates in an all-or-none fashion as Thorndike does in his 1933 article on the subject.[55] In this view, the amount of the reward has little to do with the learning taking place as long as the reward is strong enough to elicit the "ok" reaction.[56]

In regard to the amount of reward, the majority of the S-R theorists seem to accept Thorndike's approach since most experiments with humans have shown that learning does not always increase with increasing amounts of reward.[57]

In regard to the delay of reward, it seems that the S-R theorists

---

[54] Op. cit., p. 244.
[55] "A Theory of the Action of the After-Effects of a Connection Upon It," Psychological Review, 40 (1933), 434-439.
[56] Ibid.
[57] McGeoch, op. cit., p. 246.

are in fairly general agreement that the learning process is aided by a close association in time between the response and the reward.

Up to this point, we have dwelt on this concept of reward mainly to point up the relative importance of this idea to the marketer. *If reward is considered to be of great importance to learning as seems to be indicated by the S-R theorists, then this, along with providing the correct stimulus, should be of the greatest importance to the seller.* The other side of the reward picture will be presented in the next section dealing with cognitive theorists. Before leaving this discussion of the S-R theories, however, we will take up another important concept of the S-R theorists—that of habit and habit formation.

Habit formation.   In effect we have talked about habit formation without indicating it as such. This was done so that we might focus attention directly on this concept and its development in S-R learning theory.

Thorndike seems to have developed one of the first theories of habit.[58] According to this theory, responses made to a certain drive in a given situation may not elicit drive reduction. Therefore, these responses must be changeable. This substitution of responses is regarded as habit formation in the simplest case. The schematic on page 100 of this chapter shows this idea of habit formation, which of necessity involves random behavior or trial-and-error learning and a hierarchy of responses. This theory has been and is criticized on the grounds that it makes learning mechanical.

Hull, on the other hand, "has been interested not only in the problem of specifying, operationally, the experimental variables determining his hypothetical learning factor—habit—but also, he has attempted to guess at the 'law' describing how these variables combine to determine habit strength $(_sH_r)$." [59] In Hull's theory, four variables are named to which habit is a function. These variables are the number of reinforcements; the magnitude of reward; the time of delay of the reward; and the time interval between the stimulus and the response.[60] Hull also mentions other relations that habit has to other intervening variables. He calls these variables drive (D), excitatory potential (E), and inhibition (I).[61]

In explaining his theory of habit formation, Hull confined his discussion mainly to classical conditioning because of the simplicity of

---

[58] Mowrer, *op. cit.*, p. 16.
[59] *Behavior Theory and Learning: Selected Papers*, p. 250.
[60] *Ibid.*
[61] *Ibid.*

structuring these experimental conditions.[62] Hull's theory culminated in the following mathematical formula:

Figure 8: Hull's Habit Strength Formulation.

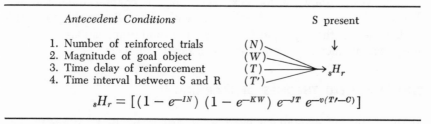

Antecedent Conditions		S present
1. Number of reinforced trials	(N)	↓
2. Magnitude of goal object	(W)	
3. Time delay of reinforcement	(T)	$\rightarrow {}_sH_r$
4. Time interval between S and R	(T')	

$$_sH_r = [(1 - e^{-IN})(1 - e^{-KW})\, e^{-JT}\, e^{-v(T'-C)}]$$

Source: Kenneth W. Spence, ed., *Behavior Theory and Learning: Selected Papers* (Englewood Cliffs, N.J.: Prentice-Hall, Inc., 1960), p. 251.

Thus, in this theory, habit strength depends on a number of variables in the connection between stimulation and response and not entirely upon the presence or absence of reward.

Other writers have defined habits a little differently.[63] While habits are not initiating forces in themselves, they are repeated response patterns accompanied by a minimum of cognitive activity. Thus, needs must be present before the habit response takes place. However, "frequency of repeating a response is not a valid criterion for determining whether or not a habit exists." [64] The strength of habit is considered to be the extent to which an individual will persist in an act after it has ceased to provide need satisfaction.

For our purposes then, habit formation has to do with the strength of connection between the original stimulus and the response. This may, hopefully, imply many things for marketers. *The development and strengthening of a desired response to a product stimulus is one of the objectives of the marketer.* More will be said about this in a later chapter.

In summary then, we should note that the S-R theorists in general hold as important in the learning process the concepts of stimulus and response, the connection between these two variables or habit formation, and also certain variables on which these concepts depend, such as reinforcement (amount or strength, and time of delay) and the inter-

---

[62] *Ibid.*, p. 251.

[63] James A. Bayton, "Motivation, Cognition, Learning—Basic Factors in Consumer Behavior," in *Marketing and the Behavioral Sciences,* ed. Perry Bliss (Boston: Allyn & Bacon, Inc., 1963). Reprinted by permission of the American Marketing Association.

[64] *Ibid.*, p. 55.

vening period between the original stimulus and the response elicited.

Also important to the S-R theorists is that to obtain the desired response with a given stimulus, an original need to respond to the stimulus must be present.

As will be shown in the next section of this chapter, other learning theorists disagree in whole or in part with the S-R position, and the work done by these people has very important implications for those interested in knowing more about consumer behavior.

COGNITIVE-FIELD THEORIES OF LEARNING [65]

At this point, an experiment cited in an article by R. K. White [66] may prove valuable to show some distinct concepts of "field" theory as opposed to the S-R view of learning. According to White, this experiment shows the "common sense" approach of Tolman and Lewin.[67]

Figure 9: Common Sense Learning.

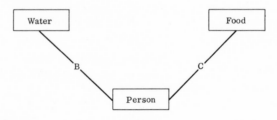

Source: R. K. White, "The Case for the Tolman-Lewin Interpretation of Learning," *The Psychological Review,* March, 1943, p. 160.

The person has had an opportunity to perceive that B leads to water and C leads to food. In the past he has always been hungry and has consequently "learned" to take path C. He is now thirsty instead of hungry. Which path will he take? [68]

White indicates that a completely consistent stimulus-response psychologist would necessarily say that the person under these conditions

---

[65] The field theories group together various varieties of gestalt, neo-gestalt, organismic, or sign-significant theories.

[66] "The Case for the Tolman-Lewin Interpretation of Learning," *The Psychological Review,* 50 (March, 1943), 157-186.

[67] While Tolman and Lewin differ in some concepts of learning and in their approaches, their individual theories may be grouped under "field" theory.

[68] *Op. cit.,* p. 160.

would choose path C, again leading to food.[69] This would of course be due to the force of habit, which would necessarily produce this response. More important according to White (from the standpoint of Thorndike and Hull) is the fact that response C is the only one which has ever been rewarded: ". . . the connection leading to this response would, then, have been repeatedly 'reinforced.' In the crucial trial, it should be stronger than any competing S-R connection and the person should go to the right." [70]

The "field" theorist in this case would say that the person would choose path B, since in the previous trials he has had the chance to "perceive" the outcome of such a response.[71] This ability to perceive or to know what the outcome of an action will be is one of the basic tenets of the cognitive theories. The person confronted with this situation would, through previous experience, have known that path B would lead him to the drive reducing object (water). As will be explained further in the latter part of this chapter, the person's environmental field or experience had been changed, thus allowing him to make an intelligent decision when confronted with different circumstances. More will be said in reference to this experiment as we continue our discussion of field theory.

In order to give some semblance of order to our discussion, it will be necessary to confine this examination of "field" theory to some basic concepts of learning. As the diversity of concepts and theories is multitudinous and intricate, we will limit our discussion to several fundamental factors.

Nonpassivity of the learner. As was explained in the preceding section of this chapter, in the simplest case the S-R theorist considers the subject to be passive. This, however, is in direct opposition to the field or cognitive theorists who maintain that "the basic implicit working assumptions of this theory are untenable. To suppose that the learner is or can be passive is ridiculous." [72] Cognitive theory holds that man's behavior is determined not only by external forces but also by internal forces which affect his learning. The position here is that "attention is focused on the individual in-the-environment context, with emphasis on how his relations to this environment change with time." [73]

---

[69] *Ibid.*, p. 161.
[70] *Ibid.*
[71] *Ibid.*, pp. 161-173.
[72] Haggard, *op. cit.*, p. 152.
[73] *Ibid.*, p. 153.

Relativistic approach to learning.   Whereas the stimulus-response theorists reduce behavior and learning to a mechanistic activity, the cognitive-field theorists maintain a relativistic approach. The basic idea here is that

> nothing is perceivable or conceivable as a thing in itself. Rather, every-thing is perceived or conceived in relation to other things. That is, a thing is perceived as a figure against a background, experienced from a given angle or direction of envisionment. Reality consists of what the individual makes of that which comes to him through his senses or other-wise.[74]

In other words, whereas the S-R associationists focus their attention on the elements of learning, cognitive-field theorists look at learning as a sum of the parts. Hilgard, in discussing cognitive-field theory, states that "the field psychologists warn against any effort to comprehend the totality of behavior in terms of component parts. The whole must always be viewed as a system to which the parts are subordinate." [75] Also, "that the whole is more than the sum of its parts represents to the field psychologist a basic viewpoint toward nature." [76]

In line with this approach to learning, studies using the field method begin with a description of the whole situation—the field—and proceed to detailed analysis of various aspects of the situation. "At no time are aspects of a field viewed as isolated elements." [77] This idea of wholeness pervades all the well-known field, cognitive, and gestalt theories. Edna Heidbreder, in her book *Seven Psychologies,* states that:

> Gestalt psychology attempts to get back to naive perception, to im-mediate experience "undebauched by learning"; and it insists that it find there not assemblages of elements, but unified wholes; . . .[78]

Wolfgang Kohler, one of the "founders" of gestalt psychology, defines gestalt in two ways as used in Germany: "Sometimes it denotes shape or form as a property of things; sometimes it denotes a concrete indi-vidual and characteristic entity, existing as something detached and having shape and form as one of its attributes." [79]

---

74 Bigge and Hunt, *op. cit.,* p. 340.
75 Ernest R. Hilgard, *Theories of Learning* (New York: Appleton-Century-Crofts, Inc. © 1948), p. 9.
76 *Ibid.,* p. 10.
77 Bigge and Hunt, *op. cit.,* p. 348.
78 *Op. cit.,* p. 331.
79 Wolfgang Kohler, "Gestalt Psychology Today," in *Documents of Gestalt Psychology,* ed. Mary Henle (Berkeley, Calif.: University of California Press, 1961).

Kurt Lewin, another field theorist, defines this concept of whole-ness in terms of "life space" made up of the person and his environment or his "psychological field." [80]

The important point to remember here is that the S-R theorists largely confine their discussion and concepts to the parts or elements of the learning process, while the "field" theorists attempt to explain learning and behavior in terms of the sum-of-the-parts, or the totality of the situation at present. Thus, as stated by Bigge and Hunt: "Cogni-tive-field theorists inveigh against use of such mechanistic terms as reflex arcs, connectionism, conditioning, associationism, and reinforcement." [81]

Purposive behavior. According to the field theorists, behavior is not directly observable; it must be inferred.[82] Thus we have a basic dif-ference in the idea of behavior itself. To the S-R theorists, behavior is directly observable, while to the field theorist this is not necessarily true. Accordingly, a change in behavior is an indication that learning has been taking place, but the change in behavior is not the learning. *Learn-ing is more adequately defined as development of insight or under-standing.*[83] Insight, says Bigge, "means the way one senses or sees things in a situation. It is a basic sense of pattern or relationship." [84] Kohler puts the concept of insight this way:

> In its strict sense, the term refers to the fact that, when we are aware of a relation, this relation is not experienced as a fact by itself, but rather as something that follows from the characteristics of the objects under consideration.[85]

According to these psychologists, the person uses these insights to pursue a goal. In other words, behavior in a person is purposeful. Tied closely with the concept of insights and purposeful behavior is the idea of in-telligence. Thus the field theorist views an intelligent person as one who acts as if he were pursuing a goal or purpose and has some insight as to how to reach it. Nonintelligent behavior, on the other hand, in-volves the pushing or pulling of an individual as an inert object.[86] This

---

[80] Kurt Lewin, *Principles of Topological Psychology* (New York: McGraw-Hill Book Company, 1936), Chaps. 6 and 18.

[81] *Op. cit.*, p. 355.

[82] Gardner Lindzey, *Handbook of Social Psychology* (Cambridge, Mass.: Ad-dison-Wesley Publishing Company, 1954), Vol. II, Chap. 3.

[83] Morris L. Bigge, "A Relativistic Definition of Stimulus-Response," *Journal of Educational Psychology*, December, 1955, p. 458.

[84] *Ibid.*

[85] *Op. cit.*, p. 6.

[86] Bigge and Hunt, *op. cit.*, pp. 360-361.

again reflects the passive versus the nonpassive learner. Intelligent behavior is purposeful and does not depend upon trial-and-error methods of solution.

Kurt Lewin, in his work with topological and vector analysis, presents what is probably one of the easier formulations of learning behavior to comprehend. Using mathematical concepts and constructs, Lewin has developed a theory based upon the person and his environment which is incorporated in his concept of "life-space." [87] It is diagrammed below.

Figure 10: A Life-Space.

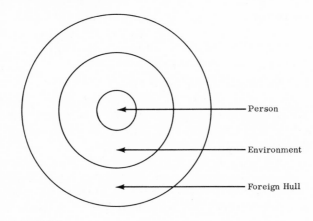

Source: Morris L. Bigge and Maurice P. Hunt, *Psychological Foundations of Education* (New York: Harper & Row, Publishers, 1962), p. 351.

The foreign hull represents the potential perception in contrast with the functional perceptions of a person's unique field.[88] The life-space itself reflects the total pattern of factors or influences which affect behavior at a certain moment in time. Behavior means a change in the life-space which is psychological.[89] A person's life-space represents the total world in which he lives. This may include his precepts, knowledge, and beliefs; his forward and backward time perspective; and abstract ideas as well as concrete objects.[90]

---

[87] *Ibid.*
[88] *Ibid.*, p. 351.
[89] *Ibid.*
[90] *Ibid.*

Lewin's basic formula of behavior, $B = f(P,E)$, indicates that behavior is a function of the state of the person and of the environment. These two states, according to Lewin, are interdependent, that is, the state of the person depends upon the state of the environment and vice versa.[91] Together, these two elements make up the life-space. Therefore, behavior, as formulated, depends upon the total life-space.

Hilgard explains learning in terms of this life-space as follows:

> A problematic situation represents an unstructured region of life space. We do not know how to get from the givens to the goal. We feel insecure until the region becomes structured. When it does become structured so as to permit problem-solution, we have learned.[92]

Thus we can see that learning according to field theory is a change of structure of the life-space or in our cognitive patterns. It is a development of insights or a reorganization of perceptions.

This change in the structure of cognitions, perceptions, or life-space (depending upon the theory adopted) may occur with repetition. But the fact of repetition does not have the same importance to the field theorists as to the S-R theorists. The important thing here is that the structure gets changed, not that repetitions occur.[93]

Owing to the fact that the "field" as used by the field psychologists denotes the present conditions as opposed to past or future conditions, "Behavior depends on neither the future nor the past but on the present field." [94] For example, the life-space, according to Hilgard, "is a construct, like other scientific constructs, to account for the psychological situation at a given moment." [95]

Field theory implies that as we learn, we increase knowledge, and thus our life-space becomes more highly differentiated. Or, in other words, we know facts in their relationships; we know what leads to what.[96] This condition of knowing what leads to what then determines how we react in a situation; this is not determined, as the associationists imply, by the connection between stimulus and response. We intelligently seek a goal instead of being led to a response in a situation by the force of habit.

---

[91] Kurt Lewin, *Field Theory in Social Science* (New York: Harper & Row, Publishers, 1951), p. 62.

[92] *Op. cit.*, p. 218.

[93] *Ibid.*

[94] Bigge, *op. cit.*, p. 459.

[95] *Op. cit.*, p. 215.

[96] *Ibid.*, p. 218.

One experiences through acting and perceiving the consequences of his acts. Every experience both takes up something from those experiences which have gone before and modifies in some way the quality of the experiences which follow.[97]

Field theory and habit. As opposed to the associationists' position on habit, the field theorists generally regard habit as an action arising through a person's reacting on the basis of insights he possesses.[98] Habit, in this case then, enables one to behave intelligently without thinking. In other words, his insights are organized in such a manner that he knows which actions will lead to what results, and he can act accordingly.

COMPARISON OF S-R FIELD THEORIES USING WHITE'S EXPERIMENT

To summarize what has been pointed out in this chapter, let us return to White's experiment concerning the choice of one of two paths leading to goal objects. Previously, the person as diagrammed in Fig. 9 (page 102) has had a need for food due to the condition of hunger. He has thus had a stimulus of hunger and through learning (according to the associationists) has responded with the response designated by C on the diagram. This response was accomplished by trial-and-error methods, and elicited after repeated trials. By taking this path leading to food repeatedly and being rewarded by lowering the urgency of the original need, the bond or connection is strengthened between the stimulus and the response. Habit is thus formed, and the person, confronted by this stimulus condition again, will almost automatically respond by taking path C. Thus we have the stimulus ....habit.....response type of learning.

At this point, however, if conditions change and the person is thirsty instead of hungry, White says that the associationist would predict that the person's response to this situation would be to take path C instead of B, which would lead to the correct goal object. This would be so because only response C has been rewarded.

In the same situation the field theorist would predict that the person would choose path B the first time and go directly toward the goal of water. How does he explain this? White, using the theory of the field psychologists, explains this in part by forming two postulates.

---

[97] Bigge, *op. cit.*, p. 462.
[98] Bigge and Hunt, *op. cit.*, p. 360.

The first he calls the "perceptual learning" postulate which states that "when a particular piece of behavior in a particular situation is once perceived as a path to a particular object, a more or less permanent 'knowledge' of this relationship usually results. As a rule this knowledge is available to the organism when the same situation is again presented." [99] This postulate is derived by White from the theories of both Tolman and Lewin and is admittedly "a gross oversimplification of two extremely complex problems—the problem of learning and the problem of recall or utilization of acquired knowledge." [100]

His second postulate he terms the "path-goal" postulate. "If there is a motive or a 'need,' the goal of which is a particular object, and at the same time there is available the knowledge that a particular piece of behavior is a path to that goal-object, then that behavior will tend to occur." [101] Applying these two postulates to the situation at hand, we can see the following explanation for the field theorists' prediction of behavior B. In the beginning of the experiment, the person had, through trial-and-error, perceived that path B led to water and while this had not been the required response, the knowledge thus acquired "changed the cognitive structure of the psychological environment." White's second postulate, based on Lewin and Tolman's theories, would explain the fact that the person entered path B the first time by saying that there was a "need" (thirst), the goal of which was a particular object (water) and that there was available the knowledge that a particular piece of behavior (choosing path B) is a path to the goal object. Thus behavior B will tend to occur.

This example, while simple, tends to point up some of the fundamental differences between associationist and field theories of learning. The nonpassivity of the learner is evident, along with the concept that learning is not necessarily a change in behavior or overt act. In regard to this, White states that, "the perceptual learning postulate refers only to the acquisition of 'knowledge,' and not, as S-R psychology does, to overt responses. Also, 'perceptual learning' implies a sort of association between 'ideas,' but not between a situation and an overt act." [102]

And finally, this illustration points up the concept of the field theorists that the behavior depends on two interdependent factors—the person and the environment; in the above case, needs and knowledge. Applying Lewin's basic formula $B = f(P,E)$, we can see that if either one of the

---

[99] *Op. cit.*, p. 162.
[100] *Ibid.*
[101] *Ibid.*, p. 168.
[102] *Ibid.*, p. 164.

two variables—need or knowledge—is absent or zero, then behavior will not be forthcoming.[103]

Applied to the experiment above, if there is no perception or "knowledge" that water lies at the end of path B, then we cannot assume that the subject will make any response in that psychological environment. And conversely, if the subject has such knowledge, but no need, then there is no reason to expect that any response will be made.

In other words, again pointing up a fundamental difference—that of wholeness as opposed to elements—a stimulus or a need alone cannot elicit a response of behavior. Behavior is elicited only when the cognitive structure or life-space is restructured, thus permitting the perception of the action toward that goal object.

MODELS OF LEARNING

From our two main theories of learning there has emerged a series of "models" used for the purpose of explaining, describing and, in some instances, predicting learning behavior. These models are usually confined to a few major factors or variables of the learning system. It is important to remember that a model is really nothing more nor less than a highly structured or well-formulated theory. However, "model" is a term which seems to arouse less reaction than the term "theory," which is sometimes considered anathema to "practical" men of affairs. The following models of learning are presented in as simplified a manner as possible consistent with the dictates of practical reality. From these models of learning we can, hopefully, deduce some important insights and generalizations regarding consumer behavior. Such an undertaking is attempted in Chapter 5.

The Hullian model. One of the most utilized and discussed models of learning is Hull's behavioral model, formalized in his book, *Principles of Behavior*.[104] While differing greatly in methodology from the later statistical and stochastic learning models, many of these were influenced by Hull's theory and formulations.[105]

The usefulness of Hull's system has not been its application in

---

103 *Ibid.*, pp. 171-172.
104 Clark L. Hull, *Principles of Behavior* (New York: Appleton-Century-Crofts, 1943).
105 R. R. Bush and R. Mosteller, *Stochastic Models of Learning* (New York: John Wiley & Sons, Inc., 1955), p. viii.

practice but rather its value in attempting to structure the theory of learning, thus providing a definite basis from which to establish some fundamental learning principles. While critical of Hull's explanations and constructs, Hilgard has said that, "whatever its deficiencies in detail, the system which Hull proposes has set a model for other theorists to emulate." [106] He goes on to say that "the formal character of the system is what one expects of science." [107]

Hull's basic theory of learning follows generally what was outlined in the early part of this chapter as the Stimulus-Response school of thought. His basic stimulus is that of an innate drive. For learning to occur, the response must be rewarded. The reinforcement strength along with the magnitude of the goal object, the time between the response and the reward, and the time delay of reinforcement are the four variables interacting in the stimulus situation which determine the strength of habit. Hull's behavior event begins with the stimulus provided by the external world and ends with the response.[108] The intervening processes in his system according to Hilgard are "scientific constructs rather than observables." [109]

The actual Hullian learning model consists (in very simplified form) of four variables which he has termed "initiating drive" (D); "incentive potential" (K); "habit strength" (H); and "stimulus-intensity-dynamism" (V). These four variables reacting in a multiplicative manner produce (E), or "reaction potential," which does not equal behavior as such, but which is implied to be close enough for use in marketing applications.[110]

The reason for this inequality is the fact that E (Hull uses $_sE_r$ to denote reaction potential) may be below the so-called "threshold value" or that value of D which is insufficient to elicit a response.[111] And Howard seems to be correct in his assumption for our purposes since no use could be made of the theoretical system if there is no reaction potential for the product. That is, if the drive is low enough so that no response can be elicited, then the relations of the variables should not concern us too much.

This relationship of the variables in Hull's system can be stated as an equation of the form [112]

[106] *Op. cit.,* p. 113.
[107] *Ibid.*
[108] *Ibid.*
[109] *Ibid.*
[110] John A. Howard, *Marketing: Executive and Buyer Behavior* (New York: Columbia University Press, 1965), p. 101.
[111] Hilgard, *op. cit.,* p. 88.
[112] Howard, *op. cit.,* p. 101.

$$E = D \times K \times H \times V$$

where E = reaction potential (assumed here to be equal to behavior)
        D = drive (measured in strength)
        K = incentive potential (value of the goal object)
        H = habit strength (function of reinforced responses)
        V = stimulus-intensity-dynamism (strength of the stimulus) [113]

Howard considers V to be of particular significance since "presumably much advertising and personal selling effort could be included as exerting their effect through V." [114] This significance is dulled somewhat by the qualification that Hull in referring to stimulus-intensity-dynamism is talking strictly in terms of physical intensity which differs from intense appeals, etc. However, the validity of Howard's statement has not been proved one way or the other. Another means of affecting the reaction potential is through D or the initiating drive.[115] By affecting consumers' drives for status and prestige, the seller or advertiser may be able to increase D, and, if all other variables remain constant, increase E. In fact, arguments could be made for influencing any one or all of the variables. And, because of the multiplicative nature of the system's equation, it can be seen that if any one of the variables is equal to zero, then the reaction potential (E) must also be zero. That is, if the initiating drive is zero (no drive at all), then there will be no reaction; if there is no incentive potential, there will be no response; if there is no stimulus-strength, there will be no reaction or response, and if H is equal to zero, then E will also be zero.

Several simple hypothetical applications of this model have been made.[116] In the first application, the drive (in this case, hunger) was increased holding all other variables constant. The result of this application (while hypothetical) was to show that as D increased, E increased also (although not in proportion). Reaction potential in this application stood for the purchase of X units of food. Thus as the drive (hunger) increased, the number of units of food purchased increased.

In the second application, drive was held constant by stating it as a three-hour hunger period for all shoppers. In this instance the variable V was changed by presenting the consumer with various sizes of cans of the food product. It was theorized in this application that the larger can was purchased, on the average, more often than was the smaller can. If this were the actual case, it could be suggested that by knowing the

---

113 See Hilgard, *op. cit.*, p. 89, for a schematic representation of the system.
114 *Op. cit.*, p. 102.
115 *Ibid.*, p. 103.
116 *Ibid.*, p. 104.

level of drive, a means of determining the most applicable size of product to market under those drive conditions might be found. This, of course, could be carried out on the basis of price, quality, or a number of controlled product attributes.

The problem, of course, is the assumption that the other variables will be held constant. Only under carefully controlled experimental conditions would this be applicable—at least at this point in the development of the model. Some means of accounting for all of the relevant variables will have to be derived. First of all, however, the actual variables involved will have to be discovered and structured.

While theoretical in nature, the Hullian learning model does present some very interesting areas for further exploration and research. In fact, Howard has cited a few applications under field conditions, but concludes:

> Unfortunately, the applications of experimentation under field conditions have contributed little to a systematic body of knowledge about buyer behavior, because in no one of the works . . . was there an attempt to relate either the design of the study or human behavior; the work was noncumulative.[117]

It is toward a "systematic body of knowledge of human behavior" that the recent literature on learning is pointed. Since the late 1940's and early 1950's, work in the field of learning models, and particularly "stochastic" or probabilistic models of learning, has picked up momentum and seems likely to progress even further as theorists attempt to systematize the myriad theories of learning into a usable framework of behavior.

Stochastic models of learning. At this time, the condition of stochastic model research seems to be little better than that of the learning theorists. Many learning models of this type have been developed over the last twenty-five years; some with more or less general applicability to many learning situations due to their wide parameters and some with more specific, closely defined parameters having few applications.

The developments in learning models have been along three lines with various theoretical bases for their development. Abstract models, urn models, and psychological or theoretical models are the main groups.[118] In all three cases, the models are mathematical and statistical

---

117 *Ibid.*, p. 106.

118 Frank Restle, "A Survey and Classification of Learning Models," in *Studies in Mathematical Learning Theory,* ed. Robert R. Bush and William K. Estes (Stanford, Calif.: Stanford University Press, 1959), Chap. 20.

in method—the difference being in the amount of theory upon which the constructs are based. Restle has stated:

> With respect to the amount of theory underlying models, we have at present to deal with three main levels: the abstract model, algebraic in form; the urn model, in which a theory (physical model) is used to justify a mathematical form, without serious commitment to the theory as psychologically meaningful; and "stimulus element" and "cue" theories, in which the equations arise from psychological interpretations of the situation and in which the underlying theory is believed to be at least a good approximation to reality.[119]

He further indicates that the choice of the type of model used—abstract, urn, or theoretical—will depend upon the immediate need. Because of this "immediate need" we will confine our discussion to the types of learning models which seem to have some applicability to marketing problems. A simple classification of these models along the lines suggested above is probably not feasible for this discussion since some of the earlier abstract models, along with more refined theoretical models, may have some use or possible future applicability to marketing.

The Bush and Mosteller model.   One model that has been applied in simple form to marketing problems is derived from Bush and Mosteller's simple learning model.[120] This simple model, which has been expanded in recent years,[121] is based upon reinforcement concepts whereas some other models, notably Estes' model, have attempted to formalize association theory.[122] The model utilizes experimental data and, through mathematical and statistical measures, attempts to predict or state the probabilities of a certain event occurring again. The events are divided into the perception of a stimulus; performance of a response or instrumental act; occurrence of an environmental event; and the execution of a goal object.[123] The environmental act, according to Bush and Mosteller, is the presentation of a reinforcing stimulus. Though not explicitly stated in the model, a state of motivation or drive is inferred from observing the goal response.[124]

---

[119] *Ibid.*, p. 419.

[120] R. R. Bush and F. Mosteller, "A Mathematical Model for Simple Learning," *Psychological Review*, September, 1951, pp. 313-323.

[121] Bush and Mosteller, *Stochastic Models of Learning*.

[122] W. K. Estes, "Toward a Statistical Theory of Learning," *Psychological Review*, January, 1950, pp. 94-107.

[123] Bush and Mosteller, "A Mathematical Model for Simple Learning," p. 313.

[124] *Ibid.*, p. 314.

In this model as well as in those of Estes, Estes and Burke, and, in fact, all of the stochastic models in some form or another, behavior is measured as a probability.[125] In Bush and Mosteller's model the probability p_1 is the probability that the instrumental act will occur during a specific time period h. "This probability will change during conditioning and extinction and will be related to experimental variables such as latent time, rate, and frequency of choice." [126]

Probability p_2 is increased or decreased after the occurrence of the response due to the environmental events (reinforcement) or the effort expended in making the response. The magnitude changed in probability p_2 after the response took place.[127] Thus, if the probability was zero, it could not be reduced any further, or if unity, it could not be increased.

It is this change in the probability after a response that is important. This change must be described since this reflects the amount of learning that has taken place. In this simple model, they have made the important assumption that the "change is independent of the still earlier values of the probability." [128] That is, they are describing the change in terms of the *last* probability before the response. This assumption of course limits the effect of previous learning or experience, thus limiting the usefulness of the model. However, this has been taken into account in some more recent models, therefore expanding the parameters and making the model more useful. The problem, however, has not been entirely eliminated.

Using mathematical operators and making another important assumption—that of a linear relationship—Bush and Mosteller's basic equation for their model is as follows:

$$Qp = p = a(1 - p) - bp$$

where a and b are parameters: a standing for those factors which always increase the probability of occurrence and b representing those factors that decrease probability (a and b each must lie between 0 and 1). The assumption of a linear operator is based on small changes—"if the change is small we would expect that this assumption would provide an adequate first approximation." [129] When there is no reward, $a = 0$; b is associated with punishment or the work involved in making the response.

---

[125] W. K. Estes, "Toward a Statistical Theory of Learning," and W. K. Estes and C. J. Burke, "A Mathematical Model for Simple Learning," *Psychological Review*, April, 1953, pp. 276-283.

[126] Bush and Mosteller, "A Mathematical Model for Simple Learning," p. 314.

[127] *Ibid.*

[128] *Ibid.*

[129] *Ibid.*, p. 316.

By applying this operator to experimental data, the probability of occurrence of the response on the next trial can be estimated, thus to some extent measuring or predicting probable behavior in the next time period. The operator Q is repeatedly applied to some initial value of the probability p. Each application of the operator (Q) corresponds to one occurrence of the response and the subsequent environmental events (reinforcement or punishment).[130]

The limitations of this simple model seem obvious and were recognized by Bush and Mosteller in their paper. No attempt was made at relating the parameters a and b to experimental variables such as the amount of work or reward, the strength of the drive, or past response history.[131] The lineal assumption limited the effectiveness to small changes in probabilities and the applicability was limited to experimental conditions where the response was the same in each instance—as was the reinforcement or work involved in making the response.

The model also was used to describe an extinction trial by using an operator E of the form $Ep = p - bp = (1 - p)b$; and, if applied successively in n trials, the equation becomes $E_p^n = (1 - p)_p^n$.[132] The usefulness of this formula is in describing curves of experimental extinction, since the parameter b is used alone. Again its applicability is limited to specific experimental data.

Further refinements and applications were made in Bush and Mosteller's model which to some extent have reduced the limitations to the simple model. Again, however, these refinements make possible the model's application only to specific experimental conditions, not, as we would like, to general marketing problems. This specificity of application is again referred to by Bush and Mosteller in their 1955 book, *Stochastic Models of Learning.* Here they state that:

> The system we describe in rather general terms is applied to a number of particular experimental problems, but we make no pretense at completeness or finality and shall feel much rewarded if we provide a start on a good approach.[133]

While limited, one application which has been tried with some success in the field of marketing has been that of the general form of Bush and Mosteller's model "in choice situations with risk." [134] A number of re-

---

[130] *Ibid.*, p. 315.
[131] *Ibid.*
[132] *Ibid.*, p. 316.
[133] *Stochastic Models of Learning*, p. vii.
[134] *Ibid.*, p. 2.

searchers interested in marketing have used variations of this type of model in attempting to predict consumer brand choice and brand switching.

In the succeeding chapter, we shall examine these stochastic models of learning in connection with brand-switching problems as we turn now to the application of learning concepts to our main concern, consumer behavior.

FIVE

Application of
Learning Concepts to
Consumer Behavior

Few sources are available which attempt to define strictly the role of the learning process in the marketing of goods and services. However, what has been written in this area suggests that too little attention has been given to this subject and that, with further research and experimentation, the application of some of the basic principles of the learning process will provide a very useful tool to the marketer and advertiser.

Two approaches to the application of these principles to marketing situations (via consumer behavior) are apparent in the literature. What has been done in the first instance is to redefine some of the elements of marketing, using the terminology of the learning theorists. *This, coupled with the explanation of consumer behavior in part as a learning process, has, through observation and some empirical evidence, shown some of the relationships between learning and how some marketing procedures may affect this learning process.*

It is important to note that at this point in time there is no universal "law" of learning which can be applied to marketing problems. That is, when confronted with a problem situation, we cannot say that if we apply formula X, result Y will occur. Some evidence exists, however, that by applying certain "principles" of learning and by thinking through marketing problems using those principles which would seem to apply, we can gain some insight into the problem and the possible solutions.

An area of increasing interest, which is basically an attempt to systematize these principles into a more structured system, is that of stochastic learning models. While some models of learning processes have been attempted throughout the history of the development of learning theory, it was not until the 1940's and 1950's that any significant advances were made. This is true particularly in the mathematical and statistical methods used in dealing with these models.[1]

Hull's model of habit formation was an attempt at formalizing these learning principles into a useful model using four variables which acted upon behavior.[2]

LEARNING ELEMENTS IN PRODUCT CHOICE

According to Gerald Zaltman, "a customer's mind moves through a series of stages before he makes a purchase decision." And, "as a rule, the movement from initial awareness to adoption is not instantaneous; there are a number of intermediary stages."[3] In an earlier chapter we saw that a person must be motivated by some physiological or psychological need or drive. Needs were viewed as pluralistic in that there were more than one of such drives (in some instances) initiating a person's behavior.

The stage before a person becomes aware of a product, then, is that of an underlying need which causes the consumer to seek out some way of reducing that need. These drives may be innate or, according to Miller, motives may be learned during the socialization process.[4] This position is in line with the stimulus-response group of theories as outlined in the previous chapter.

The gestalt position holds that "the organism has one basic tendency and striving—to actualize, maintain and enhance the experiencing organism."[5] Therefore, according to this view (which incidentally, reflects the cognitive theory idea of "wholeness"), instead of many needs or motives, it is possible that all of the physiological and psychological needs may be described merely as aspects of this one fundamental need.

---

[1] Robert R. Bush and William K. Estes, *Studies in Mathematical Learning Theory* (Stanford, Calif.: Stanford University Press, 1959).

[2] C. L. Hull, *Principles of Behavior* (New York: Appleton-Century-Crofts, 1943).

[3] Gerald Zaltman, *Marketing: Contributions from the Behavioral Sciences* (New York: Harcourt, Brace & World, Inc., 1965), p. 23.

[4] Neal E. Miller, "Learnable Drives and Rewards," *Handbook of Experimental Psychology*, ed. S. S. Stevens (New York: John Wiley & Sons, Inc., 1951), pp. 435-472.

[5] Carl R. Rogers, *Client Centered Therapy* (Boston: Houghton Mifflin Company, 1951), p. 487.

Whichever view is adopted, the fact remains that some sort of initiating drive is present in any purchase decision. And, furthermore, this initiating drive produces behavior that is goal-directed in an attempt to satisfy the initiating force. Rogers adheres to the idea that this goal-directed behavior takes place in the individual's experienced and perceptual field, which to him is reality.[6] Thus, if a person perceives a product as a source of satisfaction of his initiating drive, he will purchase that product. This idea is presented also (in varying forms) by Zaltman, Bayton, and Howard.[7]

According to the gestalt theory of cognitive learning, the "perceptual" or "cognitive" field of the individual may become the prime interest of the marketer, for this is the area in which there is an opportunity to influence or change the consumer's behavior. By changing or adding to the cognitive field of the individual buyer, the seller may be able to influence this person's product choice. This change of the cognitive field is, to the cognitive theorists, learning; thus the seller must more or less "teach" the consumer to prefer his product or brand over those of competitors.

In essence, this process would seem to be the same in either case. That is, the learning process, whether it consists of elements as taught by the S-R theorists or as a whole, as advocated by the cognitive theorists, has the same effect. *The end desire of the marketer is to influence this process in some way so as to maintain the individual as a buyer or to sway new individuals to adopt his product.*

Zaltman, in his discussion of learning, has divided the process into cognitive and affective learning.[8] Cognitive learning involves the cognitive activities of thinking, judging, perception, and memory. Bayton does not include this under learning. He defines these cognitions as purposive and regulatory in that they give direction to the satisfying of needs.[9] While the two are in agreement definitionally, they differ in their classification of the process. Whether it is viewed as a part of the learning process itself or as a separate step in the behavior sequence will not actually change its importance or usefulness as a concept. It is during this cognitive process that the person becomes consciously aware of the product.

---

6 *Ibid.*, p. 491.

7 Zaltman, *op. cit.*, pp. 19-25; James A. Bayton, "Motivation, Cognition, Learning—Basic Factors in Consumer Behavior," in *Marketing and the Behavioral Sciences,* ed. Perry Bliss (Boston: Allyn & Bacon, Inc., 1963), pp. 45-53; John A. Howard, *Marketing: Executive and Buyer Behavior* (New York: Columbia University Press, 1963), p. 96.

8 *Op. cit.*, p. 19.

9 *Op. cit.*, p. 48.

The second learning process described by Zaltman is that of affective learning which takes place after the consumer is aware of the product and begins to "like the product." [10] This "affective" learning process essentially involves the elements of the learning process from a S-R theoretical point of view. The emphasis in the literature seems to revolve around these elements and their application to the marketing situation. This may stem from the ease of defining parts as opposed to the whole process as is done by the cognitive learning theorists. And, as we shall see later, for the purposes of model building this is the most easily structured theory.

RELEVANT LEARNING PRINCIPLES

By returning to some of the principles of learning described earlier, many relationships may be visualized with apparent applications to the field of marketing.

Goal objects.   The goal object, defined in the marketing context, is any product or service which provides or is expected to provide the ability to reduce or eliminate a need. Or as one writer has stated:

> A product that satisfies a physiological need . . . or a psychological need (such as prestige) thus becomes the reinforcement agent, or as it is often called, a goal object.[11]

The expectations of the product, or goal object, are an important part of the learning process as applied to marketing. Whether the goal object does in reality provide such satisfaction is another matter—a matter of the greatest importance to the seller for "what is bought is not the product itself, but its image in the mind of the consumer." [12] In other words, the product, functioning as a goal object is, in the eyes of the consumer, a bundle of expectations. These expectations, of course, vary from consumer to consumer depending upon needs, the strength of those needs, and consumers' expectations as to what the goal object will do for them (what satisfactions will be derived from its use).

According to Bayton, the provision of the appropriate goal object is the most critical aspect of the entire sequence: "it is with the use of the goal-object that degree of gratification of the initial needs will

---

[10] Zaltman, *op. cit.*, p. 19.

[11] *Ibid.*, p. 21.

[12] Kenneth Groesbeck, "Shape Product Image to Mesh with Buyer's Mind," *Advertising Agency*, August 1, 1958, p. 29.

occur." [13] The obvious implication of this is that the product purchased by the consumer for the purpose of reducing need had better live up to the expectations of the consumer if repeat sales are to be expected. This idea, of course, ties in with the principle of reward or reinforcement which will be discussed as we proceed.

Cues. In the search for a goal object, the consumer must have some means of differentiating between products or brands of products. Cues provide the means of differentiation. [14] Cues are the product characteristics or the characteristics of an innovation. [15]

According to the usual economic demand theory, the consumer has a wealth of information concerning the markets, particularly about products. Unfortunately, however, this may be less true in the real world. Often, the consumer faces a purchase decision with a notable lack of information as to the product characteristics. For example, when a product's quality is in doubt, the consumer may rely on its price to infer quality. [16] In this case the consumer is substituting one cue (price) for another (quality) and provides himself with a set of expectations regarding the quality of the goal object.

The importance of cues in the learning process may be shown in cases where learning fails: [17] "If the cues are too obscure . . . it is impossible to make the correct response with precision," [18] the inference being that cues or product differentiations must not only be present but must actually be differentiating aspects of the product which are strong enough to elicit the wanted response (in this case, purchase of the given product). These differentiating attributes of the goal objects may be in the form of brand names, packages, a certain price-size relationship, quality, or any other product attribute or combination of attributes. [19]

One of the important things to note about cues is not only that they should represent product differences but that these differences do exist. For example, changing the color of a product creates a differentiation or different cue. However, an increase in the selection of this product by consumers will depend upon their expectancies of that product to reduce their need. If a change in color of a goal object does not

[13] *Op. cit.,* p. 53.

[14] See N. E. Miller and J. Dollard, "Four Fundamentals of Learning," in *Theories of Motivation in Learning,* ed. Richard C. Teevan and Robert C. Birney (Princeton, N.J.: D. Van Nostrand Co., Inc., 1964).

[15] Zaltman, *op. cit.,* p. 21.

[16] D. S. Tull, R. A. Boring, and M. H. Gonsier, "A Note on the Relationship of Price and Imputed Quality," *Journal of Business,* April, 1964, p. 186.

[17] Miller and Dollard, *op. cit.,* p. 48.

[18] *Ibid.*

[19] Zaltman, *op. cit.,* p. 21.

add to the drive reducing expectancies, or the consumer's perceived value of the product, sales theoretically should not increase because of this cue change.

Cues are the directing forces in consumer behavior. Cues determine the timing of a consumer's purchase, the place of his purchase, and the product or brand of product he will choose among alternatives. Therefore, the importance of cues in the consumer learning process is far-reaching. Cues affect the response made in relation to these cues. Therefore, "within limits, customer expectations may be influenced by advertising or other sales promotion methods." [20] Thus these cues are acting as weak stimuli, although technically they are not considered to be stimuli. [21]

Whole products as well as certain differentiating characteristics may also serve as cues. For instance, a product which differs in function from any other product may serve as a cue since its differentiating aspect is its use, which in effect is the essence of the product.

A recent experiment by J. R. Taylor has suggested that as the number of items increase, the consumer becomes less sensitive to changes in items. [22] Several important implications may be apparent here although further study and experimentation are probably needed. The first is that with a rising number of products on the market, each being promoted heavily, the consumer is faced with an increasingly difficult decision to make. According to this study, this increased number of products is associated with concentration upon the most frequently chosen alternative. [23] Along with this is the implication that a change in a cue such as price in one product affects the customer's choice less than when there are only a few alternatives. [24] Thus in a market situation where the seller is faced with a number of competitors with similar products, a change in a cue such as the price of the product will have to be fairly large (intense) and probably heavily promoted (thus changing another cue—that of promotion). The action to increase sales, of course, will depend upon the product and market conditions. What in effect has happened is that the information per item declined as the number of items increased, thereby setting up an inverse relationship between the number of items and information. [25]

---

[20] Richard N. Cardozo, "An Experimental Study of Customer Effort, Expectation and Satisfaction," *Journal of Marketing Research*, August, 1965, pp. 244-249.

[21] Howard, *op. cit.*, p. 99.

[22] L. K. Anderson, J. R. Taylor, and R. J. Holloway, "The Consumer and His Alternatives: An Experimental Approach," *Journal of Marketing Research*, February, 1966, pp. 63-68.

[23] *Ibid.*, p. 65.

[24] *Ibid.*

[25] *Ibid.*, p. 67.

In summary, then, we can say that cues are differentiating aspects of products (or products themselves in some cases). The cue directs the response of the purchaser. The ability to direct behavior will depend upon their relative strength and the change in those cues. Expectation of the consumer will to some degree depend upon the cue value and will influence the ability of cues to initiate the desired response.

Response. According to Howard, "a response roughly is an organism's reaction to a cue." [26] Therefore, the act of purchase is a response to the original stimulus or drive and the purchase of a specific product or brand of product is a response to cues which guide the purchase behavior.

Reinforcement or reward. Reinforcement, one of the basic elements in the stimulus-response theory of learning, strengthens the bond between the stimulus and the response. Reinforcement takes place when the original drive is reduced or, in the case of drives such as prestige, increased. Applied to marketing, these principles suggest that the purchase response must be rewarded or reinforced to provide a more adequate bond—an increased probability that the response will again be elicited when the stimulus conditions once again present themselves.

The ideas of response and reinforcement are closely entwined. That is, the response depends to a large degree upon the reward of that response, and the ability to reinforce a response depends upon the elicitation of that response. "If a response occurs only infrequently, it is difficult to find an occasion when it occurs and can be rewarded." [27] A major problem facing marketing is the attempt to elicit the first response so that it can be rewarded.[28] Since specific responses depend upon cues to give them direction, it may be assumed that the strength and type of cue used by the seller would provide or attempt to provide this response. Once again, then, the importance of providing the right cues of the greatest intensity and strength can be stressed. What these "right" cues and right "intensity and strength" of cues are, however, is left to further research. At present, as mentioned earlier, the explicit answers to these questions are not readily available for the marketer's use.

Hierarchy of responses. By arranging responses in the order of their probable occurrence, some insight may be gained as to the probabilities of selecting one product or brand over another. This involves a

---

[26] *Op. cit.*, p. 100.
[27] *Ibid.*
[28] *Ibid.*

concept generally termed the "hierarchy of responses." [29] The consumer may have within the realm of possibility more than one response in mind (awareness of several goal objects) which he assumes will satisfy a need. These are ranked according to the expectations this person has as to the ability of these various responses to adequately extinguish or reduce the need. For instance, when confronted with the physiological need of thirst, the consumer is faced with a variety of goal objects which can reduce this need. These objects can then be ranked according to his expectations of them. This ranking will depend upon other factors such as the intensity of the drive. If the need is an intense one, he may choose the most readily available means of reducing his drive; if it is less intense, he may wait until he can obtain another means of reducing the need. Another factor might be the intensity of the cues, such as price, taste, availability, brand, etc.

The first response elicited will be to purchase that product or brand which the consumer expects will provide the best solution to his problem. If, however, the response is not rewarded adequately by this first purchase, the consumer will tend to purchase the next most likely product (response #2). This order of responses is termed the resultant hierarchy.[30] The process will continue until a product is found that will adequately reward the response.

Based somewhat upon this hierarchical concept of response, a number of studies have been made along the lines of predicting consumer brand choice. Alfred Kuehn and Ralph L. Day have used a probabilistic model approach in an attempt to set up a framework within which to predict consumer responses.[31] The main method used here was to ascribe probabilities to various factors influencing brand choice.

Applications of stochastic models to brand choice situations.   In a 1962 *Journal of Business* article, it was suggested that probabilistic studies of brand choice should maintain as goals, two things: (1) to gain insight into the behavioral processes that underlie the observed patterns of brand choice, and (2) to provide a framework for predicting the effect on brand choice of such elements in the marketing mix as changes in relative price, distribution and promotion.[32] To this we might

---

[29] For an excellent discussion of this "hierarchy," see N. E. Miller and J. Dollard, *Social Learning and Imitation* (New Haven, Conn.: Yale University Press, 1941).

[30] *Ibid.*

[31] "Probabilistic Models of Consumer Buying," *Journal of Marketing*, October, 1964, pp. 27-31.

[32] Ronald E. Frank, "Brand Choice as a Probability Process," *Journal of Business,* January, 1962, pp. 43-56.

add changes in quality or any other factor influencing brand choice (supply structure and the importance of the product in the consumers' consumption patterns have been suggested).[33]

Kuehn and Day described the use of models in brand choice situations, using a generalized form of stochastic model based on associative learning under conditions of reward.[34]

> When the learning model is applied to the brand choice situation, the relevant "trials" are purchases of the product class. After each trial, the probability of the purchase of a particular brand on the next trial is revised in view of the choice made on that trial. If the brand in question was purchased, the probability of its purchase on the subsequent trial will normally be increased. If a brand is rejected, (another brand is purchased), its probability of purchase on the next purchase occasion will normally be reduced.[35]

Recognizing the fact that the consumer will never reach a situation where there is absolute certainty of a purchase of a specific brand, or an absolute certainty that he will not purchase another brand on the next occasion, the model has parameters set so that the probability of purchasing a brand on the next trial does not reach 0 or 1. This follows the form of Bush and Mosteller's incomplete learning, incomplete extinction model.[36] The use of the model thus far, Day and Kuehn report, is in studying patterns of consumer behavior and evaluating the effect of merchandising activity by studying recent purchase records of consumers.

William F. Massey has stated that "the problem of describing and predicting this type of behavior is reduced (using stochastic models) to one of specifying the relevant probability law governing the consumer's choice among competing brands under a given set of personal and environmental conditions."[37] He suggests that where a deterministic model dealing with brand switching would have to be too complex, "many features of observed brand switching behavior are consistent with relatively simple probability models."[38]

While this may be true, the fact remains that these models are not as yet refined enough to account for all of the many variables that are in-

---

[33] John A. Farley, "Why Does Brand Loyalty Vary Over Products?" *Journal of Marketing Research,* November, 1964, pp. 9-14.

[34] *Op. cit.,* pp. 27-31.

[35] *Ibid.,* p. 29.

[36] *Ibid.,* p. 30.

[37] "Order and Homogeneity of Family Specific Brand Switching Processes," *Journal of Marketing Research,* February, 1966, pp. 48-56. By permission of the American Marketing Association.

[38] *Ibid.,* p. 48.

volved in any consumer behavior. And, while they are consistent with many of the observed features of brand switching, it does not as yet seem possible to accurately predict this process.

Hertiner and Magee in 1961 conceptualized consumer behavior as a Markov process.[39] This model, they said, "is satisfying to the intuition, generally consistent with published data, and suggestive of possible marketing tactics." [40] This first-stage Markov process advocated by Hertiner and Magee has the limitation of assuming that the probabilities depend on the brand previously purchased, but not the family's purchase history prior to that time.[41] This again nullifies the effect of prior experience. Lipstein, in his more recent article, also suggests the use of this first-order Markov chain model in predicting consumer behavior.[42]

Basically, this type of model is similar to our original simple model as can be seen in A. S. C. Ehrenberg's explanation of this model:

> Markov brand-switching models aim in general to deal with repeat-buying and brand switching behavior, primarily for frequently bought nondurable consumer goods. . . . Transition probabilities are analyzed for equal periods of time within the particular product field thus providing the proportion of repeat buyers and brand switches for the next time period.[43]

The main assumption is that each repeat-buying or brand-switching proportion has to remain constant or stationary from one period to the next. If this assumption is applicable, says Ehrenberg, then the theory is applicable. He lists as the problems involved in using this type of model, the following:

1. Omitting to ensure that the data are of a technically suitable form to be modeled by the model.
2. Omitting to examine the crucial assumption involved.
3. Omitting any self-critical appraisal of the various concepts and analytical steps in the approach.
4. Omitting to gather any generalized empirical knowledge of repeat-buying and brand-switching behavior as such.[44]

---

[39] Jerome E. Hertiner and John F. Magee, "Customer Behavior as a Markov Process," *Operations Research,* January-February, 1961, pp. 105-122.

[40] *Ibid.,* p. 105.

[41] Massey, *op. cit.,* p. 48.

[42] Benjamin Lipstein, "A Mathematical Model of Consumer Behavior," *Journal of Marketing Research,* August, 1965.

[43] "An Appraisal of Markov Brand-Switching Models," *Journal of Marketing Research,* November, 1965, pp. 347-363. By permission of the American Marketing Association.

[44] *Ibid.,* p. 361.

Going even further, Ehrenberg denies the need for a brand-switching theory based on a stochastic-probabilistic approach. In fact, he states that "there is already ample evidence that the probabilistic interpretation would be impossible." [45]

What we are left with then is a variety of attempted applications of these methods to brand choice and brand-switching situations which, in fact, may not really mean anything of value. This is left to further research. It is possible, however, that through increased use and refinement of these general models, some relevant applications may be made to marketing problems of this and other types. For this to take place, however, it seems evident that:

> A useful dynamic model of consumer brand choice behavior must provide a method of revising the individual's set of purchase probabilities to show changes induced by the passage of time, new product experience, and exposures to merchandise influences. *No simple structure can adequately reflect these complex changes.*[46]

Frank has indicated that further research will be necessary to construct more complex models to include the variables not evident in present models and to study market situations where abrupt changes such as the introduction of a new brand have occurred.[47]

The gradient of generalization. Bayton, in his discussion of learning, uses the term "generalization gradient" in referring to the ordering of goal objects.[48]

> One goal object, because of its associated expectancies, can be assumed to have maximum appeal within the set of goal objects. The alternatives then can be ordered in terms of how their associated expectancies approximate those of brand A.[49]

In Fig. 11, it can be seen that in generalization of goal objects, "mere ordering is not enough—the 'psychological distance' between positions must be determined also, and the factor determining these distances is similarity of expectancy." [50]

In the first column in Fig. 11, it is shown that brand A is assigned the highest expectancy (may be based on cues associated with A), and

---

45 *Ibid.*
46 Kuehn and Day, *op. cit.*, p. 29.
47 Frank, *op. cit.*, p. 56.
48 *Op. cit.*, p. 52.
49 *Ibid.*
50 *Ibid.*

Figure 11: Gradient of Generalization.

Brand A		Brand A
Brand B		
	or	Brand C
Brand C		Brand B

Source: James A. Bayton, "Motivation, Cognition, Learning: Basic Factors in Consumer Behavior," *Marketing and the Behavioral Sciences,* ed. Perry Bliss (Boston: Allyn & Bacon, Inc., 1963), p. 52.

brand B, the next highest; brand C is at the bottom of the list. The spacing between A, B, and C indicates the closeness of expectancies. In the first case, the expectations of the consumer as to the likelihood that either brand A or brand B will satisfy his need are very close. In the second case, however, the expectancy is that brand A will provide a reward much more readily than either brand C or B.

The important points to be derived from this generalization concept are the implications of these gradients upon product substitution and product discrimination. To illustrate this point, let us revert to the cue-response-reinforcement concepts presented earlier. Expectations depend upon a pattern of cues; these cues in turn direct the response, and reinforcement strengthens the pattern of cues in the sense that this same cue pattern will tend to elicit the same response in the future. Howard, however, states that this process of reinforcement "strengthens not only the tendency for that pattern of cues to elicit that response, but also the tendency for similar patterns of cues to elicit the same response." [51]

We can see here a possible problem for the marketer and advertiser. If two responses (purchase of goal objects) are very close in expectation, the value of their cues will in all probability be close also. If this is the case, then substitution can readily take place. Small changes in cue patterns from one product to another may be enough to cause changes in expectations and changed responses leading to the purchase of another brand. Therefore, it would seem advisable for the seller to have a pattern of cues unlike his competitors so that the expectations associated with his product will not be "generalized" to include the brands of his competition. The seller wishes to maintain "discrimination" toward his product,[52] discrimination being the consumer's preference for his product above all others. This discrimination will persist as long as

[51] *Op. cit.*, p. 106.
[52] For a more detailed description of discrimination, see Zaltman, *op. cit.*, pp. 135-138.

the individual is rewarded in response to this brand's pattern of cues while not rewarded by the response of another brand.[53] This can change, however, with changing cues of competing products.

Another important aspect of the generalization gradient has been stated by Howard:

> The generalization principle also argues that a company's product should be readily available. If it is not, the buyer is encouraged to settle for a similar brand, since he encounters both the delay and the effort of looking elsewhere.[54]

He further points out in his discussion that the degree of generalization depends upon the strength of the drive. That is, as the need is increased, the generalization of cue patterns among competing products is increased, with the effect that products will be more easily substituted. According to this effect the seller who advertises may increase the learned drive and therefore create a tendency for consumers to purchase other brands instead of confining their purchases to his product.[55]

The main effort of the seller by the use of advertising, sales promotion, price factors, quality, packaging, in fact his whole cue pattern of communication is, or should be, to present a product to the consuming public which will gain awareness through the cognitive processes, and direct the response through the use of cue patterns to obtain sales of his product, which, as a goal object, must reward the response; this process will tend to strengthen the pattern of cues and the probability of a repeated response. In terms of the S-R theory, this will result in the strengthening of the bond between stimulus and the process and provide for habit formation. The stronger this bond becomes, the less likelihood of a loss of product discrimination.

Habit formation. Howard maintains that "habit strength is said to depend *only* upon the number of reinforced trials." [56] This is not true, however, in the formation of habits. Habit refers to the elimination of cognitive activity connected with making a response. This reduction may be caused by repeated reinforcement, but the act of a repeated response to stimulation is not a valid criterion for determining whether a habit exists.[57] The crucial factor seems to be the reduction of cognitive activity. Thus the seller should be attempting to reduce this activity by providing continuous reinforcement to the response.

---

53 Howard, *op. cit.*, p. 107.
54 *Ibid.*, p. 108.
55 *Ibid.*
56 *Ibid.*
57 *Ibid.*, pp. 104-105.

Continuous reinforcement is important since, as shown earlier, a response which is not rewarded leads to extinction of that response. Pavlov in his experiments defined this by showing that without reinforcement a response would tend to diminish.[58] The number of reinforcements in a given number of responses is still under study, and various findings are set forth in the literature.[59] Extinction of a response by zero reinforcement or with negative reinforcement again provides competitors with an opportunity to challenge your product's position.

We have attempted to show in the last few pages what has been done and is currently being done in applying some of the principles of learning theory to consumer behavior. While not conclusive owing to lack of universally applied "laws" of learning, evidence does seem to indicate the applicability and relevance of learning theory to marketing theory.[60]

THE BRIDGE BETWEEN THE IMAGES: LEARNING

Modern marketing is the business field which probably ranks highest in ability and willingness to adopt and adapt theories and discoveries which originate in other disciplines. This is evidenced in part by the early incorporation of the stimulus-response approach into buying behavior theory. With the discovery of self-images and product images, marketing practitioners have come to place increased emphasis on the means by which image-conscious consumers can effectively be directed to the appropriate product image. The means by which this direction is achieved can be greatly improved by the use of learning theory.

An individual is endowed at birth with three behavioral qualities. The first has already been explained—primary drives. Secondly, he has a small number of specific reflexes. This refers to definite responses or reflexes which result from specific stimuli. Thus a child should retreat from hot objects. The last endowment is called an innate hierarchy of responses. An individual usually demonstrates an ordered preference for responses to strong stimuli. He may resort to facial contortions to gain attention; if this fails, he may then begin to cry. In this last example, the stimulus could have been the sight of a parent. A cue differs from a stimulus in that it guides or directs the action of an individual. Strong stimuli, or drives, provoke actions but do not exhibit any influence on

---

[58] Ernest R. Hilgard, *Theories of Learning*, rev. ed. (New York: Appleton-Century-Crofts, 1955).

[59] Howard, *op. cit.*, pp. 115-117.

[60] For a quick summary, see Philip Kotler, "Behavior Models for Analyzing Buyers," *Journal of Marketing*, October, 1965, pp. 40-41.

that action once it is provoked. A cue is a directed drive, which is in turn a strong stimulus.

Learning can be defined as a change in behavior, caused by the association of a given cue with a given response. As can be readily understood, learning cannot take place before a given response results from a given cue. An individual must first respond before he can recognize that the response is correct.

Learning first begins with a cue; any number of responses is likely to result on this occasion. However, the likelihood of a response is governed by the amount of previous learning the individual has experienced. If no learning has occurred, the responses are performed in the order of the innate hierarchy of responses. With some learning, an initial hierarchy of responses determines the probability of various responses happening. After the individual has learned the response, it occurs in the resultant hierarchy. While learning causes changed behavior, there is always some chance, however small, that other responses will result.

Language has an enormous amount of influence on an individual's behavior because words become linked to specific responses. Not only do words serve as cues, but they also serve to specify which hierarchy of responses will be resorted to when action is in order. A "terrifying" situation would call for an entirely different probability of responses than one which a person labels as "entertaining."

The process of learning is effected when a reinforcement, or reward, is present to make the association of a cue and a response a desirable one. This association is strengthened by repeated reinforcements. Reinforcements serve to lower the drive which prompts action. Reward can only take effect when drives are operational. Consequently, reward often becomes impossible when the drive is eliminated through continuous reinforcements. A drive which is nonrecurring presents a difficult learning situation, unless the stimuli can be externally increased in strength.

In a similar vein, if reward is withheld from a response to a cue, in time the response will fail to materialize when the cue is presented. This tendency is called extinction. Sometimes after a response becomes extinct, it will reappear as a result of a cue without previous reinforcement. Appropriately this is termed spontaneous recovery.

Often an individual will respond identically to a cue which differs from an original cue; this is referred to as generalization. Conversely, when differing responses result from nearly identical cues, the element of discrimination is present; this permits the respondent to detect the slight variations in the cues and to modify his behavior with appropriate reactions.

Quite simply, buying can be conceptualized as being a learning process. The buyer is moved by drives in accordance with his needs and their degree of satisfaction. Determining what his needs are cannot be done accurately without a serious market research effort. Not only do needs and the resultant drives have to be analyzed, but the consumer's image of himself and available products must be studied. Once this groundwork has been accomplished, the learning process begins. The consumer must be informed effectively of the product which will reward him. Since an active consumer has experienced learning of various degrees, he will respond to various opportunities to buy (cues) in accordance with an initial hierarchy of responses. He may purchase the designated product, or he may respond in a different and undesirable fashion. If the product meets his needs and reduces the motivational drives, reinforcement takes place. When the consumer continues to buy the product in response to a cue, be it any stimuli presented by the marketer, the learning process is complete.

ADAPTING LEARNING CONCEPTS TO MARKETING
AND COMMUNICATION PROGRAMS

Steuart Henderson Britt, one of the early critics of the "list of motives" explanation of consumers' buying behavior, has given twenty principles of learning which can be used by marketers in designing marketing communications programs.[61] Established experimentally by psychologists, these rules should enable a marketer to more fully appreciate and use messages within a behavioral framework.

> 1. "Unpleasant things may sometimes be learned as readily as pleasant things, but the most ineffective stimuli are those which arouse little or no emotional response."

This means that the conditions most conducive to learning are rewarding ones; unpleasant conditions are not as desirable, but they are better than neutral conditions. The blaring television works, but more effective are free samples given with appropriate messages. Messages which leave no impression are only an expense.

> 2. "The capacities of learners are important in determining what can be learned and how long it will take."

[61] The following has been adapted from Steuart Henderson Britt, "How Advertising Can Use Psychology's Rules of Learning," *Printers' Ink* 252, September 23, 1955, pp. 74, 77, 80.

It is important that marketers know their audiences. Bright people can grasp the significance of messages much more quickly than can those of lower intelligence. Needless to say, underestimating audiences' intelligence can result in unnecessary communication efforts; conversely, an audience of lower intelligence will require more work and expense to learn the significance of what is conveyed. If the marketer does not realize this, he may believe his communication is a failure, whereas success may be only a short distance away.

3. "Things that are learned and understood tend to be better retained than things learned by rote."

While extensive drill is important in getting the facts across, messages are remembered more easily if they are understood. Mere repetition can get a message across, but this is much more expensive.

4. "Practice distributed over several periods is more economical in learning than the same amount of practice concentrated into a single period."

Advertising campaigns are relevant here. Audiences will remember and understand messages more easily if the campaign lasts longer. A shorter more concentrated campaign is not likely to be as effective as the one which is stretched out over longer periods.

5. "When teaching people to master technical skills it is better to show the performance in the same way that the learner would see it if he were doing the job himself."

In presenting materials they should be designed so that they show over-the-shoulder shots, the view that the learner would have if he were actually the demonstrator. Similar are messages which are written with the "you" attitude.

6. "The order of presentation of materials to be learned is very important."

In addition to the significance attached to the pattern of message components, sets, there is another consideration here. Of the total message, points presented first and last are remembered better than those in the middle. Thus, if the marketer wishes to present four reasons for buying his product, he should place the two most important points first and last in his message.

7. "If material to be learned is different or unique, it will be better remembered."

Messages which stand out usually are remembered more readily than those which are commonplace. Unusual sounds, sights, colors, and product attributes all serve to dominate the more ordinary stimuli in consumers' minds. The object of the marketer here is to present consumers with cues which differ from those regularly used by competitors so that generalization does not occur; generalization is a problem since consumers tend to ignore the barrage of messages which they receive daily from many marketers.

8. "Showing errors in how to do something can lead to increases in learning."

This point ties in with Britt's first principle: unpleasant things can lead to learning. A specific use of this principle applies to television commercials where a young woman is shown stranded on a highway with a flat tire—seemingly because she or her husband did not buy the correct make of automobile tires. She purchased incorrectly and suffers the consequences. Similarly, some coffee commercials show the results (a dissatisfied husband) of a housewife's not buying the correct brand of coffee. What not to do can be as effective as showing what to do.

9. "Learning situations which are rewarded only occasionally can be more efficient than those where constant reward is employed."

This principle refers to the fact that often free samples and premiums come to be expected by consumers, and when these rewards are taken away after a long period of time, consumers feel cheated. The objective of premiums and the like is to have the consumers learn the merits of the product, which provide the reinforcement in this process. Extended deals often result in becoming the reinforcements themselves in the learning process, rather than just the product's qualities.

10. "It is easier to recognize stimuli than it is to recall them."

Since it is easier to recognize products and messages than to recall them, the implication is that these elements should be made easy to recognize. Simple and easily seen messages should be used at the point of sale. Also, the placing of a product in the most obvious location on the shelves among its competitors is advised here.

11. "The rate of forgetting tends to be very rapid immediately after learning."

Consequently, it is important to continue communicating messages to consumers, especially in the earlier stages of campaigns. Also, this point should be well remembered by marketers who find considerable brand switching being done by their consumers. If the product image is not the cause, it would be worth the marketer's time to use premiums or free samples to reinforce the earlier learning process undergone by the brand switchers. Perhaps a few more contacts with the product would complete consumers' learning once this stage of mere recognition is passed.

12. "Messages attributed to persons held in high esteem influence change in opinion more than messages from persons not so well-known, but after several weeks both messages seem equally effective."

Unless the marketer wants to mount a very expensive and long-range campaign in associating his product with a public figure, the use of expensive testimonials is not advisable. Less well-known people should prove as effective and more economical.

13. "Repetition of identical materials is often as effective in getting things remembered as repeating the same story but with variations."

Psychologists have investigated the effectiveness of using identical materials versus similar materials to promote learning. Their conclusions point to the fact that repeating the same message is just as effective in establishing a learning pattern as is the presentation of differing messages containing the same information.

14. "In a learning situation, a moderate fear appeal is more effective than a strong fear appeal."

Marketers can use fear to enhance learning, but care must be taken to avoid the possibility that consumers will reject the whole message if the fear appeal is too great. This is somewhat similar to the eighth principle, which says learning can be increased by showing how not to do something.

15. "Knowledge of results leads to increases in learning."

To increase learning marketers should tell consumers exactly what results or benefits they will receive from using the product. Vague references to "the many advantages" that the consumer will have from the use of the product will not be as effective as the presentation of specific details.

16. "Learning is aided by active practice rather than (by) passive reception."

Participation greatly improves the learning process. For marketers this means that participation in contests such as "I like _____ because . . ." aids in establishing learning. Also, when products are placed in showrooms so that potential customers can "get the feel" of the product, the learning process is facilitated.

17. "A message is more easily learned and accepted if it does not interfere with earlier habits."

Marketers who follow this principle will show how their products enable consumers to do familiar jobs *better* than before, rather than *differently*. For instance, a new kind of power mower should be shown in terms of how much faster, neater, and easier it cuts grass than other mowers, rather than stressing mere differences between the new and the older machines.

18. "The mere repetition of a situation does not necessarily lead to learning. Two things are necessary—'belongingness' and 'satisfiers.'"

Messages should not contain irrelevant material; this tends to be distracting with the effect of impeding the learning process. Irrelevant arguments or unnecessary points should not be included in the message. Furthermore, messages should include what are called "satisfiers"— rewards for making the messages pleasing. Touches of humor, compliments for the reader, genuinely interesting facts, and the like increase learning.

19. "When two ideas are of equal strength but of unequal age, new repetition increases the strength of the earlier idea more than that of the newer idea. If there are two ideas of the same strength but of unequal age, the older idea will not be forgotten as rapidly as the newer idea."

For the marketer this principle is useful in estimating the amount of advertising needed to offset that of competitors. For two brands of different ages which are equally associated with consumers' needs, equal amounts of repetition will most likely benefit the older brand. Consequently, the newer brand will probably need more repetition than the older one in order to supplant it in consumers' minds.

20. "Learning something new can interfere with the remembering of something learned earlier."

What this means is that it is better to present consumers with one idea at a time rather than introducing several ideas at once. For example, consumers are more likely to learn messages from television commercials when they are sponsored by only one marketer for his product than if several marketers present commercials. The later commercials interfere with the messages given earlier. Increasing interference is incurred with increased similarity of the commercials. It is advisable not to present similar products on shows or radio programs which are too close together. This principle tends to support the existence of economies of scale in mass communication.

IN SUMMARY

The importance of the learning process to consumer behavior is apparent. However, until such time as the various theories of learning can converge into one systematic all-inclusive theory which can be applied in any given learning situation, the application of these theories to consumer behavior, and specifically to marketing problems which involve an estimation of consumer behavior, will continue to be inconclusive. Learning itself is an individual process; therefore, difficulties are present in any attempts to apply what is shown from one individual's behavior to the behavior of a mass of consumers. More research and compilation of data will be needed which show the proportions of the consuming public that are apt to behave in a certain manner.

The behavior of an individual in a dynamic market situation cannot readily be inferred from the results of a carefully controlled experimental situation. The variables involved are too extensive to be experimentally controlled, thus leading to greater problems in field experimental situations.

The development of learning models is a step in the right direction in attempting to account for these variables, but as yet these efforts have provided only indefinite answers to the myriad problems confronting the manufacturers and distributors of consumer goods. Hopefully, the increased interest in these studies may, over the years, provide useful insights into the "black box" of consumer behavior.

Obviously, the greatest need at this point in time is an increased effort to develop "principles" of learning so that further steps may be taken in building a useful and applicable theory of learning in the marketing situation. Motivation research seems to be only the first step in a series of developments that will be needed to further this aim.

Let us now turn our attention in Part Four of this study to the role of Marketing Communication and its effect on consumer behavior. As we shall soon discover, communication may very well be the central task of the organization. Communication deals with information flows. And this flow must be at least bidirectional. Information regarding products, prices, promotion, place of activities, and other pertinent information must be disseminated to consumers, suppliers, and resellers; at the same time, information flows from these same groups must be received by our organization and evaluated for both policy and strategy implications.

Our knowledge of consumer behavior and especially of how consumers *learn* will most assuredly affect our communication strategy both in terms of message construction and in media selection.

PART FOUR

MARKETING COMMUNICATION: A BEHAVIORAL ANALYSIS

SIX

The Communication Process

The title of this chapter has been chosen with particular care. As a matter of fact, "communication" and "process" are highly complementary terms. A process is a systematic series of actions directed to some end. Thus, we might have a marketing process, a management process, or some other process. Our concern here, as the chapter title states, is with "the communication process"—the systematic series of actions directed to the end of communication. Our purpose in this chapter is to examine this process in some detail and, in the remaining chapters, to examine fully the role of communication in marketing and other business activity, to investigate some of the sociological, psychological, and cultural phenomena which affect communication and the communication process and, finally, in the concluding chapter to explore some of the problems and challenges of developing effective communication strategies which are soundly integrated into the overall marketing planning and organizational framework.

DEVELOPING A POINT OF VIEW

We often fail to recognize the supreme importance of communication in our everyday social and commercial lives.

143

Human behavior is almost always the result of some form of communication. Communication is so pervasive and so much a part of our lives that we take it as readily for granted as breathing. Communication, therefore, is the determinant of much of behavior; the receiving of stimuli and the formation of mental and physical responses are a part of the living state of the organism. As a matter of fact, communication ceases only with the death of the organism. Our opinions, thoughts both public and private, attitudes, moods, predispositions, and cognitions are the products of myriad communications—some direct and loud, others subtle, subdued, and indirect.

Because communication is so important in all walks of life, all branches of the social sciences, and more recently many of the professional applied fields, are becoming increasingly concerned with it, and are studying and adding to the general fund of knowledge about it. Our focus and orientation is that of the student in a professional school of business administration. We wish to know, for pragmatic purposes, how communication functions as well as how it is structured. The advancement of science itself depends in considerable measure upon communication. Science, at least in one sense of the term, is the set of symbols that scientists use to communicate their knowledge to other scientists. And the advancement of science in marketing depends in large part upon our ability to understand the consumer and to link him more closely to our decision processes—in short, we need to better understand the communication process and to incorporate the consumer into our communication network. In order for man, and the systems and institutions which he creates, to survive and function adequately in an ever-changing world, the state of the organism and the state of the environment must be able to mold and direct the organism's behavior. The adaptation process or the act of accommodation is facilitated through communication in terms of messages, signs, and language.

Words are signs that conveniently replace the objects or ideas they represent. It would be misleading, as we will learn later, to imply that this representational character of words distinguishes them sharply from all other stimuli to which we respond. Listeners respond to spoken words in the same way they respond to other energies that impinge upon their receptor organs.

At the same time, stimuli do not present themselves in random, unorganized ways. It is an important psychological problem to discover the conditions under which stimuli are responded to as stable configurations. This is a basic problem related to verbal behavior and communication because without such organization we can achieve no agreement as to the objects our words represent. For example, as we have not yet presented a formal definition of the word or concept of communication, there is likely to be considerable variance between what the writer has in mind and what is conjured up in the mind of the reader. Words have only an arbitrary significance.[1] They signify only what we have learned they signify. The fact that we say "store" instead of "retail operating unit" is a matter of social coincidence and convenience. Verbal signs that are organized into linguistic systems are usually called verbal symbols. In order that we learn to respond correctly to certain words, it is usually necessary for another organism to intervene and reward us each time we respond correctly.

Once a given group or system has adopted a set of symbols, which we call vocabulary, and rules for combining them, which we call grammar, the conventions are no longer quite so arbitrary. What we have then by way of communication processes and systems is a set of mutually agreed upon concepts.

Definitions.   Let us see how, through usage and consensus, this word "communication" has taken on arbitrary significance. Several definitions and their authoritative source are as follows:

> Communication: The transmission of information, ideas, emotions, skills, etc. by the use of symbols—words, pictures, figures, graphs, etc.[2]
> Communication: The process of transmitting meaning between individuals.[3]
> Communications: The study of who says what to whom in what settings, by which channels and with what purposes and what effects. It deals with messages designed to influence human behavior, the media that carry such messages, and the markets that respond to such messages.[4]
> Communication: In essence, it implies the sharing of thoughts, feelings or appreciative perception.[5]

There is, as there obviously should be, a high degree of similarity or commonness among these various definitions. As a matter of fact, the word "communication" comes from the Latin *communis* which means common. Therefore, when we communicate with someone we are try-

---

[1] For a more comprehensive treatment of these ideas, see George Miller, *Language and Communication* (New York: McGraw-Hill Book Company, 1951).

[2] Bernard Berelson and Gary A. Steiner, *Human Behavior: An Inventory of Scientific Findings* (New York: Harcourt, Brace & World, Inc., 1964), p. 527.

[3] Charles Wright, *Mass Communications* (New York: Random House, Inc., 1959), p. 11.

[4] Edgar Crane, *Marketing Communication* (New York: John Wiley & Sons, Inc., 1965), p. 10.

[5] Wilbur Schramm, "How Communication Works," in *The Process and Effects of Mass Communication* (Urbana, Ill.: University of Illinois Press, 1955), p. 3.

ing to establish a "commonness" with someone. We have just concluded, hopefully, an act of communication whereby you are convinced that the essence of communication is to get the sender and the receiver tuned in, so to speak, on the same wave length for the purpose of exchanging information and perhaps even, under certain circumstances, for the purpose of altering beliefs or behavior.

If you concur and find the conclusions regarding communication both as a word and as a symbol logically consistent and satisfactory, we have accomplished at least two things. First, we have communicated and, second, we have demonstrated the arbitrary significance of words. We now can see that words signify only what we have learned they signify. We could, if necessary, become arbitrary to the point where we would settle for only one of the definitions to the exclusion of the others. Inasmuch as they are all quite similar in meaning, it appears unnecessary to do so.

KINDS OF COMMUNICATION

Communication as an act or process can be dichotomized into two major kinds. The first is referred to as mass communication and the second as personal or face-to-face communication.

Mass communication receives its name in the main from the kinds of media which are employed for the purpose of disseminating information. Mass communication, in other words, employs the mass media—newspapers, magazines, books, films, radio, and television. The characteristics of the mass media are suggested by the terms themselves: massiveness, or ability to communicate from a single source to large numbers of people, and what has been called mediativeness, or ability to communicate through a mechanical device such as print or a TV screen, making for an impersonal relationship between communicator and audience.[6]

Another distinguishing characteristic of mass communication is that it is directed toward a relatively large, heterogeneous, and anonymous audience; messages are transmitted publicly, often timed to reach most audience members simultaneously, and are transient in character. Furthermore, the communicator tends to be, or to operate within, a complex organization that may involve great expense.[7]

In contrast to mass communication, personal or face-to-face communication is defined as communication whereby sender and receiver

---

[6] Berelson and Steiner, *op. cit.*, p. 528.
[7] Wright, *op. cit.*, pp. 12-13.

interact on a face-to-face or personal basis. Personal conversation, therefore, on either a face-to-face basis or via telephone, is communication. However, it is not massive and not necessarily mechanically mediated.

Generally speaking, mass communication evokes images of television, radio, motion pictures, and newspapers. But these technical instruments should not be mistaken for the process with which we are concerned. A nationwide telecast of a new product to thousands of consumers in their homes is mass communication. A closed circuit showing of this product to a sales group in a test market city is not.

In short, communication is the process of transmitting meaning between individuals, and mass communication is a special kind of communication involving distinctive operating conditions, primary among which are the nature of the audience, the communication experience, and the communicator.[8]

Marketing firms, as was pointed out in an earlier chapter, are of necessity interested in both mass communication and personal communication. As a matter of fact, given the increased complexity and sophistication of marketing activities and the widespread spatial and temporal separation of marketers and consumers, mass communication has become one of the principal means of communication and promotion. Broadly speaking, mass communication activities are generally subsumed in the marketing organization under the heading "advertising and promotion" whereas personal communication of an external nature is subsumed under "personal selling or sales management."

EFFICIENT COMMUNICATION

In human societies, the communication process is efficient to the degree that rational judgments are facilitated. This in no way implies that we have unlimited rationality or omniscience, but rather that we have a bounded rationality which implements value goals and facilitates the decision-making process. In democratic societies, rational choices depend on enlightenment, which in turn depends upon information and communication, and especially upon the equivalence of attention among leaders, experts, and rank and file.

We are concerned with communication as a tool or means of developing improved marketing strategies in order that we may better serve our existing and potential markets and thus enhance our chances

---

[8] *Ibid.*, p. 13.

of making higher profits and utilizing our resources more fully. Inasmuch as some marketing communications attain these ends, they are efficient. Much marketing communication, however, for numerous reasons including both ignorance and greed, is anything but efficient.

One can distinguish between consequences, or what might be called functions of a given activity or process, and the aims or purposes behind the activity. Thus, marketing communication may strive for all the noble and well-meaning objectives listed above, yet the consequences of that activity may fall short of the stated objectives. Clearly, objectives and consequences need not be identical. Merton terms consequences that are intended *manifest functions* and those that are unintended *latent functions.*[9] Thus, marketing communications which bring about consequences which are unintended would clearly fall in the latent function category. It is certainly true that in marketing communication, as in other areas, not every consequence of an activity has positive value for the social system in which it occurs, or for the groups or individuals involved. Consequences that are undesirable from the point of view of the welfare of the society or its members are called *dysfunctions.* Any single act may have both functional and dysfunctional effects. Therefore, efficient marketing communications would be concerned with bringing about the manifest functions or objectives of the communication system and eliminating or minimizing the dysfunctions of that system.

THE PROCESS

Earlier it was stated that a process is a systematic series of actions directed to some end. Naturally, the communication process is concerned with the transmission of information or appreciative perception. A convenient way to break down the communication process and to look at the individual series of actions is to answer the following questions: [10]

Who?
Says What?
In Which Channel?
To Whom?
With What Effect?

---

[9] Robert K. Merton, *Social Theory and Social Structure,* rev. ed. (Glencoe, Ill.: The Free Press, 1957), Chap. 1, "Manifest and Latent Functions."

[10] Harold D. Lasswell, "The Structure and Function of Communication in Society," in *Mass Communications,* ed. Wilbur Schramm (Urbana, Ill.: University of Illinois Press, 1960), pp. 117-130.

The scientific study of communication tends to concentrate upon one or another of these questions. In reality, the field of communication is rather well specialized on the basis of this breakdown. Scholars who study the "who," the communicator, look into the factors that initiate and guide the act of communication. This aspect of communication is called control analysis. Other areas of specialization within the field of communication include content analysis, media analysis, audience analysis, and effect analysis. Our point of view, inasmuch as it is managerially oriented to the firm, will be largely source oriented (who) in purpose and receiver or audience oriented (to whom) in terms of substance. This, of course, reflects only our interest in terms of the structure of communication. From the standpoint of the socioeconomic system, communication has at least three manifest functions: (1) the surveillance of the environment; (2) the correlation of the parts of society in responding to the environment; and (3) the transmission of the social heritage from one generation to the next.[11]

Inasmuch as marketing communication is a part of our total socioeconomic system, the manifest functions of marketing communication must at least be compatible and contribute to the overall attainment of these functions or objectives.

THE IDEALIZED COMMUNICATION SYSTEM

The communication process as a series of systematic actions is directed to the end that information is passed from one place to another. Whenever communication occurs, we say that the component parts involved in the transfer of information constitute a communication system. As was learned in Chapter 1, every communication must have a *source* and a *destination* for the information that is transferred, and these must be distinct in time and space. Between the source and the destination there must be some connecting link which spans the intervening time and space; this link is called the communication channel. In order that the information can pass over the channel, it is necessary to operate on it in such a way that it is suitable for transmission; the component that performs this operation is a *transmitter*. At the destination there must be a *receiver* which converts the transmitted information into its original form. These five components—source, transmitter, channel, receiver, and destination—make up the model communication system shown diagrammatically in Fig. 12.

---

[11] *Ibid.*, pp. 128-129.

Figure 12: Communication Components.

This communication model can be simplified, however, where source and transmitter or destination and receiver are the same. The simplified version is shown in Fig. 13.

Figure 13: A Communication Model.

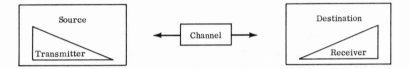

In terms of basic components, it can be seen that communication requires three elements—the source, the message or signal, and the destination or receiver. The source may be an individual, or a spokesman for a small group, or a multi-unit organization. The message may be visual or audible, face-to-face or of a mediative nature. The receiver or destination, like the source, may be an individual, group, crowd, or mob.

The communication process begins with *encoding* the message by the sender. This involves putting the information or feelings he wants shared into a transmittable form. The *code* is a pattern of energies that can travel over the connecting link. In other words, a code is simply a consensus or agreement on symbols between the two major parties of a communication act, i.e., source and destination.

The receiver's behavior at his end of the channel is just the opposite of that of the source. His responsibility is to *decode* or reconstruct the message into a more useful and intelligible form. Diagrammatically, the process just described can be seen in Fig. 14.[12]

Figure 14: The Communication Process.

[12] The diagram, as well as this section, owes much to the article by Wilbur Schramm entitled "How Communication Works" in *The Process and Effects of Mass Communications,* ed. Wilbur Schramm (Urbana, Ill.: University of Illinois Press, 1955), pp. 3-26.

One can observe that both structural and functional aspects are present in the diagrammed system. And like any system it can be no stronger than its weakest link. It is important to understand, also, that once coded and sent, the message is quite free from its sender and what it does is beyond the power of the sender to change.

In order for communication to take place effectively, it must be borne in mind that the receiver and sender must be in tune. A message is much more likely to succeed if it fits the patterns of understandings, attitudes, values, and goals that a receiver has; or at least if it starts with this pattern and tries only to reshape it or alter it slightly. Earlier we defined this process as "canalizing" which, again, means that the sender provides a channel to direct the already existing motives in the receiver. This is what is meant when advertising people speak of "starting where the audience is."

Once again, Schramm has provided us with an effective diagram for illustrating this phenomenon.[13]

Figure 15: Communication and Field of Experience.

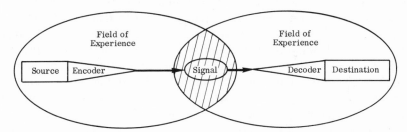

The area of intersection between the two fields of experience must be of some consequence in order for the two parties to communicate effectively. Those familiar with set theory will readily grasp the idea that if there is no intersection between the two sets or fields of experience communication will, at best, be difficult and at worst impossible. Those without an understanding of set theory should have no difficulty grasping the idea intuitively. The greater the area of intersection between the two sets of experiences, the greater the probability of effective communication. The source then, because he is the one who initiates the communication process, should attempt to encode in such a way as to make it easy for the receiver to tune in the message; to relate it to parts of his experience which are like those of the source.

---

[13] Schramm, *op. cit.*, p. 6.

Redundancy. An important concept involved in communication is that of redundancy. The encoder and transmitter has a choice at all times between sending more information in a given time, or transmitting less and repeating more in the hope of being better understood. For example, in Chapter 1, we briefly outlined the communication process but our discussion was, by design, minimal. It would have been possible to complete our discussion of the communication process then, but didactically and organizationally it would not have been too wise. Communication and learning are often facilitated by transmitting less information at a given time and repeating more often. Thus, understanding may grow as a result of a building-up process, i.e., learning simple ideas first, on which more sophisticated ideas can be structured, and the well-known psychological principle that repetition facilitates learning. The astute student will have recognized that this text utilizes both of these ideas in its treatment of concepts and in its organization.

Feedback. Another well-known communication concept introduced in Chapter 1 was that of feedback. It was stressed earlier that both sender and receiver, if two-way communication is to be established, must play dual or reversed roles. Senders, if our system is to be an open one, must be receivers, and vice versa. This concept is known as feedback. The feedback concept is an effort to recover a part of the output of a system in order to correct, modify, or control the total system. Marketing firms may oftentimes be more interested in establishing a communications system, the purpose of which is to feed back information, than in the transmission of information. Remember that a marketing message may consist of the firm's product, its distribution system, and its promotional activities. The transmission of messages composed of these elements is likely to be very ineffective if predicated on faulty perception regarding "where the audience is." It is feedback which allows us to sharpen our focus and zero in on our marketing targets.

Another example of the value of the feedback mechanism may illustrate our point more fully. Some communication systems may be developed for the manifest purpose of receiving feedback, i.e., a suggestion box. Management's goal is that of receiving information so that it can attain insight into its organization and personnel policies.

Signals. Signals are messages which are made up of signs. A sign stands for something in experience. The word "store" is a sign that stands for our generalized experience with stores. The word would be meaningless to a person who knew nothing about the world of commerce and who came from a noncommercial culture. We learn the word as a result of association. A sign will not call forth all the responses that the object itself will call forth. For example, in Brown County, Indiana, there is a replica of an old-fashioned general store filled with fixtures and artifacts of a bygone era. Throughout the store is diffused the odor of old wood, worn leather, stick candy, sassafras bark and spices. In describing this store, it (the store as a sign) conjures up delightful memories, aromas, and associations. But the sign (Brown County store) always represents the object (the reality or significate) at a reduced level of cues. By this is meant simply that the sign will not call forth all the responses that the object itself will call forth. This is a price we must pay for portability in language.

Our signal system is a kind of shorthand which enables us to categorize, locate, and store objects. As the sender transmits signals, he is receiving signals almost simultaneously, both from the person to whom he is sending and from the external environment. As he receives these signals he must interpret them and decide what portion of these signals he wishes to incorporate in his own transmission; or how his transmission ought to be altered in light of these signals. When the signals are received, they come in the form of signs. If you know the sign, you generally know that there are certain responses associated with it. These are called *mediatory responses*, because they mediate what happens to the message in your nervous system. Therefore, these responses are the meaning the sign has for you. The mediatory responses have, in a deterministic fashion, an effect on how you react to the sign. Specifically, just what you encode will depend on your choice of the responses available in the situation, connected with the meaning the responses have for you.

Learning.   The process by which the sounds of a language and signs come to acquire meaning is a part of the learning process. Communication obviously is intended to develop a commonness of feelings, agreement, mutual understanding, sharing of ambitions, and attitudes. Learning theory is, to a considerable extent, concerned with how these conditions come about. It is as difficult, however, for psychologists to agree about learning as it is for a group of theologians to agree on a definition of sin. Association theory or stimulus-response theory analyzes behavior into elements, studies the elements independently, and attempts to discover laws governing the combination of elements. It is rather typical for the association or stimulus-response theorists to emphasize the importance of learning as an explanation of behavior and to talk of the stimulus-response connections that a person acquires during the course of his life.

Cognitive or field theory, as we learned earlier, is both a protest against and a substitute for association theory. The cognitive theorists do not build the action pattern out of its component parts. Instead, they feel the parts have significance only in relationship to the whole, or gestalt. The cognitive theorists, it will be recalled, tend to emphasize the structure or configuration of the organism at the time an act is performed.

It is not necessary or tremendously important that we settle the dispute between the stimulus-response and cognitive schools of learning. From our point of view the differences are not of paramount importance. Instead, it is sufficient to determine that learning occurs when insight is obtained and changes in behavior or attitude sets are manifested and that communication is the principal means by which we attempt to bring about learning, whether it be viewed from the simple stimulus-response approach or the somewhat more sophisticated, but less tidy, cognitive or gestalt view. Most assuredly, we need much more knowledge and greater understanding of both communication and learning, as well as greater understanding concerning their interaction.

COMMUNICATION EFFECTS

Because of the uncertainty surrounding the interaction between learning theory and communication, it is difficult to talk either convincingly or conclusively about "the effect" of communication. As we shall see in the next chapter, communication has many effects or roles, and the measurement of any of these, deterministically, is subject to considerable difficulty. However, the difficulty of measuring or evaluating communication effects does not, in and of itself, abate the urgent desire of many to undertake such activity or make them less interested in its accomplishment. Nagging questions arise concerning the effect of mass communications on society as well as on consumer behavior. Do advertising and sales promotion lead to waste and inefficiency? Can consumers be misled or influenced to the point of causing them to buy unneeded or shoddy goods? Does cigarette advertising influence more young people to adopt the smoking habit than otherwise would? Only within the context of a carefully structured scientific framework can such topics be handled dispassionately.

There are two highly relevant causes which fuel the fantasies regarding communication effectiveness. The first is the extreme shortage of scientific evidence on media effects, and the second is the tone of economic and social urgency that often surrounds the questions about effects.[14]

---

[14] Wright, *op. cit.*, p. 90.

Lazarsfeld and Merton have identified four sources of the public concern about mass media.[15]

1. Many people are alarmed by the ubiquity of the mass media and their power to do good or evil.

2. Conceivably economic interest groups may use the mass media to insure public conformity to the social and economic status quo.

3. Critics argue that the mass media, in accommodating large audiences, may cause a deterioration of aesthetic tastes and popular cultural standards.

4. In many instances, it is believed that mass media have nullified social gains for which reformers have worked for decades.

It is not our task at this juncture to either support or refute the above arguments. Instead, it is sufficient to point out that communications, and especially marketing communications, are highly suspect in terms of their effect in persuading consumers to a particular point of view or frame of mind.

The "effect" of communication is largely concerned with the relationship of learning and communication. It is sufficient, for at least this stage in our development and understanding of communication, to conclude that communication has a positive effect, at least from the sender's point of view, if the receiver acts favorably to his message or request. Instead of establishing a simple and predictable relationship between communication messages and responses or effects, it is easier to describe what might be called the conditions that must be fulfilled if the message is to arouse the intended response.[16]

1. The message must be so designed and delivered as to gain attention of the intended destination. It must be available.

2. The message must employ signs which refer to experience common to both source and destination, in order to "get the meaning across."

3. The message must arouse personality needs in the destination and suggest some way to meet those needs. We take action because of needs and toward goals.

4. The message must suggest a way to meet those needs which is appropriate to the group situation in which the destination finds himself at the time when he is moved to make the desired response.

Given the attainment of these conditions, communication is likely to have some kind of effect. Communication effects, as pointed out by

---

[15] See Paul Lazarsfeld and Robert Merton, "Mass Communication, Popular Taste and Organized Social Action," in *The Communication of Ideas,* ed. L. Bryson (New York: Harper & Brothers, 1948), pp. 95-118.

[16] Schramm, *op. cit.,* p. 13.

Schramm, are the resultants of a number of forces, of which the communicator can really control only one. This is the *message*. The other three are situation, personality state of the receiver, and group relations and standards.[17]

We will turn our attention in the following chapters to a more exhaustive treatment of communications effects, or what the writer prefers to call the "role of communication," given the communication situation, personality state of the receiver, group relations and standards, and other behavioral considerations.

---

[17] *Ibid.*, p. 17.

SEVEN

The Role of Communications

As was observed in the concluding pages of the preceding chapter, the "effects" of communications are difficult to assess in a simple cause-effect framework. Instead, a more fruitful and perhaps more precise way of handling the problem of consequences and implications of communication might well be to view the phenomenon in a "role" framework. This is somewhat more in keeping with the psychological and philosophic framework developed earlier in this treatment. The role of communication is thus concerned with the entire characteristic pattern of behavior imposed upon an individual, thing, or process because of its status or influence in the overall scheme of things. A word of caution is in order here. The concept of role is interactive and interdependent. Thus, the *role* or characteristic pattern of behavior imposed upon a process or concept because of its status or influence in the overall scheme of things can be viewed in something of a converse order. A thing's status or influence can, in turn, be affected or influenced by its role. Communication, as a process, much like a person as an individual, has not one role, but usually several. A man may be a father, husband, brother, teacher, or reformer. All these "roles" call forth characteristic patterns of behavior. Thus, communication may be used to disseminate facts, persuade, reinforce, or convert. This implies also a range in the characteristic set of behavior patterns produced both intentionally and unintentionally by the communications process.

UNDERSTANDING COMMUNICATION'S ROLE

Our knowledge about the role or effects of communication has been fairly adequately, if not precisely, outlined by Berelson in the statement that "some kinds of *communications* on some kinds of *issues*, brought to the attention of some kinds of *people* under some kinds of *conditions*, have some kinds of effects." [1] This is not, operationally speaking, much of a valid conclusion or a predictive tool for marketers or communications researchers. And the task of both of these groups has been, of late, an increasing and more scientific attack upon the general problem of analyzing the role of communications, both in the more general social context and in the expanding world of commerce. Twenty years after Berelson's statement concerning the "role" of communication, we are still engaged in research studies and speculation regarding the expanding role of communication. And despite the added intensity and sophistication of our research studies and methodology, we can today assert little more, and with little more assurance, accuracy and predictive value, than did Berelson.

Consequently, the discussion which follows must necessarily be of such a nature and couched in such qualifications as to be tentative rather than assertive. Our analysis necessarily leads to suggestive prescriptions which, however, must lack conclusiveness. In keeping with our skepticism regarding direct cause-effect relationships, we arrive at the point where the "hypodermic effect" is refuted in favor of a "situational, functional," or what Klapper calls "phenomenistic," approach which he defines as "a shift away from the tendency to regard mass communication as a sufficient cause of audience effects, toward a view of the media as influences, working amid other influences, in a total situation." [2] This viewpoint, if not entirely the same as our framework of existential behavior developed earlier, is at least similar to and consistent with it. This view regards the role and effect of communication as the observation of *existing* conditions or changes, followed by an inquiry into the factors along with communications which produced these conditions or,

---

[1] Bernard Berelson, "Communications and Public Opinion," in *Communications in Modern Society*, ed. Wilbur Schramm (Urbana, Ill.: University of Illinois Press, 1948), p. 172.
[2] Joseph T. Klapper, *The Effects of Mass Communications* (Glencoe, Ill.: The Free Press, 1960), p. 5.

as was stated earlier, the range of the characteristic set of behavior patterns produced by the communication process. The communication process is thus viewed as a set of influences, working in conjunction with other influences, in a total system or existential situation. Klapper thus defines the phenomenistic or existential attitude regarding communication effects as a situation whereby "attempts to assess a stimulus which was presumed to work alone have given way to an assessment of the role of that stimulus in a total observed phenomenon." [3]

This approach appears to make possible certain generalizations regarding communication as a process and the role of this process. These generalizations are by no means verified to the point where they would warrant the label "law," or scarcely "principle." Instead, at least until more conclusive evidence is gathered, they might more nearly be called "testable hypotheses." Some, of course, have progressed further in terms of the usual tests of validity and therefore might possess a greater operational usefulness. Others, however, represent only vague impressions and are highly conjectural and of doubtful operational validity. Again, let it be pointed out that the usefulness of the generalizations will vary depending on the purposes to which they are put. As guideposts for acquiring a greater understanding regarding the process and role of communications, they are of inestimable value. Likewise, as a basis for incorporating our understanding of communication into an overall framework of marketing strategy and theory, they would appear as at least the bare framework for such an undertaking. The generalizations which have emerged as a result of the phenomenistic or existential study of the communication process as reported by Klapper are as follows: [4]

1. Mass communication ordinarily does not serve as a necessary and sufficient cause of audience effects, but rather functions among and through a nexus of mediating factors and influences.

2. These mediating factors are such that they typically under mass communications are a contributory agent, but not the sole cause, in a process of reinforcing the existing conditions.

3. On such occasions as mass communication does function in the service of change, one of two conditions is likely to exist. Either:
    a. the mediating factors will be found to be direct; or,
    b. the mediating factors, which normally favor reinforcement, will be found to be themselves impelling toward change.

4. There are certain residual situations in which mass communication seems to produce direct effects, or directly and of itself to serve certain psycho-physical functions.

---

[3] *Ibid.*, p. 5.
[4] *Ibid.*, pp. 8-9.

5. The efficacy of mass communication, either as a contributory agent or as an agent of direct effect, is affected by various aspects of the media and communications themselves or of the communication situation (including for example, aspects of textual organization, the nature of the source and medium, the existing climate of public opinion, and the like).

The reader is cautioned at this juncture that to some degree the presentation of Mr. Klapper's preliminary, yet impressive, sophisticated, and to a considerable extent documented, generalizations has had at least these probable "effects"; *facts have been presented* which, depending on the phenomenistic or existent situation either (1) reinforce existing beliefs, (2) create opinion on new isssues, i.e., the role of communication, or (3) convert the reader from previously held beliefs, attitudes, and opinions regarding the role and effectiveness of communication. The lay person commonly believes that communication has a considerably more direct and profound effect on the receiver than the above generalizations assume.

In order that we may proceed to examine the range in the characteristic set of behavior patterns produced by the communication process, as outlined by the above generalizations, the reader is urged to re-read and examine them. We shall then proceed to investigate more fully this set of behavior patterns, first within a general communication framework, and later, within a more behavioristic consumer framework as it relates to the marketing strategy development of the firm.

It is a widely held lay opinion (and also true) that the aim of most communication is to persuade. Persuasion is the act or process of attempting to induce something or to bring about some known reaction. But what are the ranges of reactions which communication as a persuasive force attempts to bring about? The remainder of this chapter is largely concerned with this problem. Persuasive communication attempts to induce or win people over to particular courses of action. But what about the range of behavior which falls in the category of "particular courses of action"? What are the alternatives available to the receiver of the communication message? Are these alternatives acceptable to the communication source and transmitter in light of his (or their) goals and objectives? In short, in discussing the role of the communication process we are necessarily concerned with the effects of communication, the previous qualifications and generalizations notwithstanding. We have tentatively discovered that instead of direct cause-effect relationships, there are only mediating effects, depending on other related phenomena. We shall continue our discussion of effects within this context and attempt now to assess (1) the possible range of effects within (2) the context of the other related phenomena.

THE RANGE OF POSSIBLE COMMUNICATION EFFECTS

Communication, as a persuasive tool, is most often used to affect the learning process. Earlier we discussed learning and concluded that the term, used very broadly, means the acquisition of skills and understandings and involves a process of perceptual reorganization. As in measuring the effects of learning, we discover that such effects can lead to very minor attitudinal changes or to completely reversed opinions and insights leading to observable and manifest behavior characteristics—conversion. We might just as well be discussing the possible range of effects for communication, and actually we are because, as has been repeatedly demonstrated, the communicator is utilizing his knowledge, at least as he understands it, of the learning process in order to accomplish his communication goals. Once again, it must be repeated that communication is the *means* of implementing the learning process. Communication, therefore, can be instrumental in accomplishing three levels or sets of characteristic behavior results: (1) minor attitude change and reinforcement, (2) creation of opinion on new issues, and (3) conversion—significant changes in thought and behavior.

Reinforcement and minor change. There is an overwhelming amount of evidence, both from the researcher's laboratory and the world of commerce, which strongly suggests that communication is far more effective as an agent of reinforcement than as an agent for change or conversion. As a matter of fact, in light of the direction of changes in relation to communication as mentioned earlier, Klapper has stated that "it would appear to be no exaggeration to say that the efficacy of mass communications in influencing existing opinions and attitudes is inversely correlated with the degree of change." [5]

Our task here, given the remaining work to be done, can only be to survey briefly the three levels of change or, as we have called them before, the range in the characteristic set of behavior patterns produced by the communication process, and to look within each of these categories at some of the phenomena responsible for both the type and intensity of the communication response. Our treatment will be hardly more than a survey and description. We shall postpone a full analysis of these findings and their implications until Chapter 8, when we will explore from the marketing point of view the area of consumer behavior and communications. Our purpose here is to develop a basis and famil-

---

[5] *Ibid.,* p. 15.

iarity of concept in order that we may proceed with more rapid and thorough understanding later.

The human mind is hardly a *tabula rasa* or blank slate upon which messages are indelibly inscribed by the communication process. As a matter of fact, we are at any one moment the product of countless communication messages, plus a host of other mediating factors including heredity, intelligence, life style, group norms, and culture. Therefore, the idea that we receive messages of any kind with an "open mind" is a rather absurd suggestion. On the other hand we may, correctly speaking, be somewhat open to the *reception* of messages, even if we are not necessarily open to the *perception* of messages. In fact, we generally "see" only what we "know" or have been conditioned to see.

A man's perception is fashioned by his existence. A description of the Detroit riots during the summer of 1967 would vary considerably if solicited from (a) a social worker in the area, (b) a Negro active in the looting, (c) a nonactive, but sympathetic Negro, (d) H. Rap Brown, or (e) George Wallace. In short, each of these reporters would be largely predisposed to see what his predispositions told him to see.

Thus, the communication process is affected by the psychological phenomenon described in earlier chapters as perception, and perception together with its influence as a mediating factor of communication is in turn affected by a group of phenomena known as *selective perception, selective exposure,* and *selective retention.* Human dispositions are the sum total of all the propensities of a person. Predisposition implies that the propensities to behavior are fairly well fixed within certain probabilistic limits. Consequently, our predispositions, which are brought about by a multitude of contextual factors, cause us to selectively expose ourselves to the messages which are compatible with our own predispositions or life style. We subject ourselves to the messages and appeals which we want to hear, and this results, to a considerable degree, in a constant reinforcing of our predispositions. Normally speaking, over time we tend to become more rigid in our behavior patterns instead of more flexible.

Not only do we selectively expose ourselves to the media, messages, and appeals which support our predispositions, but we selectively perceive that which we want to perceive. Media messages and appeals which are in conflict with our norms of behavior and our predispositions are controverted, in the event of exposure, to positions more nearly compatible with our own. This phenomenon is known as *selective perception.* We tend to see, hear, and believe only those things which we wish to see, hear, and believe. Our perceptual mechanism converts to positions of greater congruence those things which are unpleasant or incongruent with our predispositions. This, too, tends to build a strong case for the reinforcement and minor change effects of mass communication. Finally, our predispositions induce us to retain only that which is congruent or compatible with our life style. This is known as *selective retention*. Ideas, concepts, messages, and appeals to which we have been subjected are rapidly forgotten if they do not tend to reinforce our existing opinions and predispositions.

Thus we see that our predispositions give rise to selective exposure, selective perception, and selective retention. These phenomena have the tendency, in turn, to *reinforce* our existing opinions, norms, or dispositions. Therefore, one of the more probable effects of communication is that of reinforcement, or the inducement of minor attitudinal changes.[6]

Our attitudes and predispositions do not spring forth full blown, however, and remain forever transfixed. Man is a learning animal and he does change over time. Sometimes the changes are profound and considerable. This rarely happens, however, unless there is a marked change in the environment or culture. The reasons why man's attitudes or predispositions change over time are far from obvious and are not yet completely understood. We have some knowledge of the process, but what we don't know would fill a far larger volume than what we know. Only a most succinct treatment of a few of the factors mediating the change in predispositions is possible here. Predispositions, as we have said, grow out of one's existence. Earlier it was stated that man is what he is and what he has been. We are members of a society and very few of us are social isolates. We live, think, act, and behave in a group or societal situation. We are further disposed to do these things within a milieu in which others live, think, act, and behave in a fashion similar to our own or in a fashion to which we aspire. Consequently, our attitudes, opinions, and predispositions are to a considerable extent those which come to us via the selective processes just discussed and which reflect the attitudes, opinions, and predispositions of the groups to which we belong. Thus, the group tends to act as a filter which aids the selective process. We ape the manners and the behavior of the group. Individuals have countless group memberships—political, social, religious, and racial, to name only a few. The group tends to aid reinforcement of existing predispositions in a number of ways.[7] They make possible selective exposure and the provision of arenas for the dissemination of the content of sympathetic communication. That is, two individuals in group inter-

---

[6] For well-documented examples and research into these phenomena, see Bernard Berelson and Hazel Gaudet, *The People's Choice* (New York: Columbia University Press, 1948).

[7] Elihu Katz and Paul F. Lazarsfeld, *Personal Influence: The Part Played by People in the Flow of Mass Communication* (Glencoe, Ill.: The Free Press, 1955).

action discussing commonly held views are likely to reinforce their own respective positions. Argument and discussion most often tend to bring our own opinions and prejudices into sharper focus.

Sometimes, given the nature of our own personality, its strength or weakness, its dominance or submissiveness, we discover that we take our cues regarding predispositions and attitudes from *opinion leaders,* or that we ourselves may be opinion leaders on certain issues or in a particular sphere of issues. The opinion leader is generally a "super normative" member of the same group as the followers, but he is likely to be more exposed to communication, and perhaps even more articulate in his dissemination of the group norms or attitudes. The opinion leader is most often a force for reinforcement and minor change, as opposed to conversion. The opinion leader, like any leader, is one who follows the same path of action as the group, but is a little further advanced than his followers. Sometimes, it would appear, the leader is one who discovers the direction in which the group wishes to go and then proceeds to get in front of them. The point is this: Conversion is not often the aim of the opinion leader nor the result of his actions. To be an opinion leader, one must first be a member of the group and hold the basic attitudes and predispositions of the group. An individual with attitudes and opinions contrary to the group norm is not likely to become either a member of that group or an opinion leader. Thus if he espouses causes which are alien to the group, and if his objective is conversion, he is not likely in the first place to become a member of the group or an opinion leader within the group; and even if he should meet the first two qualifications, it is not likely that he can convert the will of the group to his own.

Individuals are subject to influence and change of attitudes as a result of communication persuasion depending to a considerable extent upon how important they perceive the issue to be. Issues which are essential to their own self-images or the perpetuation of their life styles are often referred to as "ego-involved" attitudes. Such attitudes are extremely difficult to change. Therefore communications aimed at converting ego-involved attitudes are quite likely to fail. Conversely, communications designed to bolster or reinforce ego-involved attitudes have a high probability of success.

The creation of opinion.   Individuals generally have neither open nor closed minds. They have not made up their minds about all things for all time. New issues are constantly arising out of the dynamic forces of the world of society and commerce. One practitioner of the blackest side of mass communication, Joseph Goebbels, Hitler's Minister of Propaganda, stated that "Whoever says the first word to the world is always right." [8]

Many persons today, though with far less sinister motivation, both believe and practice this communication dictum. The basis for this position is that mass communications can play an important role in fostering and developing attitudes and opinions concerning issues on which individuals have no opinions or attitudes. However, one must be cautious in pursuing this line of reasoning too far. In an age of mass communication miracles where whirling satellites make instantaneous communication from the local to the international scene not only possible but actually operational, the number of truly "new" issues which are likely to confront an individual is apt to be quite small. So-called new issues will tend to have decided areas of similarity to issues already considered and for which we have built up a reservoir of attitudes and predispositions.

However, when issues arise for which the individual or group has no particular feeling one way or the other, communication is believed to be widely efficient in creating opinion or in developing what we have called predispositions. Under these circumstances communication is likely to have more of the so-called hypodermic effect, whereby the communication receiver or the audience is inoculated with a message which supposedly predisposes it favorably toward the given position of the message source.[9] Research of a completely determining nature on the role of communication in the creation of opinion on new issues has yet to be done. However, several important though somewhat conjectural explanations are available. Often the individual is at the point where he is indifferent on certain matters, and in such instances where the subject has no firmly held opinions, communication is likely to play an instrumental role in the formation of opinions on the relevant issue. Where opinions are already formed, the mediating factors listed earlier —the selective processes, group norms, and opinion leaders—are likely to filter and greatly affect the communication messages directed toward receivers, and thus a communication contrary to the predispositions of the individual and the group is likely to be rejected outright. Where the message is compatible with the predispositions of individual and group, it will tend therefore to reinforce the existing predispositions. On

[8] Leonard Doob, "Goebbels' Principles of Propaganda," *Public Opinion Quarterly*, 1950, p. 435.

[9] Irving L. Janis and M. Herz, "The Influence of Preparatory Communication in Subsequent Reactions to Failure," summarized in Carl I. Hovland, Irving L. Janis and Harold H. Kelly, *Communication and Persuasion* (New Haven, Conn.: Yale University Press, 1953), pp. 114-116.

new issues or on issues on which the individual and the members of his group have not taken positions, or on which they have arrived at a state of relative indifference, communication, because it is not hampered or mediated by the selective processes or group predispositions, is allowed to get through to the receiver uncontaminated, and he is likely to at least partially formulate opinions on the basis of the communications.

Conversion: the "about face" in communication. The role of communication, as we have learned thus far, is not always to convert or bring about a complete reversal on the part of its subjects. We have learned also that communication is more effective in bringing about reinforcement of existing opinions and predispositions and creating opinion on new issues than it is in changing a subject's mind about a matter or issue on which he already possesses opinions and predispositions. However, as we also saw in our discussion of learning theory, man often receives what we call "insight" into an issue, and this insight quite often comes in the form of communicated information, causing the individual to reverse his stand or position. It goes without saying that the more ardent the individual's feelings on a given issue, or the more ego-involved the issue, the more difficult conversion is likely to be. However, conversion does occur, even though less frequently than reinforcement and minor opinion change.

Conversion is not well understood. The process, which might best be called a phenomenon, lies at the very heart of the individual's behavior mechanisms. Communication is seldom, if ever, solely responsible for conversion; instead, much like reinforcement though in a somewhat introverted fashion, it requires extra communication factors working in a mediating fashion to bring about the desired effect. However, in the case of conversion as opposed to reinforcement, the extra communication factors appear to be less active, or working in an imperfect manner. For example, the selective processes may actually sensitize an individual to change. An upward mobile whose reference groups are rapidly changing and whose group norms are therefore fuzzy and not well defined to the newly arrived member of the group may be alerted to change or conversion by communication. Individuals already impelled toward change would, conceivably, selectively expose themselves to the communications which offer a fresh insight or point of view or which are congruent with their new outlook.[10]

Group norms may become, at least for certain issues, considerably

    [10] Bernard Berelson, Paul F. Lazarsfeld, and William N. McPhee, *Voting: A Study of Opinion Formation in a Presidential Campaign* (Chicago: University of Chicago Press, 1954).

less important and thus less effective in the conversion processes. An individual may find his personal aspirations no longer closely tied to his existing group memberships, and he may therefore be more inclined "to go it alone" on particular issues. The discussion and repartee which are so much a part of group membership may tend to bring into sharper focus the goals and objectives of the group and may further tend to reveal a growing discrepancy between the group and the individual's predispositions and opinions. Also not to be overlooked is the fact that not every issue germane to the individual is germane to the group or groups to which he belongs. Certainly, for issues on which the group has taken no stand, the individual remains somewhat naked in his defense of the communication messages to which he is subject.

The role of personal influence and opinion leaders can be highly effective in the whole range of roles for mass communications and will be dealt with at considerable length later. However, it has been shown that personal influence tends to exercise a more direct and important effect toward change than does mass communication when both such influences are present.[11]

As a matter of fact, it has been rather conclusively shown that conversion—real change in attitude and behavior—is most often the product of personal influence, face-to-face communication, reinforced by the mass communication media, i.e., a two-step flow or double-barreled communication effect.[12] The gist of this hypothesis is that the mass media reach the opinion leaders and the opinion leaders reach the masses. But whether the mass media work simply to reinforce the predispositions and opinions of the opinion leaders or as a force for conversion remains something of a moot point.

One or two additional points regarding the process of conversion would appear warranted. As was previously discussed, some individuals appear by dint of personality to be more persuasive than others, and their persuasiveness appears to be related more to their own self-image or self-esteem than to their actual intelligence. The degree of persuasiveness appears also to be "topic free," that is, regardless of the topic or issue, the highly persuasive personality remains the highly persuasive personality.[13]

There is an impressive array of documented studies which show that facts may be widely disseminated via communication without pro-

[11] Katz and Lazarsfeld, *op. cit.*

[12] Elihu Katz, "The Two-Step Flow of Communication: An Up-to-Date Report on an Hypothesis," *Public Opinion Quarterly,* XXI (1957), 61-78.

[13] Carl I. Hovland, Irving L. Janis and Harold H. Kelly, *Communication and Persuasion* (New Haven, Conn.: Yale University Press, 1953), p. 175.

ducing the behavioral changes sought. Any advertising manager would sorrowfully substantiate this assertion. Oftentimes communications are designed around facts which are stated explicitly, while the opinion or behavior to which they are supposed to lead are not. The danger here is that, once again, the selective processes will take over and read into the facts the message or appeal which our predispositions lead us to interpret.

There are many stratagems for facilitating conversions. Boring from within, the idea of planting an idea within a group or individual and letting him convince others within his reference group of the merits and advantages of a given issue or cause, can be an effective means of facilitating conversion. The stratagems of the camel's head in the tent, the red herring, and fabianism are all longer-run methods or techniques for bringing about conversion.

THE COMMUNICATION SITUATION

It was stated earlier in this chapter that the communication process is viewed as a set of influences working in conjunction with other influences in a total system or existential situation. We have therefore, in the preceding pages, attempted to describe and analyze these sets of influences working amid other influences in a total or existential situation. Our task is not yet completed, however, inasmuch as we have not dealt explicitly with another set of interacting variables affecting the role or persuasiveness of communicating, namely, the communication and its aspects in and of itself. The communication situation is lacking in precision regarding both its definition and description. In short, the situations in which communications occur have been found to be related to the effectiveness of persuasion, or the degree of effectiveness in bringing about reinforcement, opinion change, or conversion. However, certain aspects of the communication situation have been categorized and partial explanations of their role in persuadability documented. The communications situation consists of (1) the source of the communication, (2) the medium through which it is transmitted, and (3) the content of the communication itself.[14]

Earlier we viewed the communication process in terms of: [15]

Who
Says What

---

[14] Klapper, *op. cit.*, pp. 98-99.
[15] Harold D. Lasswell, "The Structure and Function of Communication in Society," in *Mass Communications,* ed. Wilbur Schramm (Urbana, Ill.: University of Illinois Press, 1960), p. 117.

In Which Channel
To Whom
With What Effect

Now our task here is to examine briefly how effects are brought about by the "Who" or source, speaking through a particular channel or medium, given a particular message that "Says What."

Source effect.   The audience is most likely to have opinions and predispositions regarding the source of the communication, and this audience image of the source will probably affect the communication's persuasive intensity. Sources viewed as authoritative, trustworthy, reliable, etc., are likely to be viewed favorably and in turn favorably dispose the audience for messages emanating from this source, even though the qualifications of the source are not in the area of its message dissemination—for example, an actor who becomes active in state or local politics. Normally, however, highly specialized sources appear to be more effective for congruent specialized audiences than are more general sources for specialized audiences.

Media effects.   The media or channels of communication can themselves be an effective force for bringing about desired results in the range or characteristic set of behavior patterns produced by the communication process. Many people are somewhat in awe of the mass media, and messages carried over such media are likely to have a persuasive effect on certain listeners or viewers. The fact that a known personality endorses a particular issue makes for certain positive communication effects. The additional fact that this personality endorses the issue on network television may, other things being equal, only add to the persuasiveness of his given message. The different media or channels of communication are in turn affected by the selective processes of both individual and group, depending on a host of psychological, sociological, and other factors including life style and the relative position in the family life cycle. People with more education generally tend to watch less television and a different mix of programs than their less well-educated counterparts. Commuters tend to listen to more radio than those who do not commute. Generally speaking, as we noted earlier, personal appeal or face-to-face contact is more effective as a persuasive tool than various forms of mass communication including print, radio, and television.

Conclusive evidence attesting to the persuasive ability of the various mass media has yet to be brought forth. Suffice it to say that each of the media possesses certain qualities and characteristics which, depending on the nature and characteristics of the audience, the goals and objectives of the communicator, and the structure of the message itself, make for a given probability of persuasive success.

Message effects. The actual content and the structuring of the message itself are known to have an effect on the persuasiveness of communication. Messages which are clearly stated, simple in construction, and without ambiguity have a better chance of clearly conveying the attitudes and wishes of the sender or source, and thus a greater likelihood of bringing about the desired communication objectives. The highly educated receiver is likely to be suspect of only one-sided messages, and therefore two-sided messages are likely to be received and acted upon more favorably by this type of receiver. On the other hand, the less educated receiver will probably be less responsive to the two-sided message, perhaps because of an induced state of confusion. People can, perhaps, be presented with too many facts which appear subject to too many interpretations and offer too many alternatives or choices. On the other hand it would seem safe to conclude that the middle majority probably prefer a choice between something and something rather than something and nothing in their communication messages.

Pointed communications appear to be more successful in their intent than nondirectional messages. For example, communications which convey facts, draw conclusions, and suggest courses of action are likely to be more effective than those which present only facts and allow the audience members to draw their own conclusions. The reason again can probably be found in the selection process and the fact that certain audience members need to be told what they are supposed to see, hear, or read and, specifically, what the things they have seen, heard, or read imply in terms of attitudes, opinions, or behavior.

Fear appeals have been shown to be less effective in persuading the audience to certain prescribed attitudes and behavior than appeals which are tempered with reason and calmly emphasize a given threat.

Repetition which does not harangue and annoy the receiver has been found to be an effective means of increasing the persuasiveness of communication. This no doubt results from the reinforcing tendency of repetition. A thing heard or seen repeatedly is more likely to become both (1) more familiar and (2) more believable.

Given the propriate strivings of individuals discussed in Part Two, it would appear somewhat obvious that communications or messages which offer to the receiver a means of insight into the implementation of his existing needs hierarchy or "becoming" will probably be more successfully persuasive than communications which undertake to arouse new needs and then suggest ways of satisfying them. This idea or concept is known as "canalizing," and it involves in a theoretical sense the notion of matching means to ends.

Possessed now with some significant knowledge about the role of communications, or the range in the characteristic set of behavior patterns produced by the communication process, we proceed in the next chapter to develop, explore, and analyze the basic dimensions of marketing communications.

EIGHT

The Structure of

Marketing Communication

Our approach, at least up to this point, has been largely a functional one. That is, the approach to consumer behavior has focused on a system of action—learning theory and communication—where the emphasis has been on identifying the interaction between these two concepts and on determining how and why the system of action operates in a particular manner. Thus, our approach to consumer behavior via learning theory and communication has tended to stress the interrelationships and interdependencies between these concepts. Our approach might further be termed "holistic" because of our preoccupation with the system as a whole. Remember that the system with which we are concerned is the marketing communication system with the firm as one vital link or subsystem in this system, along with the consumer, as an objective abstraction, operating in a group environment and behaving according to a set of behavioral axioms or propositions. A fundamental presumption which underlies our functional approach is that the operation of any system, behavioral, communicating, or otherwise, is likely to change over time and that the essence of science is its dynamic, not static, aspect. This characteristic poses something of a dilemma, however, for the scientific researcher. Oftentimes, given a rapidly changing or dynamic system, he is forced to make both his observations and his deductions, figuratively speaking at least, on the run.

172

Our objective, then, is to learn something about a given system of action, the marketing communication system, which in its simplest form consists of the firm, messages, channels, and consumers, all bound by given temporal and spatial constraints. The idea of a system has been discussed previously, but it will be recalled that it embraces the concept of a whole consisting of related component parts. Sometimes there is great complementarity, and thus congruity, among the parts. At other times, with other components, the system is likely to be wracked by divisive, incongruent, and if not incompatible at least hostile components. A given system is often composed of a series of behavior sequences which are more closely linked than other behavior sequences. Such a sequential set of components is referred to as composed of subsystems, which implies that they are closely linked even though they do not constitute an independently functioning entity in time and space.

To repeat, the emphasis thus far throughout this treatment has been more functional than structural. However, as has been pointed out, both function and structure are embraced in the subject matter of scientific study.[1] The functionalist is guided in his scientific inquiry by a basic dictum, however, which is that function basically determines structure in group behavior rather than the reverse.

It is time now to look at marketing communication from its structural standpoints as well. It is necessary to at least describe the existing structural relationships of marketing communications. We need to examine such questions as: "What is the relationship between communication strategy and marketing strategy? What are the structural components of a message? What is the relationship between signs and significates? What constitutes a marketing communications system?" The more functional question, "How can marketing communications, utilizing our knowledge of individual and group behavior, be made more effective?" will be treated in subsequent chapters. Our ultimate goal in studying both learning theory and communication, in a managerial sense and from a marketing point of view, is to develop principles of action which can make the purposeful behavior of both firm and consumer more successful.

MARKETING MIX TO COMMUNICATION MIX

Figure 4, in Chapter 1, depicted the relationship between learning and communication. For our purposes now, the lower half of this schematic

[1] Wroe Alderson, *Marketing Behavior and Executive Action* (Homewood, Ill.: Richard D. Irwin, Inc., 1957), p. 17.

diagram can be particularly useful in showing relationships between the marketing mix and the communications mix. As a matter of fact, there is some serious doubt if we are really talking about two concepts at all or if, instead, we have just renamed, at a later stage of application, the marketing mix by calling it the communications mix. One writer, in summarizing the importance of communications to marketing, stated:

> Marketing effectiveness depends significantly on communication effectiveness. The market, in reality, is energized (or activated) through information flows. The way a buyer perceives the market offering of the seller is influenced by the amount and kind of information he has about the offering and his reaction to that information.[2]

Is marketing, then, primarily a series of information flows? There is much to recommend this particular point of view.

The reader will recognize the figure on page 175 as primarily a reproduction of Fig. 4 in Chapter 1. The firm is confronted with the competitive necessity of developing a marketing strategy, which was defined earlier as a comprehensive plan of action. The marketing mix consists of those elements or components around which such a systematic plan can be formulated. The *implementation* of the plan, however, requires *information flows,* and these information flows may be channeled through any of a number of communication alternatives, as listed at the bottom of the diagram. Put another way, the firm is an isolated organism until it both sends and receives information. In short, until communication takes place the firm is not triggered or activated into any kind of purposeful behavior. The market-oriented firm takes its marching orders from the market. Once the market communicates its needs to the firm (the reader will observe that the arrows in the diagram are shown with bi-directional thrust), the firm then responds to this environmental stimulus with some aspect of its marketing mix—product, price, promotion, place, or some combination thereof. It is important to understand that it is communication which prompts the firm to action. Without communication, the firm would either remain in a sodden state of inertia or flop and thrash about like any headless or nonsensory receiving organism with no pattern or purpose.

A marketing strategy can be neither wisely formulated nor implemented without a well-structured communication system. On the other hand, a communication system, no matter how well structured, is no panacea for the firm's success. It is only a contributory factor. Without good products, well priced and conveniently accessible to consumers,

---

[2] Thomas A. Staudt and Donald A. Taylor, A *Managerial Introduction to Marketing* (Englewood Cliffs, N.J.: Prentice-Hall, Inc., © 1965), p. 353.

Figure 16: Relationship Between Marketing Strategy and Communication Strategy.

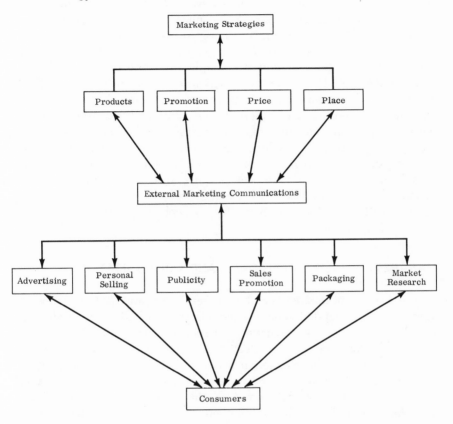

no amount of persuasive communication can guarantee the firm's success. Once again, however, it is important to point out that the guide to what constitutes a good product, well priced and conveniently accessible to consumers, is to be found through the firm's marketing intelligence system, i.e., communication.

MARKETING FUNCTIONS AND COMMUNICATION

The historical-functional approach to marketing has pretty largely been abandoned in favor of the more sophisticated and analytical managerial approach. The historical-functional approach applied in the early study of marketing was concerned primarily with the description of the marketing functions that characterized each marketing transaction. This approach is not to be confused with our concept of functionalism described at the beginning of this chapter. The functional approach to the study of marketing is concerned with an analysis (description) of the major activities or functions of marketing that must be performed by the marketing system.[3] The marketing functions are generally listed under three headings: [4] (1) Functions of Exchange, which consist of Selling and Buying, (2) Functions of Physical Supply consisting of Transportation and Storage, and (3) Facilitating Functions consisting of Financing, Risk Taking, Marketing Information (its collection, communication, and interpretation), and Standardization. As one can readily see from examining this list of the functions approach to the study of marketing, communication receives far too little emphasis as a major mediating factor affecting the overall marketing process. Only Marketing Information is considered in the realm of, or contributing to, communication whereas in actuality, as we have seen earlier and as we shall explore subsequently, communication is a far more pervasive concept than marketing information narrowly conceived.

MANAGEMENT SYSTEMS APPROACH AND COMMUNICATION

As was briefly outlined earlier, the marketing operation can logically be viewed as an integrated action system affected by both internal and external forces. From this viewpoint, the success of such an action system depends not only on proper selection of each element and submix, or component, but on the interaction between them. Boyd and Levy argue forcefully that "the market mix is in reality, a communications mix in which all activities interact—sometimes in a mutually reinforcing way, sometimes in conflict with one another—to form an image that can be favorable or unfavorable." [5]

Perhaps this assertion is a bit too strong. Marketing is not just another name for communication and vice versa. Instead, taking the management systems approach point of view, a stronger argument, and therefore one which is more logically appealing, is that marketing strategy consists of a series of submixes or subsystems which are highly interactive. Figure 17 visually relates these subsystems into a larger integrated and holistic concept. The marketing system shown in Fig. 17 is an input-output system. The various submixes or systems are the inputs

---

[3] Rayburn D. Tousley, Eugene Clark, and Fred Clark, *Principles of Marketing* (New York: The Macmillan Company, 1962), p. 13.

[4] *Ibid.*, p. 14.

[5] Harper W. Boyd, Jr., and Sidney J. Levy, *Promotion: A Behavioral View* (Englewood Cliffs, N.J.: Prentice-Hall, Inc., © 1967), p. 20.

Figure 17: Marketing System and Subsystems.

Source: Adapted from William Lazer and Eugene Kelly, "The Retailing Mix: Planning and Management," *The Journal of Retailing,* Spring, 1961, p. 38.

which flow through the marketing firm in an effort to attain the outputs realized by the organization. The philosophy which underlies the marketing system, then, is that of strategy. The firm and its management are interested in the composite of all effort which can be programmed for the adjustment of the firm to its environment.

The most apparent and observable of the various subsystems or components of the marketing system is the goods and service system. The goods and service component constitutes the firm's product offering, along with the special conditions or terms under which the product can be secured. The product constitutes a bundle of expectations from the consumer's point of view and, as will be explained shortly, the product can do a great deal to communicate a given message to a given consumer.

The physical distribution component is oftentimes a more obscure, and therefore less observed, aspect of the overall marketing system. However, it has been the increased analysis of marketing activities from a systems point of view which has brought to light the importance of the physical distribution component. The systems approach emphasizes that efficient or optimum relationships between inputs and outputs of a system result only from system balance. Therefore, an effective and efficient total marketing system implies balance among the various subsystems. This subsystem is composed in turn of two vital components: the channels component and the physical distribution or logistics component. The channels component is concerned with store, plant, and warehouse location, and the sequence of activities among these physical entities and other marketing functionaries such as middlemen. The physical distribution component is concerned with the economical storing and moving of goods from a logistics point of view.

The communications system is concerned with developing information flows between the firm and its environment, which includes primarily consumers and competitors. Nothing is so important to the firm as the knowledge or information which it possesses about markets, product offerings, consumer tastes, wants, and behavior, or competitive plans. With the widespread specialization and division of labor of modern mid-twentieth century industry, the firm is oftentimes far removed from its customers and markets in both time and space. It is the specialization and division of labor which permit economies of scale, mass production and mass marketing, but only if the task of coordination between sophisticated production units and equally sophisticated consuming units is accomplished or facilitated by communication. Without communication to accomplish this coordination, economies of scale leading to mass production and mass marketing would be impossible. The provision of information about the marketing firm and the goods and services available constitute the important second half of the communications system. The first half, of course, is concerned with the gathering and retrieval of information concerning market opportunities.

In summary, the systems approach to marketing emphasizes the interdependency of the various subsystems and planning. Planning is deciding in advance what needs to be done. One can plan astutely only by possessing superior marketing information or intelligence obtained through communication. On the other hand, effective execution of marketing plans depends upon ideas and constructs well articulated and transmitted to consumers and facilitating agencies. This too, then, is a part of our communications system.

It would be neither logical nor accurate to reduce the complex bundle of activities which we call marketing to little more than a series of acts labeled communication. To make something everything is at the same time to make it nothing. Communication, however, is vastly important to the economic well-being of an enterprise. Only recently has the importance and validity of this relationship begun to be explored and understood. Communication is much like atmosphere; it sustains life or it doesn't, and in turn it has an effect upon the size, character, and behavior of the organisms which it supports.

While marketing is more than communication, it is important to remember that communication is far more important to the development and implementation of strategy than earlier marketers were willing to concede. A far more accurate appraisal of communication would be that nearly every aspect or function of marketing is in some way dependent on the communication process or that the function or activity is concerned with communicating some message or signal, either to or away from the firm. Marketing is to a considerable extent a phenomenon of group behavior, and as we learn more about both individual and group behavior, we become even more aware of the role of communication in such behavioral activities as perception, cognition, motivation, the formation and persistence of groups, the analysis of group structure and function, and the internal and external adjustment of groups to meet changing conditions.

The marketing firm as a communicative agency becomes a highly important nexus in the communication process. To a considerable extent, then, nearly everything a marketing man does becomes a means of communicating something to someone.

The product, for example, may tell prospective purchasers a great deal about the quality and integrity of the firm's production and engineering processes. It may at the same time, because products are symbols and therefore have the potential of connoting all sorts of meanings, project a message or image which is not totally in keeping with the company's intended objective. To many consumers, products have images or personalities, and, like the human personality which is a bundle of characteristics, a product personality profile can be constructed on the basis of such characteristics as product attributes, price, channels through which it is sold, and promotional campaigns used, including appeals and media. Depending on the predisposition of the market segments for which a product is intended, such product personality profile is likely to elicit a host of consumer responses. Attempts of marketing firms at branding are also efforts directly involved with the communication of symbolic ideas. Some brands of major appliances and automobiles are known to elicit a set of particular attitudes, associations, expectations, and responses. By the same token, packages are designed to communicate a number of messages to buyers and potential buyers. Much of the message may be purely informational in nature such as weight, ingredients, and caloric content. A significant portion of the message may be more subtly presented by showing the contents as a part of a well-planned, nutritious meal in a smartly styled social setting with trim, neat, well-dressed people as a part of the overall setting. This might very well entice potential buyers with the belief that the contents of the package are easy to prepare; light and not fussy; nutritious, but not filling or conducive to gaining weight; or that the item is served and eaten by chic, modern, sophisticated members of an upper echelon social class.

Price, too, is a highly important communication device. Not only does it tell the person how much he must pay to acquire a given item; it is something of an index of quality and therefore projects considerable "knowledge" to the potential buyer.

It is a well-known fact that retail stores and their particular decorative motifs can have a profound effect in attracting or repelling a given class of clientele. Consumers, generally speaking, seek out stores which have an image or personality consistent with their own self-image or cognitive style. Pierre Martineau has noted this affinity between customers with given life styles and self-images and stores which seem to complement or enhance these attitudes. He has stated that "some stores intimidate her; others may seem beneath her. A store may be acceptable for one type of good and not for others. A shopper may go to one department store for bargains, children's clothes, or housewares, and to another one for gifts or personal items." [6] Store designers, architects, and layout engineers today recognize the possibility of creating moods and attitudes via lighting, color, and spatial manipulation. Thus we see that communication is a vital part of the whole spectrum of marketing activity, and while promotion is the major means or vehicle for external marketing communications, other aspects of the marketing mix are concerned with communication as well. Promotion is really designed to communicate knowledge to the consumer about our products, prices, and places of business; and therefore promotion as a form of communication can act as a powerful mediating force in the success of our overall marketing strategy.

Communication as a pervasive marketing activity raises many problems with which decision makers must contend.[7] The first problem, and, given our present state of knowledge, the one which is subject to greatest control, is that of technical accuracy. Has the intended message been accurately transmitted? Has the proper type size and face been employed? Has the salesman transmitted truthful information? Did the media faithfully reproduce our message? The second problem, and the one least subject to control because of our high state of ignorance regarding it, is the semantic problem. Communicators at all levels are faced with the

---

[6] "The Personality of the Retail Store," *Harvard Business Review*, January-February, 1958, p. 47.

[7] Edward L. Brink and William T. Kelley, *The Management of Promotion* (Englewood Cliffs, N.J.: Prentice-Hall, Inc., 1963), p. 52.

difficulties and misunderstandings to which all human communication is subject. The difficulties of using language as a communication symbol are well documented in the literature. The possibility of error or ambiguity in interpretation is always paramount. A personnel manager once received a letter of recommendation regarding a young college graduate which stated, "I can't recommend this young man too highly." Seldom, if ever, do we either receive or perceive a complete message. Instead we receive only parts, or what are called "bits" of information, which we fit together by means of our own cognitive process. The context in which messages are received, our own attitudes, group norms, culture, etc., affect the meanings or patterns which we make from these parts. Thus the whole is completed by what we have called gestalt or insight. To continue with the above example, the personnel manager, if he has a favorable interview with the young man, is likely to conclude, regarding the letter of recommendation, that the respondent was greatly impressed with the young man and therefore eager to praise him adequately. An unfavorable interview or additional letters of recommendation tending to be unfavorable are likely to lead to a different conclusion, both about the original recommendation and the young man himself.

COMMUNICATION STIMULI

Let us turn our attention now to a somewhat more meticulous analysis of the structure of communication, especially as it relates to the field of marketing. Numerous definitions of communication were given in an earlier chapter but the basic meaning of communication centers around the main idea that communication is "the process by which an individual transmits stimuli to modify the behavior of other individuals." [8] Given the purposive intent of marketing, this definition appears quite apt. Thus, marketing communication is concerned with transmitting stimuli for the purpose of affecting and/or modifying consumer behavior and of receiving stimuli for the purpose of making our transmissions more effective. The principal means of marketing communication is language. The words, phrases, and expressions of a language are all stimuli. When strong enough, these stimuli are signs, or symbols, which prompt action. At the same time languages are composed of cues. For example, a linguistic stimulus consisting of an unrecognized word should not cause action, especially in the absence of other stimuli. On the other hand the word (sign) "warning" should evoke an undetermined response. The

---

[8] Carl I. Hovland, Irving L. Janis, and Harold H. Kelly, *Communications and Persuasion* (New Haven, Conn.: Yale University Press, 1953), p. 12.

word (cue) "stop" is supposed to lead to an exact response. A large part of the inculturation process of the individual from childhood to adulthood is composed of learning widely accepted responses to the stimuli provided by language.

The basic attempt in using language is to meaningfully and accurately express reality. Thus, when cues and signs are meaningfully interrelated in communication, language serves as a model. A well-developed model is an abstraction of reality where reality itself is too cumbersome or complex to communicate. Recall that we cannot communicate a mood or emotion. We can only encode our feelings about the emotion or mood and communicate it in the form of language.

Reality is the significate of language in total. A significate is the object, condition, quality, or activity which is portrayed by signs and cues. "Sale" is a word which tries to describe a condition wherein goods might be purchased at reduced cost but which in some contexts also means "cheap." In short, words are nothing more than bundles of conceptualizations, the conceptualizations in turn being a function of culture and other social and psychological phenomena.

At the same time, there is far more to communication than just language. Stimuli can be transmitted otherwise than by words. Stimuli for communication purposes can be transmitted through any of the human senses including hearing, seeing, feeling, smelling, or tasting.[9]

The symbolic significance of products and product attributes was mentioned earlier. To illustrate the above point, it is generally understood that darker colors imply more respectable products whereas pastel colors are symbolic of gaiety and youthful frivolity. Science is associated with products of technical merit and high quality.[10] It is these nonverbal aspects of communication which have only recently come to the attention of marketers. Because many of the stimuli involved with products are perceived by the consumers regardless of their purpose, it has been only realistic to use them to full advantage in the communication process.

One of the important aspects of communication structure is that of pattern or organization. The stimuli which are used to influence or affect buyer attitudes and behavior must be arranged in a meaningful manner in order to achieve optimum effect. The intended meaning of the stimuli is lost when they are presented randomly without order and organization. It is for this reason that the message or the stimuli arrangement must be carefully analyzed before consumers receive it. Messages

---

[9] Colin Cherry, *On Human Communication* (Cambridge, Mass.: The MIT Press, 1957), p. 4.

[10] Sidney J. Levy, "Symbols by Which We Buy," in *Advancing Marketing Efficiency*, ed. Lynn H. Stockman (Chicago: American Marketing Association, 1959), pp. 411-412. By permission of the American Marketing Association.

can be broken down and studied in terms of their three structural components: isolates, sets, and patterns.[11]

The distinguishable components of messages are sets. When sets are broken down into their smallest parts, isolates are uncovered. A marketing communication in the form of an advertisement can be studied in terms of sets. The isolates of the advertisement would therefore include the words, illustrations, and colors used in the advertisement. Another aspect of marketing communication might be the distribution network used by the manufacturer. The isolates here would include the stores' interior and exterior appearances, the clienteles, the competing products available, and the kinds of stores in which the products are found.

The final element of a message is the pattern or arrangement of the sets. The manner in which sets are arranged changes the meaning of the message. "Patterns are those implicit cultural rules by means of which sets are arranged so that they take on meaning." [12] Messages which are spoken, and in which the words, gestures, and bodily movements are sets and the simplest sounds are isolates, have different meanings from culture to culture even when the same pattern is used. In the United States the face-to-face speaking distance is usually considered to be five to eight feet. In Latin American countries, however, this distance is normally much closer. Therefore, when Americans transact business in these Latin American countries, they are often considered cold and aloof. On the other hand, North Americans feel cramped and uncomfortable in such close proximity to their communicators. The result of this cultural variation is a somewhat undesirable and unintentional interference in the communication process.[13]

It now becomes more readily apparent why so much of marketing activity can be logically construed as communication. In any given distribution system, the marketer can alter the messages he sends by rearranging the distribution system so that different sets are used. A policy shift from exclusive agency distribution to more extensive distribution channels may alert consumers as well as channel members and competitors of the increased availability of the product and of changes in production philosophy or technique, or that the product is now more conveniently available.

The analysis of messages by sets and isolates must proceed on a

---

[11] Edward T. Hall, *The Silent Language* (New York: Fawcett World Library, Premier Books, 1961), p. 93.

[12] *Ibid.*, p. 111. Reprinted by permission of Doubleday & Company, Inc.

[13] Edward T. Hall, "The Silent Language in Overseas Business," *Harvard Business Review,* June, 1960, pp. 87-96.

relative basis. The messages can be analyzed at one level at one time; messages cannot be studied in terms of sets and isolates in anything like an absolute manner. A given advertisement, product, or distribution system can be analyzed as sets. At the same time, however, these systems can also be analyzed as complete messages or isolates.

When advertisements are viewed as single messages, the arranged words, illustrations, and symbols contained within the advertisements themselves are sets. The sets can be broken down into many isolates such as size of type, the letters in the words, the color of the paper, etc. Conversely, advertisements can be considered to be isolates which are only part of the total communication effort of the marketer. Other isolates besides advertisements in this case would be the product price, the distribution system, and the method of distribution employed.

All this, then, leads us to a very important and significant marketing generalization: All marketing communication proceeds by means of signs, which are stimuli; as a result of association with the significate; they evoke in the customer some part of the total behavior elicited by the significate; and with these the producer or marketer tries to influence the behavior of customers who are buying significates.[14]

It is therefore clearly in the interest of the marketing manager to know how, when, where and what signs (promotional appeals, product attributes, distribution systems, etc.) to use to influence or trigger the customers to buy the significate (the product or service under consideration).

THE MARKETING COMMUNICATIONS SYSTEM

Having thus examined and explained in considerable detail the structural components of messages, let us look now more closely at the structural aspects of a marketing communications system. Figure 18 diagrams the major components of such a system.

The reader will observe that the communications system here described and diagrammed is in the form of a pyramid which has three major components: the marketer, the consumer, and the product. The base of the pyramid is information—the crux of any communications system. Observe that information flows in two directions—both to and from consumer to marketer.

Marketing communication originates with the consumer, at least in a buyer's market. After messages, which can be either signs or cues

---

[14] Gerald Zaltman, *Marketing: Contributions from the Behavioral Sciences* (New York: Harcourt, Brace & World, Inc., 1965), p. 104.

Figure 18: A Marketing Communication System.

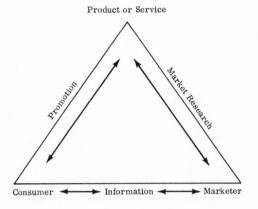

depending on their content and the importance attached to them, are received and interpreted by the marketer, he devises a communication strategy based on this market research. The research data are used by the marketer to change his behavior in accordance with these stimuli. Contained in the market research data are important facts about consumers, their life styles and self-images. Based upon his knowledge of attitude formation, group norms, status, social class, and other factors,[15] the marketer will begin to formulate important aspects of his marketing strategy including price, promotion, and product considerations, together with such other marketing aspects as the market segment(s) to which he wishes to appeal, and the type and number of distribution outlets.

The next component of the marketing communication relationship is the product. Products were discussed earlier in the construct of messages. However, a distinction must be made between products and products as messages. When a marketer communicates to consumers, he relates to his products. In doing so he uses various signs to portray the actual product, which is the significate. When a salesman speaks of boats, he is using signs to portray a kind of water conveyance. Newspaper and magazine advertisements show pictures of many products. Once again, these are signs portraying the significance of reality. It is the product in the sense of being a significate that is a component of the marketing communications system. When products are envisioned as signs, they become messages carried by the communications system. The messages

---

[15] We shall explore these phenomena more fully in the next chapter entitled "Communications and Consumer Behavior."

travel about the system in accordance with the pattern set by the components—the consumer, the marketer, and the product.

In terms of messages, the product, its distribution system, the personnel involved, and the advertisements are all sets of the message which forms the basis of the product image. It is this aspect of communication which is affective. That is, promotional communication is designed so that a favorable affective interpretation results. This means, of course, that communication not only aids in the creation of a product image but also has a purely informational purpose. In this latter aspect, communication, as has been so often stated in this study, facilitates the learning process. Informative communication tells the consumer that a given product is available, where it can be purchased, and how it can be used. The promotional or what was called affective aspect of marketing communication can be exemplified by the giving of a name to a car which denotes speed, power, and fashion; by designing it as such; and by showing it in advertisements with backgrounds and illustrations which enhance the image which is being portrayed.

This affective influence of communication can be seen in Bulova's attempt to secure a place in the market for higher-priced men's watches. Long a leader in the medium-priced field, Bulova conducted a market research study to determine what characteristics men and women, who purchase 60 percent of all men's watches as gifts, desire in high-quality watches. The results revealed that accuracy, reliability, and appearance, in that order, were the most popular characteristics. After designing the watch according to these specifications, and pricing it from $175 to $2,500, the name for this new watch was decided upon. The winner was Accutron, although Sonac and Satellite received consideration. The market research director at Bulova, Alexander D. Goodman, said concerning this affective selection, "Accutron conveyed several impressions (accuracy, electronics, scientific achievement, space age, and newness) that our studies indicated would be well received by men particularly, and by women to a somewhat less degree." Bulova's president commented on the result, "We have no doubt Accutron will soon rank among the top six or seven fine watches for men on the domestic market." [16] Quite naturally, the introductory advertisements stressed accuracy, reliability, and appearance.

Considerable emphasis has been placed on the image-building process of communication. It must be pointed out, however, that the product and its image are inextricably related. If a product image does not fit the product, it is in all likelihood doomed to market failure.

---

[16] Peggy Boomer, "Male Market: Big, Rich, But Tough," *Printers' Ink,* July 20, 1962, p. 23.

The major aspect of marketing communication is concerned with what might be called "pure unadulterated information." Informative communication, which tends to be the major characteristic of marketing communication, television commercials notwithstanding, has as its objective the implementation of the consumer's learning process in which the consumer associates a product and its image with his needs and self-image. One writer put it thus: [17]

> The increasing volume of industrial research and the consequent new products place demands on the buyer for learning adaptive behavior. Even with given product offerings, changes in such dimensions as price, advertising, and availability require learning.

It is increasingly evident therefore that in any economy characterized by affluence and a virtual explosion of consumer products the consumer must learn adaptive behavior in order to maintain any semblance of awareness and understanding. As is true of most organisms, consumers adapt by receiving sensory stimuli, much of which is information.

Because most informational communication is rarely evaluated without a subjective influence, the marketer cannot wholly divorce informational communication from promotional communication. The goal of the marketer is to establish the learning process whereby the consumer responds to cues so that he continually buys the marketer's products. The cues must be in the form of informational communication which must convey that the product exists that will satisfy the customer's needs and that it can be bought at certain places. Once the product is used satisfactorily, reinforcement and cognition take place, thus strengthening the learning process so that the consumer knows what product to buy when the need arises.

COMMUNICATION AS A MARKETING FUNCTION

Perhaps it is time now to more fully recognize the importance of communication as a part of total marketing activity. If marketing functions are those activities which are endemic to the marketing process, then no activity is more important or more pervasive than that of communication. As has been pointed out by Duddy and Revzan, communication plays an important role in three major areas of marketing: [18]

---

[17] John A. Howard, *Marketing: Executive and Buyer Behavior* (New York: Columbia University Press, 1963), p. 253.

[18] Edward A. Duddy and David A. Revzan, *Marketing: An Institutional Approach* (New York: McGraw-Hill Book Co., Inc., 1947), pp. 104-112.

(1) Buying and selling
(2) Price determination
(3) Organization

Communication is without doubt the adhesive which binds the economic market forces together and forms a network of information flows that provide the basis for knowledgeable behavior of all members of our market system. Another earlier and distinguished marketing theorist came close to recognizing the importance of the communication function in marketing, even though he gave it a slightly different name. He acknowledged the extreme importance of communication when he stated, "The (communication) function in marketing has to do with the searching out of the market for the purpose of finding who the potential customers or the potential sources are and then of making and maintaining connections between those who have goods to offer and those who may want them." [19]

A marketing communications system such as we have described and analyzed in this chapter represents a vast network of relationships, each of which is goal seeking and programmed for the purpose of looking for satisfaction on the basis of certain cybernetic principles. These principles or axioms of behavior are not fully formulated or understood. Many are rooted in abstruse areas of the social sciences, especially psychology and sociology. We will turn our attention to these areas in the next chapter.

---

[19] Edmund D. McGarry, "The Contactual Function in Marketing," *The Journal of Business,* April, 1951, pp. 96-113. © by The University of Chicago Press.

NINE

Communication and Consumer Behavior: Social-Psychological Considerations

Our investigation into the phenomena of consumer behavior has, thus far, led us in several directions and to some important and meaningful insights. Our attention has at varying times focused upon the general psychological processes which affect behavior, namely, perception, motivation, thinking, learning, and remembering. And these basic psychological concepts have been used as important building blocks for a scientific theory of consumer behavior as it is affected by communication. There is an important difference between what might be called practical and scientific knowledge about consumer behavior. The major objective of science is not primarily to control and predict but to understand. Effective control is a reward of understanding, and accuracy of prediction is a check on understanding.

The marketer, the promotion manager, the account executive, can usually ascribe reasons for his successful control and prediction. However, like a savage engaged in a primordial rain dance, his "explanatory" generalizations are steeped in the lore and superstitions of his culture. This kind of understanding fails to meet the dictates of true science. This failure to differentiate between the scientific understanding of behavior and practical know-how about behavior has some truly unfortunate consequences. First of all, it inhibits a more thorough and ongoing study of consumer behavior because of the mistaken belief that we already know enough. And, secondly, it discourages most attempts to create a *theory* to encompass the facts we do *know* or have at our command because the theories have no practical value. The "practical" value of theory, however, is beyond measurement. There is, perhaps, nothing so valuable or practical as sound theory.

Our efforts to develop a *theory* of consumer behavior have centered around the role of learning theory and communications as they affect behavior, given certain underlying philosophical-psychological assumptions. Foremost among these assumptions is that consumer behavior is an interpersonal behavior event and that any interpersonal behavior event begins with the arousal of wants in the participants. Each phase of the event succeeds, in chain-like reaction, the preceding phase in a consistent manner, as action in the event tends toward goal achievement.

It is for these reasons that consumer behavior, as a proper subset of human behavior in general, is subject to a host of influences which have already been classed and discussed under psychology, sociology, and anthropology. Consumer behavior

> . . . can be regarded as a series of events in which the conditions of one time period are the primary determinants of the activities and conditions of the next time period. It can be conceived as a goal sequence in which an apparent goal becomes a stepping stone to some further goal, each chosen in turn because it represents the greatest of pleasures or the least of pains. There is no great intellectual effort involved in imagining causal effects that flow backward from the future, forward from the past, inward from the surrounding world or outward from some deep organic process.[1]

How aptly this excerpt *outlines* at least the dimensions of a theory of consumer behavior and *underlines* the importance of the central and crucial concept of *interaction* in studying consumer behavior phenomena. Interaction lies at the heart of consumer behavior and is the basis of the interpersonal behavior event. The interpersonal behavior event is also an integrated act. It reflects the integrated influence of the individual's wants and goals upon his emotions, thoughts, perceptions, and memories. Imagine two women driving into the city for a day's shopping activity. They *talk* about their plans for the day, they *worry* about the possibility of limited parking space, they *fantasize* about purchases they would like to make but cannot afford, they *anticipate* with eager enthusiasm the luncheon they propose having in a chic and sophisticated restaurant,

---

[1] W. T. Tucker, *Foundations for a Theory of Consumer Behavior* (New York: Holt, Rinehart & Winston, 1967), p. 1.

they *remember* their last trip to the city and the excitement and satisfaction which it engendered—all this as they *drive* along at 70 m.p.h. on the freeway. All of their activities are integrated and organized by the goal of getting to the city to shop, and all of these activities are a part of the consumer behavior complex.

Consumer behavior is the *raison d'être* of business. All business decision making is predicated on certain known or assumed facts regarding consumers. All the firm's schedules and budgets, all the long- and short-range plans, are conditioned by, and again predicated on, given assumptions regarding consumer behavior. The firm's output of goods and services must of necessity be oriented to the needs and wishes of consumers— food is to eat, clothes are to wear, cars are to drive, etc. Thus consumer behavior becomes the sole justification of business enterprise. The reactions of the firm and the consumer are inextricably linked together. The actions of each are in reference to the other. The actions of each are at once a result of and a cause of the actions of the other. In the case of lower animals engaged in such interaction which forms an interpersonal event, the interaction consists largely of a series of bodily movements. In the case of human beings, however, "body language" has given way to verbal language. Man interacts primarily by using words and developing communication systems.

Thus far, we have explored in considerable detail something of the nature of the formation of communication systems, the communication process, and the role of communication in altering and affecting consumer behavior. We have learned that the role of communication in affecting behavior is seldom a direct one but instead works indirectly through, and is in turn affected by, a series of mediating factors. It is our task throughout this chapter, first of all, to lay sufficient groundwork for understanding the interactive and integrated nature of consumer behavior and communication and, secondly, to spend some time developing the ideas, or what have been called the mediating factors, which are, in essence, the leaven of the consumer behavior phenomena.

A SOCIAL-PSYCHOLOGICAL FRAMEWORK

Our emphasis upon the interactive and integrated nature of communication and consumer behavior can be more fully developed and understood within a framework of social psychology.[2] Bear in mind that our

[2] For a comprehensive and most literate treatment of social psychology, see Kimbell Young, *Social Psychology*, 3rd ed. (New York: Appleton-Century-Crofts, Inc., 1956) and David Krech, Richard I. Crutchfield and Egerton L. Ballachey, *Individual in Society* (New York: McGraw-Hill Book Company, 1962).

treatment of communication and consumer behavior has repeatedly dramatized the importance of interdependence. Communication is affected by consumer behavior, i.e., group norms, attitudes, opinions, expectations, culture, etc. But on the other hand, consumer behavior, i.e., group norms, attitudes, opinions, expectations, culture, etc., is in turn affected by communication. This is not quite like saying that something is caused by everything. Instead it recognizes that complex phenomena such as consumer behavior are affected by a host of seemingly complex considerations. Just *how* and to *what* degree consumer behavior is affected by certain complex phenomena is not yet determinate. But it is perhaps better to have a *theory* which lacks precision and neatness but offers possibilities for understanding than one which is logically neat or even tautological but bears no relevance or resemblance to the real world. For example, economics treats consumer behavior with a high degree of mathematical precision but in doing so assumes away the really important questions of behavior, namely, motivation and the problem of changing tastes.

As was mentioned much earlier, consumer behavior is really rooted in the area of social psychology. Both learning theory and communication are fundamental to the area of social psychology, and in light of our central thesis that consumer behavior is largely the product of learning and communication, it is appropriate that we develop somewhat more fully our major framework of analysis.

Social psychology is concerned with the study of the interactional processes of human beings. Broadly defined, interaction refers to the fact that the response—gesture, word, movement, or gross body movement—of one individual is the stimulus to another, who in turn responds to the first. The basic model is the dyad $A \rightleftarrows B$ in a recurring condition of interstimulation and response contact. For example, we might generalize the model to the following dyad $F \rightleftarrows C$ which we would interpret as F = firm, C = consumer, whereby each in turn is affected by the actions and behavior of the other. Social psychology is interested in three basic interactional relationships: person to person, person to group, and group to group. The first of these, often called interpersonal relations, is limited as to the number of individuals who can be involved. The visual, auditory, and other perceptual processes, as well as the communicative process of each individual, must be capable of involving in more or less direct contact all the others who make up a given social unit.

In the second basic relationship—person to group—there is usually a group name or symbol with which the individual identifies himself. For the individual, his role in the group carries with it a sense of varied expectations. The relationship is often more conscious and deliberate than in the interpersonal situation. Yet there is an awareness of mutual participation, and a sense of solidarity often develops.

Finally, social psychology is also interested in group to group relationships. The group is viewed as a congeries of interacting individuals and as such it may be considered and studied as a unit just as logically as one may consider and study the individual as a unit. Marketing can be viewed as the study of the interactional processes of these three categories: (1) person to person, (2) person to group, and (3) group to group. Personal selling activity is largely concerned with the first two of these categories, and the operation of the mass media in the formation of consumer opinion and attitudes is concerned with category three, or large secondary groupings.

The basic interactional level of marketing is *communication*. This takes the form of expressive gestures and symbolic interaction which call into play speech and writing. Marketing activity within a framework of social psychology is largely interested in the give-and-take between the individual and his fellows, or what has been called the dialectic of personal growth.

Social psychology subsumes, as does our theory of consumer behavior, two major characteristics of human action. First, human action is motivated or goal-directed; secondly, human action is integrated—that is, the individual's wants, emotions, and cognitions operate in concert to influence his actions. It makes no difference whether we are studying the behavior of a man in the laboratory or the haberdashery, his performance on an intelligence test or his churchgoing habits; we are, in effect, studying the behavior of a man as a participant in interpersonal behavior events. The effects of a man's past, present, and anticipated behavior events influence each of his activities, no matter how simple or apparently remote. Therefore, consumer behavior as affected by learning and communication is a social phenomenon subject to all the mediating forces bearing on all social action and behavior.

We shall now examine more fully these mediating forces which affect communication, and thus consumer behavior and action.

THE TWO-STEP FLOW OF COMMUNICATION

Our discussion thus far leads us to the point of a flat assertion. *Communication does not directly affect consumer behavior but may positively or negatively affect behavior given the presence or absence of certain mediating factors and their interaction.* Nowhere is this assertion or generalization shown to be more valid than in the two-step theory or flow of communication. As the name implies, "two-step" means that communication and resulting behavior or attitudinal changes are the function not of one factor but of two or more. The developers of the two-step flow theory contend that influences stemming from the mass media first reach "opinion leaders," or what might be called key influentials, who in turn pass on what they read and hear to those of their everyday associates for whom they are influential.[3]

The two-step flow of communication theory has many interesting implications and appears to fit within the logical framework of analysis developed thus far. This theory underlines the central thesis that people are greatly influenced by the give-and-take that exists in a particular existential or social milieu and, further, that the influence of the mass media is considerably less than generally assumed. The concept of the audience as a large homogeneous mass of disconnected individuals hooked up in direct cause-and-effect linkage with the media, but not to each other, cannot be readily reconciled to the two-step flow of communication model which implies complex networks of interconnected individuals through which mass communications are channeled.[4] It ought to appear somewhat obvious then that mass communication messages as they move through the various media and, in turn, through the opinion leaders and key influentials, are subject to considerable modification, filtering, and distortion. The theory further provides several additional concepts or ideas worthy of exploration in our effort to structure the relationship between communication and consumer behavior. First of all, we now must recognize the role of personal influence in the overall decision processes of consumers. The consumer as an isolate weighing and measuring so much pleasure versus so much pain in a given purchase situation is an anomaly. Instead, in a consumer decision process, one must look for the decisive factors regarding choice. To what extent was the decision individualistic or group oriented? And what are and who were the major determinants of behavior? Secondly, it would appear that some people are likely to play a more important role as key influentials than others in the transmission of information and as persuaders of certain kinds of consumer behavior. And, thirdly, how do mass communications affect the decision processes, and thus behavior, of this select group of opinion leaders or influentials? An exhaustive treatment of these questions is naturally beyond the scope of this book, but we will explore at least the fundamental dimensions of these questions implicitly as we proceed to more thoroughly examine the role of personal influence in consumer decision making.

Perhaps the significant feature of personal influence as opposed to mass communication is that people trust their friends. Mass communica-

---

[3] Paul F. Lazarsfeld, Bernard Berelson, and Hazel Gaudet, *The People's Choice,* 2nd ed. (New York: Columbia University Press, 1948).

[4] See Elihu Katz, "The Two Step Flow of Communication: An Up-to-Date Report of an Hypothesis," *Public Opinion Quarterly,* Vol. 21 (1957), pp. 61-78.

tion by its very impersonal nature is subject to considerable suspicion. The mass media are much more purposive in their intent, i.e., they have a definite axe to grind, while personal influence is somewhat less purposive or more subtle in its approach to influencing or altering opinions, behavior, or position.

Research has shown that the strength and flow of personal influence depends to a considerable extent on the individual's role and status within the group.[5] Therefore, in attempting to assay something of the relationship between consumer behavior and marketing communications we must be aware of and deal with the problem of personal influence as both a causal and mediating factor. People talk, seek advice, or allow themselves to be influenced by other people. Usually the other people are those who are very much like themselves, having the same or closely allied interests, backgrounds or life styles. Just who is likely to become a key influential, or why, is not thoroughly understood but one's degree of influence seems somehow related to three factors: [6]

(1) Personification of certain values (who one is).
(2) Competence (what one knows).
(3) Strategic social location (whom one knows).

These factors strongly suggest that a high degree of social interest is therefore involved in the process of decision making as it is affected by personal influence. That is, group norms, reference groups, class and status concepts are phenomena which affect the communication process and have a determining influence on the overall effects of communication, including personal influence on the consumer behavior decision processes.

THE REALISTIC POINT OF VIEW

In developing a communication strategy the marketer must be attuned to a particular point of view regarding the nature and behavior characteristics of his audience. There are at least two polar viewpoints regarding the audience. One is egotistical and the other is realistic.[7] The short-sighted, egotistical point of view regards the audience as a relatively inert and undifferentiated mass that can be persuaded in something like a direct cause-and-effect manner via the mass media. This point of view is egotistical because it attributes great powers to the

---

[5] *Ibid.*, pp. 62-64.
[6] *Ibid.*
[7] The ideas of this section are developed from Donald F. Cox, "Clues for Advertising Strategists, II," *Harvard Business Review*, November-December, 1961, pp. 160-182.

communicator and regards the audience as a swayable mass. In short, the two-step flow of communication model is not considered. The realistic point of view, given our knowledge of human behavior and influences on behavior, offers greater promise for the more effective use of communication inasmuch as the audience is viewed as a body of interacting individuals who may respond to a communication in a variety of ways depending on their individual *predispositions*. The realistic point of view enforces the notion that while the communicator, the communication, and the medium play important roles in the communication process, it is the cognitive set of the audience, in the final analysis, which determines *if* and *to what extent* it (the audience) will be influenced. Remember from our earlier discussion that cognitions are attitudes, values, predispositions, opinions, etc., which tend to make meaningful our perceptions. Therefore, in order for the audience to be influenced in the desired manner by a communication, several conditions must be met or developed:

(1) The message must reach the sense organs of the people to be influenced. (*Perception* must occur.)

(2) If perception occurs, the message must be compatible and accepted as a part of the person's beliefs, opinions and facts. (A high state of *congruence* must be present.)

(3) To induce favorable behavior by communication, this action must be seen by the person as a path to some goal that he has. (*Canalizing* or matching means to ends must be accomplished.)

(4) To induce a given action, it is necessary that the consumer's behavior be under control or influence of appropriate motivation, attitudes, and opinions relating to the purchase decision. (*Cognitions* must operate to provide behavior insights.)

It is obvious from viewing these conditions necessary for influence to occur that the consumer becomes, in turn, a gatekeeper or decision maker regarding the communication process and its effects. The consumer *decides* what messages to receive by deciding what kinds of communication messages or media he will expose himself to. He, in turn, decides what messages to *perceive* and what messages to *retain* on the basis of certain existential or social-psychological factors. These existential or social-psychological factors are basically the consumer's *predispositions, which are in the nature of anticipatory reactions or conditions of readiness brought about by social or existent phenomena such as group norms, attitudes, and culture.*

Our analysis of communication and consumer behavior must turn now to the discussion of how predispositions are developed and changed by these existent phenomena. First, however, let us both summarize and conclude this section with a few relevant generalizations.

A large amount of marketing communication must function either to reinforce existing attitudes and behavior or to accelerate or stimulate the behavior sequences of consumers who are already *predisposed* to act in a given manner. As was emphasized in the previous chapter, communication is not in itself a *direct* cause of audience effects, but rather works with and through various mediating factors such as audience *predispositions* and *personal influence* which themselves are subject to mediating factors such as group norms, attitudes and opinions, and culture. It therefore appears logical to conclude that the major function of marketing communication is to select consumers or target markets which are already predisposed to buy certain products and present them with appeals which encourage and facilitate cognitive learning, and thus the desired responses. It becomes painfully obvious that we must know more about how the mediating factors affect marketing communications and consumer behavior.

ATTITUDES, COMMUNICATION, AND CONSUMER BEHAVIOR

The possibility of altering consumer behavior, or affecting it favorably, depends to a considerable extent upon the marketer's ability to both structure and restructure consumers' beliefs or attitudes. It is the consumer's attitudes or organized set of belief systems which enable him to develop a set of given mental and physical reactions to marketing stimuli. Consumers either "know" or do not "know" a company, its products, or its messages. How consumers react to a firm's promotional messages will be determined largely by the consumers' attitudes toward the company and its products and by how the products "fit" into the consumers' overall system of beliefs or cognitive style.

Consumers with strong convictions against cigarette smoking are not likely to be receptive to messages encouraging smoking, or smoking-related activities. All men, to a greater or lesser degree, have some kind of reasonably integrated view of the world in which they live. This total view is called a man's belief system or cognitive style. The core of a belief system consists of attitudes and values. Values encompass the concept of preferences or choices on a scale of things that people desire or want. Values largely grow out of and are assimilated from one's attitudes. As consumers are forced to cope with the continual bombardment of communication stimuli, the repeatedly evoked cognitions, feelings and response dispositions become organized into a set of patterned emotional reactions. These patterned reactions, loosely speaking, become attitudes. As patterned reactions become more complex and as the individual tends more and more to utilize these patterned reactions as measures of the worth of objects, they in turn become values. In order for marketers to more fully *understand* and supply the objects necessary to satisfy the needs hierarchy of consumers and to better utilize principles of learning and communication to facilitate this end, a better understanding of the structure and function of attitudes as affecting consumer behavior becomes imperative.

The anatomy of attitudes. An attitude is a mental set or a proclivity to respond in a certain way when the appropriate situation occurs. An attitude has several components which are integrated to form a system. The basic components of an attitude are cognitions, feelings, and action tendencies. Given the normal processes of growth or maturation, as individuals develop, their cognitions, feelings, and action tendencies with respect to various objects to which they are exposed, become organized into solidified systems called attitudes. The objects of attitudes are both physical and mental. Products are kinds of objects about which consumers have attitudes; oftentimes ideas are objects about which consumers have attitudes. Flying, as an abstract idea, is reacted to by a host of attitudes including excitement, speed, efficiency, modernity, and *fear*. It is probably the presence of this latter attitude which keeps vast numbers of potential buyers out of the market for airplanes and commercial air travel.

The number of an individual's attitudes is probably finite, because individuals have attitudes only about objects which exist in their own social-psychological worlds. A firm unknown to everyone in the United States does not exist as an *object* for those who do not know it, and therefore an unknown object cannot elicit consumer attitudes. Firms often overlook the fact that before consumer attitudes regarding their products, services, or total company image can be measured or evaluated they must first be sure that consumers *have* the attitudes in which the investigator is interested.

Briefly, the three components of an attitude can be described as follows: The cognitive element consists of the beliefs of the individual regarding the object, and these are usually evaluative. For example, Product X is good or bad, expensive or cheap. The feeling component of an attitude is concerned with the emotions associated with the object. For example, skiing is liked or disliked. Importantly for marketers, it is this emotional loading which operates as a *motivating* factor in the purchase of some goods. The action tendency component of attitude includes the behavioral inclinations associated with the attitude. It is a certain manifest proneness to react either negatively or positively. For example, Yes, I *like* product X and *will purchase* it, or No! I wouldn't be caught dead buying *that* product. It is important, nonetheless, for marketers to understand how their objects—products, services, company image—affect the total structure of consumer attitudes, as well as the various components and their interrelatedness.

The components of an attitude can differ in several important respects. Two of the characteristics which are most prominently analyzed in terms of variance are *valence* and *multiplicity*. Valence pertains to the degree of favorability or unfavorability of each of the various components. The cognitive component may vary from very good to very bad, like the feeling and action tendency component. The quantitative measurement on some scale or continuum from unfavorableness to favorableness is referred to as valence. Multiplicity refers to the complexity of the information possessed by the individual regarding the *object* of the *attitude*. It pertains to the *range* of reactions possessed by the individual. A simple example may help to clarify this. A prospective purchaser of an automobile who is actively engaged in prepurchase search behavior may be asked by a salesman if he likes the new Dodge Charger. The man responds with an unexcited shrug of the shoulders, Yes. The object is the automobile. The consumer's belief system regarding the inquiry articulated to the salesman reflects his *attitude*. His attitude, subjectively gauged by the salesman, reflects the degree of the consumer's attitude valence. The multiplicity of the attitude, however, is unknown at this moment because multiplicity is concerned with the range and dimensions of the attitude. Is it shallow and superficial, based upon scanty and limited information, or considered and deliberate based upon careful search and analysis?

It is well known that much consumer behavior reflects a favorable or positive valence regarding consumer attitudes in relationship to certain products. A man may be favorably disposed toward a given brand of cigarettes (positive valence), but definitely not walk a mile for a particular brand if there were any other conceivable choice available to him, because of the multiplicity aspects of his attitude. The cognitive, feeling, and action tendency components of his attitudes cannot be reconciled to such unusual behavior, given his tendency for alternative uses of time and his desire to conserve energy or other resources. Multiplicity is a check on the tendency to be simpleminded in our analysis and expositions regarding complex phenomena. It encompasses the idea that a person under one set of circumstances may have a very favorable attitude toward some object; but given a change in circumstances, new or additional information, a change in environment or time, his attitude may change in both its character and its valence.

A consumer's attitudes may differ in the extent to which they are related or connected into some meaningful whole. It is a rather rare individual, or consumer, who has integrated and pieced together his total set of attitudes into a meaningful life philosophy. Instead, consumers integrate rather meaningfully sets of related attitudes regarding purchase decisions or situations into what are called attitude clusters. For instance, a consumer may have a whole set of attitudes regarding food purchases, such as what products to buy, where to shop, how much to spend, etc. Her attitudes regarding the purchase of children's clothing may be quite isolated from her food shopping attitudes, or perhaps even interconnected. It is not likely, however, that many attitudes exist in a state of virtual isolation.

Attitudes become woven into an intricate pattern and network of consumer behavior reactions—myth, folklore, ritual, legend, and clichés are all part of the consumer's behavior mechanism. A more thoroughgoing and fundamental understanding of *attitudes* and how they are formed and changed must of necessity be the cornerstone on which a theory of consumer behavior is predicated.

The formation and changing of attitudes. For expository purposes one could easily separate the treatment of the formation of attitudes from that of changing attitudes. Such a treatment would, however, suffer from a lack of reality. The subtle and complex ways in which attitudes are formed and changed is an ongoing investigation since the highly complex interrelatedness of attitudes, group associations, and culture are recognized, but not fully understood. To know something of the complex structure and characteristics of attitudes is to know a great deal, but it is not enough.

If we are to more fully understand consumer behavior and if marketing strategies are to encompass this greater understanding, we must also know something of the ways in which attitudes are formed and changed. Prediction, which is to a great extent the goal of scientific marketing behavior, demands understanding. There is hardly an individual or a group of any kind which is not interested in attitude formation and change. Every phase of the marketing program cries out for more and greater understanding of this process. Marketers spend unlimited resources in their efforts to strengthen existing attitudes, to eliminate undesirable attitudes, or to develop whole sets of new attitudes pertaining in some way to the company or its products.

The relationships and forces which result in the formation and change of attitudes are often obscure and almost always indirect. The primary force resulting in attitude formation and change is internal to the individual and centers around the complex phenomena known as personality. The particular unitizing trait of personality which is related to attitudes is that which was mentioned and discussed in Chapter 2 as the process of goal striving. It is in coping with the multitude of problems in regard to satisfying wants and achieving short- and long-run life goals that the individual develops attitudes.

The consumer's goal striving in terms of goods and services must interface with cognitions related to life style. The consumer develops favorable attitudes in relation to products which tend to foster or enhance his self-esteem or self-image. One study of attitude formation concluded that attitude objects which are seen as means of goal achievement are evaluated favorably, whereas those which are seen as sources of frustration are evaluated unfavorably.[8] The implications to marketers are obvious. Products as goal objects must be integrated into the entire goal striving mechanism of the prospective purchaser. In short, not only do attitudes give meaning to the individual's world, but they serve as means to other goal striving ends or objectives. A given attitude about dress may serve various other goals such as comfort, security, social mobility, or economy. To repeat a generalization made earlier, in order to find out something of an individual's attitudes regarding purchase behavior, it is first necessary to make inquiries as to where the individual is striving to go, or what he is striving to become.

There are a host of additional factors which affect the manner in which attitudes are formed and changed. Throughout this section it has been emphasized that communication is important as a determiner and shaper of attitudes. The attitudes of consumers are therefore both formed and altered by the information to which they are exposed. But as we learned earlier, information is seldom a determinant of an attitude except in the context of other attitudes. Information may be complete or incomplete, true or false, relevant or irrelevant. Under these various circumstances the consumer is forced to sample, weigh, and evaluate the information at his disposal.

Consumer attitudes then are formed and altered by a host of interrelated factors including goal striving, personality development, communication, group associations, and culture. Before proceeding with a more elaborate discussion of these last two determinants, let us look at some ideas related to attitude change and the implications of attitudes for marketing.

Attitude changes are of two major kinds. Most of the research centering on attitudes has been concerned with changing the sign of attitudes, or what we earlier called valence. By sign is meant positive or negative reactions to objects: I like product X or I do not like product X. This type of change is referred to as incongruent change because the direction of the change is toward the sign opposite that of the original

[8] M. J. Rosenberg, "Cognitive Structure and Attitudinal Effect," *Journal of Abnormal and Social Psychology,* 1956, pp. 367-372.

attitude. Thus, when American Motors attempts to change the outlook of the eighteen to thirty-five-year-old car purchaser (the bulk of the American market) from attitudes which are essentially negative, if not hostile, to attitudes which are favorable and receptive by introducing a swifter, sleeker, more powerful version of the Mustang and calling it the Javelin, they are attempting an incongruent change.

The second type of attitude change is called a congruent change because the direction of change is congruent with the sign of the prevailing attitude. To continue with our example of American Motors: Those who were already favorably disposed toward American Motors may be even more pleased with the company and other products in its line because of the generally favorable image which is likely to result from the introduction of the Javelin, i.e., the idea that American Motors is alert, progressive, and viable.

The research evidence is extremely limited, but superficially it appears that, other things being equal, congruent change is easier to produce than incongruent change. Incongruent change may represent too much of an "about-face reaction" to some people and cause frustrations in maintaining cognitive balance or harmony. Congruent change, because it is more consonant, harmonious, want-serving and related to propriate striving goals, probably would be easier to accomplish.

It is never easy to change attitudes if the change is likely to break the consistency or ordered pattern of total behavior responses. The individual strives for balance and harmony in behavior which, in turn, implies balance and harmony in attitudes. This would strongly suggest that an attitude which is in a state of imbalance with other attitudes in a cluster or system of beliefs will tend to move toward a state of balance or total attitudinal equilibrium.

Intelligence levels play an important role in attitude formation and change. Marketing communications have not yet solved the problem of where to pitch their mass promotional appeals. Faced with this uncertainty, the all too frequent general approach has been to direct the message to the lowest common denominator. These may be the chronic Know-nothings in the American population. One study concluded that "there is something about the uninformed which makes them harder to reach, no matter what the level or nature of the information." This something may be in part lack of intelligence.[9]

The mechanisms by which attitudes are formed and changed are exceedingly complex, and our discussion has touched upon only the most obvious and salient considerations. The social orientation of the indi-

---

[9] H. H. Hyman and P. B. Sheatsley, "Some Reasons Why Information Campaigns Fail," *Public Opinion Quarterly*, 1947, pp. 412-423.

vidual strongly suggests, however, that attitudes are largely the products of interpersonal behavior events and that to understand the process of attitude formation and change we must continue our search and investigation in the realm and setting where such events occur—the home, the office, the church, the store.

Attitudes and implications for marketing.   There can be little question that attitudes have both direct and far-reaching implications for marketing and especially for marketing communications. *An attitude is preparation for behavior.* As attitudes become more complex and integrated into overall belief systems or cognitive sets, they tend to predispose consumers in a given fashion to products, firms, retail outlets, prices, promotional and advertising appeals. Earlier, the concept of product and store image was introduced. We can see more readily now that the product or store image is nothing more than the consumer's attitudes regarding these given stores or products.

In an aggregate sense the attitudes of a large number of consumers can be surveyed in an effort to forecast and anticipate the level of consumer demand for different kinds of products.

The Survey Research Center at the University of Michigan has this as its main goal and objective. The Center is often charged by the Federal Reserve Board or other government and private agencies to undertake extensive surveys of consumer attitudes and intentions to buy large ticket items such as appliances, new automobiles, and homes. In addition to soundings concerning the degree to which consumers feel they are likely to buy, i.e., a range running from "a definite intention to buy" to "a definite intention not to buy," the respondents are also surveyed about their attitudes toward the state of the economy and other such purchase variables as their cash or near liquid asset holdings, and expected changes concerning their future financial condition.

Consumer attitudes, at least to some degree, measure one important dimension of an effective market. Effective markets are those with (1) people, (2) purchasing power, and (3) a high propensity to consume. If people's attitudes and therefore their expectations concerning future earnings, economic conditions, changing technology, etc., are unfavorable, they are more likely to restrict purchases and wait for a more propitious period. In the strict economic sense, consumption is a function of income. But a knowledge and understanding of a broader based theory of consumer behavior would immediately lead one to conclude that consumption is not just a function of current income but rather of expected income. Expected income implies that the consumer's *attitudes* about his future economic and financial well-being affect his present consumption patterns.

Consumers not only have attitudes regarding external objects; they have attitudes and cognitive sets about themselves. We called this phenomena earlier the self-image. The behavior of consumers is subject to change and influence by changing their attitudes or images regarding the external objects—products, prices, promotional appeals, firms—or by changing their attitudes regarding their own personalities or behavior, i.e., their self-images.[10] In short, influence consumers' images and you are likely to influence their behavior. The direction of influence, it must be recalled, is never easy to predict on an *a priori* basis. Where images are stable and well grounded in the cultural and group norms, almost any technique used to change them will be met with firm resistance. However, in a highly literate, knowledge-oriented, and dynamic culture such as that of the United States, it may be possible to accomplish a significant degree of change in attitudes in weeks or even months, given the widespread use of mass communication.

From the standpoint of marketing communication, the attitudes of the viewers concerning the firm or source of the communication can have a determining effect on whether or not the viewer will perceive, retain, and react favorably to the message. This phenomenon is well documented in the literature.[11]

Communication is an interpersonal event and it would therefore seem apparent that whether and to what degree a communication is effective will depend upon the way in which the sender is perceived. The attributes which the receiver evaluates before evaluating the message center around the attractiveness of the sender, his group affiliations and credibility. These findings have important implications for the marketing firm, both from the standpoint of personal selling and advertising.

Insurance salesmen are usually shown and projected as attractive, well-groomed, mature, conservative people, as men of position, stature, integrity—in short, as people you can put your trust in because they have your best interests at heart. Firms that promote via mass communication oftentimes attempt to make their promotional campaigns and appeals more acceptable by promoting the company and its institutional values as well as the individual products.

Another dimension of this concept, which is usually called "source effect" in communication, is the "sleeper effect." Studies have revealed [12] that compared with immediate opinion changes, there is, over an interval

---

[10] See Bardin H. Nelson, "Seven Principles in Image Formation," *Journal of Marketing*, January, 1962, pp. 67-71.

[11] See C. I. Hovland and W. Weiss, "The Influence of Source Credibility on Communication Effectiveness," *Public Opinion Quarterly*, 1951, pp. 635-650.

[12] Carl I. Hovland, A. A. Lumsdaine, and Fred P. Sheffield, *Experiments in Mass Communications* (Princeton, N.J.: Princeton University Press, 1949).

of some weeks, a *decrease* in the amount of agreement with the trustworthy source and an *increase* in the amount of agreement with the less trustworthy or untrustworthy source. This phenomenon is explained by the assumption that with the passage of time the identity of the communicator becomes less relevant than the content of the actual message. Put more simply, it means that with the lapse of time attitudes regarding "Who said it" become less important than attitudes regarding "What was said."

Conversely, at the outset, receivers who are initially disposed to accept the message because of the trustworthiness of the communicator generally show a decreasing acceptance of the message as this awareness of the trustworthy communicator decreases over time. The role of consumer attitudes and their effect and influence on consumer behavior are, as yet, more suggested than demonstrated. The attitudes of receivers toward the sender of messages really amount to something of an independent judgment by the audience as to whether they will be more or less influenced. This concept of "source effect" and the related concept of "sleeper effect" were recently more thoroughly analyzed in terms of their marketing relatedness by Theodore Levitt in a simulated study at the Harvard Graduate School of Business.[13] It is important to remember that this was a simulated study and something of an abstraction from reality. Nonetheless, the simulation was conducted under rigidly controlled conditions and the findings strongly suggest a high degree of relevance to real world situations. The simulated study of "source effect" and "sleeper effect" led Levitt to posit a series of questions and answers pertaining to these phenomena and industrial selling. A summary of relevant findings and conclusions are as follows: [14]

1. "Does corporate or institutional advertising by industrial product companies pay?"

    Yes! Advertising can be an effective means of creating a favorable corporate image (bundle of attitudes) and increasing a given company's ability to make sales. The strong presumption regarding advertising is that mere visibility of a company's message is in some way helpful and reassuring, provided that the impressions that are created are not negative. Generally speaking, the better a company's reputation, the better its chances of (1) getting a favorable first hearing for a new product among customer prospects and (2) getting early adoption of that product.

2. "Do well-known company salesmen have an edge over the salesmen of other companies?"

---

[13] Theodore Levitt, "Communications and Industrial Selling," *Journal of Marketing*, April, 1967, pp. 15-21. By permission of the American Marketing Association.
[14] *Ibid.*, pp. 16-17.

Yes! And customers generally seem to have a different set of expectations and reactions (attitudes) to the better known companies' salesmen. In short, customers expect more of them. There is some indication that some buyers or prospects actually attempt to help the lesser known company's salesmen.

3. "Is it better to advertise more or to select and train salesmen better?"

There is what Levitt calls a presentation effect surrounding the well done sales presentation. The smaller company may benefit more from a really effective sales presentation than from their advertising. However, the larger and more prestigious company loses the advantage of its reputation *if* its direct sales presentation is clearly inferior to that of an unknown or little known company. The general conclusion would be that the less well known and prestigious company, in terms of its communication mix, can do an exceedingly effective job for itself through more careful salesman selection and training.

4. "Is there a sleeper-effect in industrial selling?"

Yes! The research indicates that there exists in industrial purchasing a phenomenon which communication researchers call "the sleeper-effect." The favorable influence of a company's generalized good reputation does indeed erode away over time. Erosion appears to occur specifically when there is no intervening reinforcement or reinstatement of the identity of the source. Sleeper-effect, it would appear, thus tends to hurt relatively more the well-known company and relatively less the lesser known company.

We have had a rather discursive look at attitudes. Our analysis has led us to explore the nature of attitudes, what they are, how they are formed and changed, and most importantly, how attitudes affect consumer behavior. Let us turn our attention now to two other important determinants of attitudes and thus consumer behavior: the role of groups and culture.

GROUPS, GROUP NORM AND ROLE—
CONSUMER BEHAVIOR DETERMINANTS

An important, yet often neglected, determinant of consumer behavior is the influence of the groups to which the consumer belongs. The groups are instrumental in casting the individual consumer in a series of roles, some of which may actually incur conflicting modes of behavior. The groups to which consumers belong will have standards of behavior or norms to which the individual must either conform or submit to group censure or sanction. In keeping with our proposition that consumer behavior is a form of adaptive behavior, that adaptive behavior is the product of learning, and that learning is a function of communication given certain situational factors, it may safely be asserted that the groups to which consumers belong affect or bring about social learning. Social learning is concerned with the acquisition of skills, facts, attitudes, and values which occur as a result of our perennial communion with others. In short, interaction facilitates the learning process. Earlier we discussed learning theory and concluded that it is an attempt to explain how certain stimuli induce changes which in time become responses. A response may be physiological or psychological and it is designed to achieve some specified end or goal. Broadly speaking, there are two major kinds of responses. There are first of all instrumental responses whose chief function is to produce immediate modification in the relationship of the organism to its external environment. Examples of instrumental responses are eating, drinking, pushing the elevator button, or driving one's car. The second major type of response is called a cue-producing response. As the word "cue" suggests, a cue-producing response acts as a stimulus for another response. Group activity plays some role in both instrumental and cue-producing responses in social learning situations but, most importantly, group activities, reference group concepts, group norms, and status are more directly concerned with consumer behavior because of their cue-producing roles. The activities of one's groups often dictate within a rather narrow range the instrumental response choice of the individual. The group's approach to problem solving is likely to differ significantly from that of an isolated individual. And for that matter as we shall soon discover, there are few persons whose purchase decisions and market behavior are not to some degree at least affected by group activity.[15]

It is important at this juncture to make at least a few qualifying statements. One should not assume a lack of considerable autonomy on the part of individuals as they persist in their search and choice of consumer satisfactions. In the final analysis, most consumers make their own decisions about what groups to belong to as well as what products to buy and how much to spend. But when is a decision really one's own? No consumer is so uncontaminated by his contact and interaction with friends, family, or acquaintances that their influence and presence are not felt to some degree in the individual's decision making. Consumer responses are seldom ever stereotyped. Consumers from the same family or belonging to the same set of group associations or having the same life style will manifest a wide range of differences in their choice and decision behavior. Consumers develop a set of responses which are called *habit families* and constitute a response repertory. The response repertory or habit family permits the individual to make different responses to attain the same goal-directed aim. It is the personality of the individual, his cognitive set, which not only permits but demands uniqueness of behavior. Response repertories or habit families which are unique and different for every individual will cluster into patterns of similarity and conformity. It is these patterns of response repertories which ought to be the central concern of market researchers, and response repertories of consumers are molded and shaped by their group affiliations and membership.

The nature and persistence of groups. Groups are perennially among us. The Creator made the first group by sequentially creating man, then woman. From that moment in history, the impact of group affiliation on the individual has been an important factor and determinant of behavior. A group is two or more persons in a state of social interaction. The action may be physical, as between two junior varsity wrestlers vying for the championship, or it may be emotional or social-psychological, as in the relationship between a professor and a student. The key element of a group, however, is the interactional nature of its members. This means that an aggregation of individuals is not necessarily a group. For such an aggregation to take on meaning as a group, there must be interstimulation and response. Group connotes the idea of the interpersonal behavior event.[16]

For our purposes the group is best viewed as a social unit of interacting persons. The group is composed naturally of individuals, but it may also be regarded as developing or possessing distinctive characteristics of its own. In addition to the idea of interaction concerning the concept of group, i.e., each member's behavior in turn affects the behavior of the other members, there is a second distinctive aspect regarding the group concept. This is that group members share an ideology—a set of beliefs, values, and norms which regulate their conduct. It is this dimension of group behavior which is of such vital concern to the marketer.

Kinds of groups. There is a varied typology for classifying groups. The principal classification is one that views groups as being either *primary* or *secondary*. The primary group is one characterized by intimate, face-to-face association and cooperation. The principal primary groups are the family, the play groups of children and adults, and the

---

[16] See Muzafer Sherif and Carolyn W. Sherif, *An Outline of Social Psychology,* rev. ed. (New York: Harper & Row, Publishers, 1956).

neighborhood or community groups of adults and elders. The primary group, as we shall explore more fully later, covers a wide range of needs and gratifications and has a common or central locus.

The family is certainly one of the most important primary groups if not the most important. It is primary not only in terms of its role in attitude formation and the structuring and conditioning of behavior, but it is also important temporally. It is the first group to which individuals belong and, under normal circumstances, it is the group to which the member belongs for the longest period of time. Consequently, the ability of the family group to influence the personality and behavior of its members is paramount.

Other primary groups which are of nearly equal importance in shaping attitudes and behavior are the play groups of children and adults, friendship and courtship dyads, and the intimate, face-to-face work groups to which so many individuals belong. All of these associations, because of their intimate and close-knit interrelations, give rise to the possibility of influencing, altering, and molding behavior—especially consumer behavior. What we like and buy, where we shop and how often, what we spend and what we save, will to a considerable extent be affected by the almost constant indoctrination of our primary group memberships.

In addition to primary groups, there are secondary groups. Secondary groups are characterized by a much more deliberate and conscious choice. Membership is seldom ever by accident but by a rather rational appraising, matching, and sorting of group goals and characteristics in relationship to individual needs and aspirations. Face-to-face contacts are not necessarily characteristic of secondary groups. Examples of secondary groups are the organization where one works, the church where one worships, the clubs and associations where one plays. Other examples are political parties, trade unions, professional associations like the American Marketing Association, and social fraternities and associations. Secondary groups play an important accommodative role for their individual members by defining for them their status and role as members. Secondary groups are readily likened to social organizations which involve a system of integrated and interrelated primary groups formed to accomplish a stated purpose. In other words, secondary groups are social organizations, i.e., composite interrelated networks of primary groups.

There is one other important aspect of group affiliation and membership which is extremely relevant in terms of certain kinds of market behavior and that is the concept of in-group and out-group. The in-group is a human association toward which the members have a cohesive sense of loyalty, identification, and commonness of purpose and with which a larger societal segment seems to be in sympathetic accord. The out-group, on the other hand, may or may not have all these characteristics. The principal difference is that the out-group does not appear to have the sympathetic accord of a larger societal segment. Hence, they are "out" and the others are "in." The in-group is likely to manifest behavior which tends to perpetuate this sympathetic accord and the out-group which desires the approbation and sympathetic accord of the larger societal segment is likely to manifest behavior designed to (1) result in different group objectives, standards, or behavior; or (2) change the criteria of sympathy and approval of the larger societal segment.

Individuals belong to many groups, and the increased sophistication and complexity of an industrialized affluent society tends to increase the extent of one's group memberships. We are members of a family, church, political party, fraternity, race, university, community, bridge group, professional and honorary society, athletic team, or buyer's club. Our associations and exposure in these various groups and countless others predispose us to certain kinds of behavior and attitudinal responses. Our responses, and the degree to which our group affiliations affect our attitudes and behavior, are to a considerable extent the function of the goals and objectives of individual and group.

Group functions.   The function of groups is to satisfy the needs and aspirations of the constituent members.[17] Through membership in various groups the individual strives for need fulfillment. The need fulfillment will cover the entire needs hierarchy ranging from basic physiological needs such as hunger, thirst, and shelter, to the esteem needs of the individual concerned with aesthetic pleasures, the need for social approval, and belongingness. The group may protect the individual from threats as basic as extinction, or it may be the ladder for the achievement of certain social goals which necessitate cooperative effort. Not all members will belong to a given group for the same reasons, nor will the group necessarily persist in its same set of goals or style over long periods of time. Generally, however, individuals seek and continue membership in given groups to serve either their need for *power* or their need for *belonging*. Every group will provide *roles* for its members and if the role provided by one group is insufficient to meet the needs of that member, then he will generally react by seeking membership in a group which offers greater promise of need fulfillment. The group therefore becomes a means to the ends of its members. And as the group comes into being

---

17 K. D. Benne and P. Sheats, "Functional Roles of Group Members," *Journal of Social Issues,* April, 1948, pp. 41-49.

and its members interact, there is an emergent group ideology which regulates their attitudes and behavior. Not all members of the group will share with equal excitement and enthusiasm the goals and objectives of the group. However, the longer-run effectiveness of the group and its chances of continuing survival depend upon the degree to which the majority of its members agree on the goals resulting from common association. It is a well-known fact that a person will work for the group goal only if he believes that its achievement will satisfy his own wants.[18] The range of individual behavior within the group is mediated by the degree to which the members share the group goal. In effect, the members over time tend to develop what might be called a group ideology. The common ideology, in turn, creates a core of shared wants among the members and induces a common method of expressing different wants. The common ideology embraces the values of the majority of the group membership and therefore reflects the group's values, or those things which the group considers worthy. An important concept for marketers in relationship to group influence is that of group norms. Quite naturally, the norms of the group reflect the group's values. Norms are, broadly speaking, rules of conduct which specify what actions are proper and what actions are improper under given situations. The group norms become standards of measurement and evaluation which bear on perception, judgment, and conduct. Group norms become effective means of controlling group behavior; therefore marketers must be aware of the group norms of the target markets to which they direct marketing programs and campaigns. Products of an intimate personal nature have always posed problems for promotion because of the difficulty of writing copy and producing continuity which was not offensive and not in violation of certain group norms. Frequently, the most promise for marketers lies in understanding and, through communication, changing group norms.

Thus far we have spoken of group and group affiliations as if the individual were free to become or not become a member of any group. The unrestricted entry into some groups is self-evident: One is born into a family or race, and has a choice of becoming a member of a political party. Other group associations may be denied an individual as a result of his race, sex, or failure to obtain the necessary credentials. One must have an M.D. degree to obtain membership in the American Medical Association. Some groups influence the behavior of individuals who are

---

[18] S. E. Asch, "Effects of Group Pressure on the Modification and Distortion of Judgments," in *Readings in Social Psychology,* ed. E. E. Maccoby, T. M. Newcomb, and E. L. Hartley (New York: Holt, Rinehart & Winston, 1958).

not constituent members of the group. These are often referred to as reference groups.[19] A reference group may be a group in which the individual already holds membership, or it may be a group to which an individual aspires to belong. But the important and distinctive feature of a reference group is that it is a group whose perspectives and attitudinal posture are assumed by the individual. Stated another way, a reference group is a group association with whose ideology, style, and norms an individual identifies; that is, such a group influences the behavior of individuals even though they are not members of the particular group. Reference groups can be extremely important in influencing consumer behavior.

The group functions in terms of two important aspects for the individual. First of all, it designates or denotes his *status,* and secondly it assigns or delegates his *role*. Status pertains to the individual's position in the group hierarchy and is indicative of his authority or power to undertake certain kinds of behavior. Role pertains to the behavior which certain members of the group are to manifest, given their position or status in the group. Members of a group generally exercise two important kinds of behavior with respect to both role and status. Behavior which is directed toward fulfilling the dictates of a given role is called operative behavior; behavior directed toward preserving or enhancing one's position in the power structure is called positional behavior. For example, the role of a housewife in a family group may well be that of the designated purchasing agent of the group. Her purchasing behavior in carrying out this role is therefore *operative* behavior. On the other hand, in order to enhance her position in the status hierarchy of the family, the housewife may go to extra lengths to perform her role responsibilities as household purchasing agent. This amounts to positional behavior. Early in the history of instant coffee it was discovered that many housewives would not purchase this item because of a fear of being thought lazy and not having the best interests of their families at heart—a form of positional behavior related to perceived role and status.

A fitting summary statement to our remarks concerning group functions would appear to be that in all groups the roles and status of the members become to some extent different and unique, but integrated into a system which we call group structure. The group structure, in turn, affects the behavior and functioning of the group and the satisfactions which the individuals derive from the group association.

---

[19] Alberta E. Siegel and Sidney Siegel, "Reference Groups, Membership Groups and Attitude Change," in *Group Dynamics,* ed. Dorwin Cartwright and Alvan Zander (New York: Harper & Row, Publishers, 1960).

Leadership and group behavior. Members of a group are either leaders or followers. In every group situation there emerge those who are feared, respected, listened to, or sought after. These persons in the group are usually referred to as leaders, and often possess formal authority or title. In other instances, they have no formal position at all in the power structure of the group, yet they are highly persuasive members of the group and important sources of pressure and influence on the group and the behavior of individual members.

We have stated that the individual lives out his life under the influence of various groups; given the superior-subordinate nature of groups, this is to say that the individual lives out his life under the influence of various leaders or superiors. He is often told, sometimes assertively and frankly, what to do, where to go, what to wear, what to say, and what to buy. Our subordinate-superior environment from birth to the grave implies that all of us, to a greater or lesser degree, are programmed, figuratively speaking, to assume both leadership and followership roles in the various groups to which we belong. The leader is one who recognizes the goals and sympathies of the group members and is often capable of synthesizing the somewhat divergent needs of its members into a cohesive framework of action. The group is, to a considerable extent, a function of its leadership capabilities. The leader may act as an innovator in his desire to introduce new goals or objectives into the group; or he may innovate in terms of changing the group norms. The leader of a group may be the opinion leader of a given group, or he may be a gatekeeper and work toward the preservation and maintenance of the status quo. In any event, marketers must be aware of the role of the leader in group behavior. Such knowledge is important in terms of greater understanding and effectiveness concerning new product development and innovation, the role of key influentials in fashion goods merchandising, and a host of similar problem areas.

Group structure and communication. Communication systems are greatly affected by the size and structure of the group. In large formalized group structures such as the military, government, and private bureaucracies, the information flows are channeled through what is called a chain of command. The chain of command is a superior-subordinate hierarchy which makes clear who speaks to whom. In the smaller primary groups characteristic of informal organizations, communication channels and content of communication will vary with the role and status of the members. To understand both communication structure and function, we need to know the pattern or position of the groups which comprise the system. In other words, we need to know something about the role and status of the members of a communication network.

Studies of small group behavior have given us considerable insight into the nature of the communication process. Festinger and Thibaut have investigated the effects of interpersonal communication on attitudes and opinions. They discovered that belonging to a given group tends to induce changes in opinions and attitudes which make for conformity of opinion and attitude. They reasoned on the basis of their investigation that the amount of shift toward uniformity which may be accomplished is a function of the attractiveness of the group in question for its members. They further concluded that those who do not conform to the prevailing pattern of opinion and conduct tend to be rejected by others in the group.[20]

Other studies of group behavior have shown that individuals whose social behavior has been changed by hearing something tend, in turn, to relay this information to others who are believed to be affected by it. Individuals who do not conform to the group behavior pattern are likely to have fewer communications directed to them as a result of their differences from the group. In addition, persons who demonstrate nonconformist behavior characteristics and tend to be rejected by the group may serve as innovators or human wedges for splitting the group. Festinger and Thibaut, in addition to the research findings briefly discussed above, concluded that when there is a wide range of opinion in the group communication is most often directed toward those members whose opinions are at the extremes of a given range.[21] For marketers, this could well mean that effectively promoting to a given market segment group might entail discovering the range of opinions and attitudes of the group, finding who the persons are who hold the opinions with the greatest variance from the norm, and then directing messages and appeals to these individuals.

Harold J. Leavitt has demonstrated that the structure or form of the interactional connections of a group influences the communication of the participating individuals in a diverse manner. He structured four experimental patterns: circle, chain, Y, and wheel. These patterns are shown in Fig. 19.

Leavitt had twenty groups of five men each and tested them under conditions of these four patterns of communication. The experimental tasks involved passing messages back and forth with the objective of solving a problem which no one man could solve alone. His principal discoveries centered around the following propositions: Major behavior differences can be attributed to communication patterns and these affect

---

[20] Leon Festinger and John Thibaut, "Inter-personal Communication in Small Groups," *Journal of Abnormal Psychology*, 46 (1951), 92-99.
[21] *Ibid.*, p. 94.

Figure 19: Experimental Patterns of Communications.

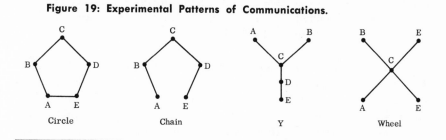

Source: Harold J. Leavitt, "Some Effects of Certain Communication Patterns on Group Performance," *Journal of Abnormal and Social Psychology*, 46 (1951), 42, Figure 4.

deviations in accuracy, satisfactions of the group members with their work, and differences in organization.[22] For example, in the circle group where there was no leader, there was little adequate organization. In the wheel group, on the other hand, there very quickly developed an organization and an effective leader soon emerged. Furthermore, the positions occupied by the individuals in the communication chain influenced their positions during the time they occupied the positions. One of the most characteristic aspects of this study was that of *centrality*. That is, those at the center of a structure were affected more thoroughly than those at the periphery of the communication chains. Apparently, when one's position is low in centrality relative to other persons in the communication network, the removed member will tend to take the follower position and be dependent upon the leader. This may partially explain the leadership-followership phenomenon discussed earlier.

One other factor of significance relating group behavior to communication is that of group norms. Inasmuch as communication involves sharing meaning, communication is virtually impossible without some mutual understanding of group norms.

> People can interact without any common body of norms, but they cannot communicate in the sense of sharing meaning through this interaction . . . Communication, in this sense (i.e., the sharing of common experiences) presupposes frames of references (norms) which are shared by the communicating persons, so that similar meanings are shared by them.[23]

---

[22] Harold J. Leavitt, "Some Effects of Certain Communication Patterns on Group Performance," *Journal of Abnormal and Social Psychology*, 46 (1951), 38-50, Fig. 4.

[23] Theodore M. Newcomb, *Social Psychology* (New York: Dryden Press, 1950), pp. 267-268. Reprinted by permission of Holt, Rinehart & Winston, Inc.

It thus appears that effective communication involves a rather extensive and deep-rooted knowledge and understanding of the nature and behavior of group-affiliated individuals.

Group behavior and implications for marketing.   The formation, structuring, and functioning of groups has many important implications for marketing. Consumer purchase behavior may be a highly individualistic process; on the other hand, there is much to indicate that it is a highly socially oriented process where group norms, reference groups, roles, and status are concepts which have important bearing on the purchaser's decision process.

The groups to which one belongs or which affect one's decision making, i.e., reference groups, affect consumer decision processes in at least two important ways.[24] First of all, reference groups affect aspiration levels of individuals. They may influence members or individuals who simply relate to the reference groups to provide aspiration guides for certain kinds of goods. Secondly, reference groups are influential in initiating certain kinds of reactions or behavior in individuals related to taboos, sanctions, etc. In short, the norms of the reference group may become guidelines which constrain an individual's market behavior. Marketers simply cannot afford to overlook the importance of the influence exerted on the individual by the groups with which he is associated. The possibility for group influence on consumer decision processes is illustrated graphically in Fig. 20.

According to the classification of Fig. 20, a particular item is likely to be susceptible to reference group influence on its purchase in three different ways. Reference group influence may operate with respect to brand or type, but not with respect to product (brand +, product −) as for example in the upper left cell, or it may operate both with respect to brand and product (brand +, product +) as for example in the upper right cell, and so forth.

It would appear that the preceding kind of reference group analysis would have strong implications for marketing and especially for marketing communication. At least two of the more important implications have been suggested by Bourne.[25]

1. Where neither product nor brand appear to be associated strongly with reference group influence, advertising should emphasize the prod-

---

[24] Francis S. Bourne, "Group Influences in Marketing and Public Relations," in *Some Applications of Behavioural Research*, ed. Rensis Likert and Samuel P. Hayes, Jr. (Paris, France: UNESCO, 1961), pp. 217-224.

[25] *Ibid.*, p. 222. Reprinted by permission of Charles Y. Glock, Director, Survey Research Center, University of California.

Figure 20: Products and Brands of Consumer Goods May Be Classified by Extent to Which Reference Groups Influence Their Purchase.

Weak—Reference Group Influence Relatively—Strong

(Left vertical axis: Weak—Reference Group Influence Relatively—Strong)
(Right vertical axis: Brand or Type)

−	+
Clothing Furniture + Magazines Refrigerators (type) Toilet Soap	Cars ° Cigarettes ° Beer (prem. vs. reg.) ° + Drugs °
Soap Canned Peaches − Laundry Soap Refrigerators (brand) Radios	Air Conditioners ° Instant Coffee ° − TV (black and white)

−   Product   +

° The classification of all products marked with an asterisk is based on actual experimental evidence. Other products in this table are classified speculatively on the basis of generalizations derived from the sum of research in this area and confirmed by the judgment of seminar participants.

Source: Francis S. Bourne, "Group Influences in Marketing and Public Relations," in *Some Applications of Behavioural Research,* ed. Rensis Likert and Samuel P. Hayes, Jr. (Paris, France: UNESCO, 1961). Reprinted by permission of Charles Y. Glock, Director, Survey Research Center, University of California.

uct's attributes, intrinsic qualities, price and advantages over competing products.

2. Where reference group influence is operative, the advertiser should stress the kinds of people who buy the product, reinforcing and broadening where possible the existing stereotype of users. The strategy of the advertiser should involve learning what the stereotypes are and what specific reference groups enter into the picture, so that appeals can be tailored to each main group reached by the different media employed.

In summary, the basic decisions marketers must make in connection with reference group theory center around the following ideas:

1. *Reference Group Relevance.* The marketer must decide if reference group concepts are applicable to a given situation.
2. *Reference Group Identification.* The marketer must identify the particular relevant reference group and its members.
3. *Reference Group Identification and Effective Communication.* Having identified the nature and relevant characteristics of the reference

group in a given situation, the marketer must then develop a program of effective communication with the groups or individuals he desires to influence.

Other studies have suggested that group formation and behavior can affect the process of innovation and especially the diffusion process for new products.[26] The relationship between gatekeeper and opinion leader can be an important determinant of certain kinds of consumer purchase decisions. For example, in the American household the male head is usually given the role of deciding what brand of coffee should be purchased even though the wife is the official family purchasing agent. The small children of the household, on the other hand, are the key decision makers or "opinion leaders" regarding choices of cereals or other breakfast foods. Consequently, innovations or new product offerings in coffee or breakfast foods must meet with the approval of these opinion leaders or gatekeepers before their success can be assured.

Other studies have suggested that social class can be an important factor in the adoption and rate of adoption of certain innovations.[27] Research in this important area has revealed that the amount of contact between innovation and potential acceptors is extremely critical in determining the degree of acceptance. It has been found that as each innovation is unique, each is compatible in different degrees with the culture (behavior) of a given group. No single class or group has been found to be conservative in reacting to innovations. Instead, the upper classes are found to be conservative in some cases, the lower in others, and sometimes both are conservative.

The concept of social class, which is a special kind of group affiliation, has received considerable attention from researchers who seek clearer implications of the concept in terms of specific marketing implications. The concept of social class has proved to be a very helpful tool for the marketing researcher–decision maker. However, it is important to remember that differences as well as similarities exist in each social class designation. Some products, for example color television sets, are not correlated with income generally, but instead enjoy markets in each social class among relatively prosperous or "over privileged" families.[28] It is also important for marketers to remember that social class, like other

[26] Thomas S. Robertson, "The Process of Innovation and the Diffusion of Innovation," *Journal of Marketing,* January, 1967, pp. 14-19.

[27] Saxon Graham, "Class and Conservatism in the Adoption of Innovations," *Human Relations,* IX, No. 1 (1956), 91-100.

[28] Richard P. Coleman, "The Significance of Social Stratification in Selling," *Proceedings of the 43rd National Conference of The American Marketing Association,* ed. Martin Bell (Chicago: American Marketing Association, 1960), pp. 171-184.

group concepts, is not a static structure. As structure changes, as it so often does for most groups, the function of those groups is likely to change. This, of course, means that the effect of the group and the manner in which the group changes or alters the behavior of its members are also likely to change.

CULTURE: THE SEEDBED OF BEHAVIOR

Our approach to understanding consumer behavior has been largely monistic. That is, we have consistently emphasized the wholeness or relatedness of the parts or determinants of consumer behavior. Our analysis began with some central propositions regarding the nature of consumers in certain kinds of existential surroundings, and we have subsequently attempted to put together into a meaningful pattern or theory the factors which affect consumer decision processes: personality, cognitions, motivation, learning, attitude and opinion formation, the formation and persistence of groups, and now culture. Throughout this process it has been repeatedly necessary for us to cross numerous disciplinary boundaries in order to examine the concepts which we feel are relevant to the understanding and explanation of consumer behavior. Our discussion has led us from philosophy to psychology, through sociology and social psychology, information and communication theory to cybernetics, and now we must briefly conclude our analysis of the social-psychological factors affecting consumer behavior by examining briefly the place of culture and the role of anthropology in explaining consumer behavior. It is *culture* which binds many of man's meaningless acts into purposeful and meaningful patterns of behavior. Culture is perhaps the single most important existential factor affecting consumer behavior, because it is the *existence* of the individual in a particular *existent* culture which accounts for certain attitudes and opinions and predisposes the individual to both general and particular kinds of behavior. It is culture which is largely responsible for the kinds of groups which emerge and the functioning of these groups in terms of given kinds of problem-solving consumer behavior. Out of culture there emerge whole patterns of perceptions, role taking, and norm giving which affect consumer behavior. A tree which spends its existence in a well-nurtured environment, safe from the fierce ravages of wind and storm, is likely to exhibit an entirely different prospect and pattern of growth than one which springs to life on the barren, rocky slope of a western mountainside. While they had the potential of becoming, if not identical, at least similar kinds of objects, the disparities in external environment brought about profound and fundamental differences in both character and appearance. The same kind of phenomena can affect consumer behavior. Different existential surroundings can bring about profound and fundamental differences in the character and behavior of consumers.

Kroeber has noted the rather remarkable effects of culture and the wide range of behavior which the American individual learns from his culture.

> That he speaks, say, English and not Chinese is the result of where he is born or raised; that is, of which language forms part of the culture in which he grows up. Similarly with his being a Christian instead of a Buddhist, casting his vote in November, observing Sunday, celebrating New Year on January 1, instead of February, eating with a fork and not chopsticks, and bread and butter and not rice . . . saying hello to his parents instead of using honorifics, steering a tractor instead of a plow, writing with letters instead of a thousand logograms, and so on endlessly. In fact, the mass of what any person receives from his culture is so great as to make it look at first glance as if he were nothing but an individual exemplar of his culture, a reduction of it abbreviated to the scope of what one personality can contain.[29]

One could readily deduce that the behavior induced by one's culture can greatly affect the consumer behavior which one manifests in solving certain kinds of consumer–culture related problems. For example, behavior related to religion has consumer manifestations. Easter is not only a time for the multitude to rejoice in the resurrection of Christ; it is the occasion for parading in new clothes, and also has significance in terms of feasts and foods, travel and visits, and other related kinds of behavior.

More subtle aspects of culture have been ignored by marketers, and only recently have these aspects and their consequences been brought to the marketer's attention. Marketers have often failed to realize that "what really binds men and women together is their culture— the ideas and standards they have in common . . ."[30]

The nature and meaning of culture. "Culture is a more or less consistent pattern of thought and action."[31] It can be viewed as an environment, framework, or social structure in which human wants, desires, aspirations, and perceptions are more or less conventionalized and directed. A *subculture* is a specialized segment of a culture. The concept

---

[29] A. L. Kroeber, *Anthropology: Race, Language, Culture, Psychology, Prehistory*, rev. ed. (New York: Harcourt, Brace & World, Inc., 1948), pp. 288-289.

[30] Ruth Benedict, *Patterns of Culture* (Boston, Mass.: Houghton Mifflin Press, 1934), p. 14.

[31] *Ibid.*, p. 42.

of culture embraces the idea or concept of modal patterns of behavior and underlying regulatory beliefs, values, and norms. Culture is an important factor in social learning because it plays such a central role in training the new members of a society in that society's life ways. It is important, once again, to emphasize that the effect of culture on the individual is not necessarily a one-way street. The individual can often, regardless of his status and rank in society, alter and change the culture of which he is a part. The paramount role of culture is that it represents a particular set of arrangements for solving the problems of the various members of the society. For the many economic problems, i.e., what goods to produce, where and how to produce them, what methods to employ and how to distribute the proceeds, the American culture dictates the use of a market system centering around competitive activity. Other cultures, notably those of some Eastern European countries, approach their crucial economic problems in terms of greater centralization of decision making, the socialization of certain factors of production, and either mutual or forced cooperation. The particular set of cultural arrangements adopted by a given society may result from numerous factors such as physical environment, previous experience and history, and natural resources. However, cultural adaptations to certain kinds of societal problems may also result from human enterprise. That is, the effect of the individual on culture and cultural adaptations cannot be overlooked.

There are at least two dimensions of culture which are noteworthy. As a matter of fact culture is much like an iceberg in that only a portion of it is directly observable. This portion of culture which is observable and therefore objective is overt culture; it consists of directly observable regularities in the verbal and nonverbal behavior of the members of the society. The less observable and more subjective aspect of culture is referred to as latent culture; it consists of the beliefs, values, and norms which anthropologists infer or invent to describe and explain observed regularities in behavior and the structuring or patterning of what might appear to be unrelated and unconnected bits of behavior.

Culture is concerned with modal patterns. That is, culture deals with average kinds of behavior. The individual is not the central focus of cultural studies. What is attempted are studies which produce generalizations about the average behavior of members of a given society. Studies which focus on the culture of a given society are of interest to the mass marketers who are attempting to merchandise goods and services to a vast homogeneous market. Other marketers are likely to be more interested in studies which focus on a smaller size group or subculture inasmuch as it is these subcultures which constitute the market segments or market targets of many firms.

Culture and values. Values are those ideas or beliefs which people esteem. Cultural values therefore are those beliefs which are held in esteem by the members of a given society. Cultural values have a definite normative aspect; that is, they tell the members of a society what they "ought" or "should" do. The cultural values of the United States have important implications for marketers.

For example, the fetish of cleanliness, the hippie movement (a very small and rapidly dwindling subculture) notwithstanding, implies a society which is receptive to a large number of products which promote this cultural phenomenon. Soap, perfumes, colognes, talcum powder and deodorants are a few of the products widely promoted in this country. In other countries, cleanliness is not considered such a national virtue and consequently such products receive far less promotional emphasis.

Behavior is also regulated by *cultural norms*. Cultural norms are a larger set of group norms, i.e., rules or standards accepted by members of a society and by the typical occupants of a given role situation. These cultural norms specify the details of appropriate and inappropriate behavior. For example, Williams has shown that the cultural *value* of cleanliness leads to decisions concerning choices of occupation and other activity on the basis of whether it permits or promotes cleanliness and that children are approved and otherwise rewarded for cleanly behavior.[32] However, in spite of a society which extols the virtue of cleanliness, our society's cultural norms militate against the mixed public bath. The cultural norms of many eastern civilizations, however, permit such an institution. Cultural norms are subdivided into two categories: folkways and mores. Norms are folkways when the behavior they dictate, if violated, is not considered vital to the welfare of the group and when a means of enforcing such behavior is not fully operational. Norms are mores when the behavior they dictate is vital to the welfare of the group and when effective means for assuring such behavior have been accomplished. Many of our habits and customs are related to cultural folkways and mores. At present, at least, cultural norms dictate that young girls' hemlines should be somewhere in the vicinity of four inches above the knees. The *folkways* permit considerable variance in this norm, but if the Dean of Women dictates that they shall be no higher than four inches, and develops sanctions to enforce her decree, then we have a cultural norm which has become part of the mores, at least for this particular subculture.

Many of the folkways and mores of a culture become so much a part of the fabric of that society that we call them institutions. An

---

[32] R. M. Williams, *American Society: A Sociological Interpretation* (New York: Alfred A. Knopf, Inc., 1951).

institution embodies a whole set of beliefs, customs, values, and norms. Examples of institutions are churches, schools, governments, and retail stores. It goes without saying that institutions play a very important role in affecting the behavior and attitudes of their members. Viewed another way, an institution might be conceived of as a gigantic reference group. The attitude of the Catholic Church, Harvard University, or General Motors on a given issue may immeasurably affect the attitudes, opinions, and behavior of a large number of individuals who look to these institutions for signals and hints as to the correctness or appropriateness of their own behavior. Culture is a dynamic concept. It changes over time, and any given culture will have a character or uniqueness all its own.

The American culture. It would be an Olympian task indeed to characterize the American culture, to describe the universal or cultural elements which Americans share. The American culture is marked by unbelievable diversity, a multitude of crisscrossing and conflicting subcultures. However, one audacious set of researchers attempted to develop a quantitative measure of degree of acculturation to what might be called the American core culture. It must be remembered that cultures do change, and that this description, because it dates back to 1948, is subject to considerable error and faulty interpretation. The list was compiled by Ruesch, Jacobsen, and Loeb and was used in connection with a scale for measuring degree of conformity to the American core culture which they, in turn, defined as "general attitudes and orientations which are shared by the majority of Americans." [33]

1. Nativity: Native born of native born parents.
2. Culture of Origin: Born and educated in American culture.
3. Attitude toward American culture: Unaware of cultural differences.
4. Attitudes toward parents and family structure: Parents are primarily friends and guides rather than punitive authority. Matriarchal family structure or authority evenly divided between parents.
5. Religion: Member of any large Protestant denomination.
6. Name: First, middle and last name according to Anglo-Saxon use.
7. Mother tongue: American, English, Scottish, Irish, Canadian-English, New Zealander-English.
8. Accent: No discernible accent.
9. Reading: Reads American papers and books only.
10. External appearance: Style of dress reflects American local standards and fashions; posture, relaxed, casual, and informal; gestures, minimal; physical culture conforms to American ideals of slender youthful appearance.
11. Choice of menu: Protein eater.

---

[33] J. Ruesch, Annmarie Jacobsen, and M. B. Loeb, "Acculturation and Illness," *Psychology Monogram,* 1948, pp. 1-40(5).

12. Preparation of food and use of condiments: Quickly prepared dishes; no sauces; no spices; catsup and other condiments added at time of meal. Food served in large pieces. Leftovers thrown away.
13. Attitude toward food: Food is nourishment, but provides no particular sensual gratification. Convenience and expediency greatest concern. Emphasis on food hygiene, vitamins and calories.
14. Non-alcoholic drinks: Coffee, milk, fruit juices, cola drinks, milkshakes.
15. Drinking habits and alcoholic beverages: No separation of sexes for alcoholic consumption. Cocktails before dinner, highballs after dinner. Preference for cocktails made of whiskey, gin, rum. Beer with food.
16. Recreation: Passive, non-organized types of relaxation; spectator sports and gambling enjoyed. No separation of sexes except for occasional hunting or fishing trips of men and sewing and knitting for women.
17. Characteristic personal traits: Sense of humor, casual, warm, conformist, playful, fair, vivacious, healthy, good sport, happy go lucky, self-sufficient, tough.
18. Ideal traits wished for: Relaxed, democratic, casual, successful, easy going, energetic, fair minded, tough, flexible, cheerful, enterprising, non-argumentative, resourceful.
19. Attitudes toward women: Women emancipated; they vote and work. Status not related to marriage. Women considered equal to men.
20. Attitudes toward public and success: Winning the public is of prime importance. Success measured in terms of money and popularity.
21. Residence: Resides in areas determined by class membership. If member of lower class, less separation from minority ethnic groups than if a member of middle or upper class. Mixes with neighborhood group.
22. Associates: If a joiner, belongs to American type of lodge, club or association without ethnic slant. Same friends as in childhood. No members of minority ethnic groups among close friends.
23. Festivities and special occasions: Celebrates official or local holidays of American character.
24. Music: Prefers popular American music; jazz, jitterbug, musical comedy, swing, boogie-woogie, Bing Crosby, Negro spirituals, etc.

Such a bold and exhaustive attempt to characterize the American core culture can have far-reaching benefits to marketers who are interested in knowing and understanding the cultural patterns, norms, attitudes, and opinions of what might be called Mr. or Mrs. Average American. Successful marketing campaigns might very well be based upon these propositions regarding the modal behavior of Americans. Effective and potent appeals for particular products, services, or institutions might very well focus upon some one or several of these cultural characteristics. However, sophisticated marketers, as was cautioned earlier, must be aware of marketing to a statistic, or a broad cultural core. Marketers who are really consumer oriented will focus their marketing programs upon something less than Mrs. Middle Majority. In such cases, these core culture characteristics might very well be studied in terms of particular market segments or subcultures in order to discern patterns or modes which more accurately characterize the market target in question. However, a mass marketer would want to be assured that his marketing programs and communications did not violate these minimum cultural characteristics.

CULTURE AND ITS IMPLICATIONS FOR MARKETING

The importance of culture to marketing can be dramatized by recalling our discussion of communication. It was stated earlier that the possibility for effective communication increases proportionately with the degree to which the fields of experience of sender and receiver overlap or intersect. This, once again, underlines the significance of the advertising dictum which states that the advertiser "must begin where the audience is." That is, communication messages and appeals which are incongruent with the cultural values, folkways, mores, and norms of the receivers are doomed to failure. Audiences, as we have learned, selectively screen messages and selectively expose themselves to messages which are at least compatible with their cultural predispositions. A newspaper advertisement showing a lovely wedding gown worn by a model in the surroundings of a Protestant church but circulated in a predominantly Catholic community will be less successful than one using a more appropriate environmental surrounding.

In one sense of the word, culture, broadly speaking, is communication. Culture is a kind of adhesive which binds together men of similar ideas, values, and behavior. Communication of a cross-cultural nature is naturally more difficult than intracultural communication. Marketers can often tell a profound story in an intracultural setting by way of a simple diagram, cartoon, illustration, a pause, a modification in tone or pitch, or some other device. However, such a device in a cross-cultural framework is likely to meet with little response or even negative response. Colgate blundered quite seriously when it introduced its trademark "Cue" into French-speaking districts of Louisiana where the word has an obscene connotation.[34]

Culture, then, is an important determinant of behavior and, as we have learned, behavior is often the function of communication. It is necessary for marketers, therefore, to understand the role of culture as it affects marketing communication. The effect of culture on communication is often paramount:

---

[34] Howe Martyn, *International Business* (New York: Free Press of Glencoe, 1964), p. 78.

It determines the time and timing of interpersonal events, the places where it is appropriate to discuss particular topics, the physical distance separating one speaker from another, the tone of voice that is appropriate to the subject matter. . . . Culture includes the relationship of *what is said to what is meant*—as when "no" means "maybe" and "tomorrow" means "never." [35]

Culture as communication has some far-reaching implications in terms of learning. The learning of tastes is largely a cultural phenomenon. What one buys, wears, or eats, where one goes and what he does are largely a matter of what he has learned to do or become accustomed to doing as a result of his inculturation. There is a strong relationship which manifests itself in terms of familiarity and liking. Not always, but often, one likes what one is familiar with.[36] Again, what one is familiar with is to a considerable extent a function of his culture.

Culture also teaches its members what artifacts or goods to cherish and revere. Our acquisitive society, which to some extent is noted for its "conspicuous consumption," places a high degree of importance on such status items as radios, television, appliances of all descriptions, and especially automobiles and homes. As we have mentioned before, culture changes and brings about corresponding changes in behavior. For example:

> . . . the consumer is not as functionally oriented as he used to be . . . The aesthetic preferences that were there have changed somewhat—we no longer go in for stained glass lamps and antimacassars, although the latter were probably more attractive than transparent couch covers; and the diversity of choices that are now possible in the ways people spend money makes for a diversity of reasons for the choices.[37]

The above quotation demonstrates the effects of culture on purchase behavior but even more vividly it demonstrates the danger of *generalizing* too much about given behavior. In 1968, stained glass lamps were one of the hottest demand items of furniture stores and decorators, and even antimacassars had begun to show signs of reemergence.

In terms of strategy design and the development of marketing programs, a knowledge and understanding of culture and subculture configurations is a *sine qua non*. "Subcultures are the relevant unit of analy-

---

[35] Edward T. Hall and William F. Whyte, "Intercultural Communication: A Guide to Men of Action," *Human Organization*, 19, No. 1 (1960), 6.

[36] Herbert E. Krugman and Eugene Hartley, "The Learning of Tastes," *Public Opinion Quarterly*, Winter, 1960, pp. 621-631.

[37] Sidney J. Levy, "Symbols by Which We Buy," *Advancing Marketing Efficiency*, ed. Lynn Stockman (Chicago: American Marketing Association, 1959), p. 410.

sis for market research. *They represent definable target groups for specific products and logical units for the segmenting of larger markets."* [38] The possibility of increasing the firm's effectiveness by product differentiation and/or market segmentation is being explored increasingly by business organizations. The presence of *cultural assimilation* and *structural pluralism* in the United States complicates the strategy formulation and design of mass marketers but, to some extent, facilitates both product differentiation and market segmentation for others. Cultural assimilation suggests that the major ethnic groups in the United States tend to share a common core culture. However, structural pluralism suggests that each of these groups retains a strong sense of identity. Hence, it becomes a reasonably easy matter to identify several major subcultures in the United States and, given their different values, needs, norms and behavior, to identify them as important market segments. For example:

By Age:
* pre-school market
* teen-age market
* college age market
* senior citizen market

By Occupation:
* blue collar vs. white collar
* professional vs. organizational
* skilled vs. unskilled

By Income:
* low
* medium
* high

By Race:
* white
* non-white

By Religion:
* Protestant
* Catholic
* Jewish

Each of the categories within each of these classifications is an important subculture and thus, potentially at least, holds out the promise of becoming an important market segment or target of special market programs in terms of either the firm's goods or service mix, its communication mix, or its distribution mix. This is to say that the culturally re-

[38] Gerald Zaltman, *Marketing: Contributions from the Behavioral Sciences* (New York: Harcourt, Brace & World, Inc., 1965), p. 8.

lated needs of the various subcultures or market segments may respond more readily to (1) products or services especially tailored to meet their specific needs, (2) personal selling or promotion which incorporates their special cultural needs into effective appeals and message design, or (3) retail stores, branches, or direct selling outlets which will reach these particular and unique market targets.

The Negro and teen-age markets as well as the senior citizen market are now of such size and importance in terms of numbers, income, and purchase behavior as to warrant careful and deliberate attention. The strong cultural assertion by more militant Negroes and black power advocates is a result of the fact that they are tired of being treated as "white niggers." They are beginning to purchase goods and develop a style of life which emphasizes and asserts their blackness and other ethnic differences.

As more and more U.S. firms turn their attention to foreign markets and international operations, the necessity for understanding cross-cultural differences increases.

Quite frequently, the major differences between domestic and foreign marketing or business boil down to the fundamental differences in culture between the U.S. and foreign businessman, or the U.S. businessman and the foreign consumer. The biggest error which U.S. marketers in foreign countries commit is to assume that "only the place is different; the customs, norms, and values of the people are the same all over." Ernest Dichter has accumulated an impressive array of cultural differences which should guide the American businessman in his conduct of affairs in foreign countries. Among these differences, he notes: [39]

* Frenchmen have an aversion to brushing their teeth.
* Germans change shirts only about once a week.
* French women are more concerned with quality than fashion.
* Natives often prefer non-local products.
* Over-attention to the body in terms of cleanliness, scented soaps, perfumes, etc. is considered immoral in many Catholic countries abroad.
* French women bathe with laundry soap instead of toilet soap.

The cultural anthropologist can be of enormous help to businessmen and marketers in enabling them to better understand consumer buying behavior, given a particular cultural environment. An example of such a contribution is offered by Winick:

A manufacturer of central heating equipment was planning to introduce central heating to an area which previously had used other heating.

---

[39] Ernest Dichter, "The World Customer," *Harvard Business Review*, July-August, 1962, pp. 113-122.

Since people generally grow up to accept a certain approach to heating which they take for granted, introduction of the new central heating posed marketing problems in coping with deeply imbedded consumer resistance to what would be a major innovation. An anthropologist was able to draw on his knowledge of the folklore and symbolism of heat and fire in order to suggest methods of presenting the new system so as to make it as consonant as possible with the connotations of heat, even though the nature of the heating method had changed radically. There was considerable resistance to the central heating, but it decreased substantially after the first year.[40]

The essence of science is to know. As marketers come to know more about consumer behavior and the determinants of this behavior, their strategy formulation, which is directly dependent upon the degree and adequacy of their knowledge, is bound to become increasingly effective.

---

[40] C. Winick, "Anthropology's Contribution to Marketing," *Journal of Marketing*, July, 1961, pp. 53-60. By permission of the American Marketing Association.

TEN

Developing

Communication Strategy

Our investigation began, as the reader may recall, with a treatment of marketing management and with a lengthy discussion of the importance and function of marketing strategy. The reader will recall that strategy was defined as "a major comprehensive plan," "the movement and countermovement in pursuit of goals," a "sequence of decision rules." These definitions go a long way to describe the dynamic and interactive nature of strategy; as a matter of fact, there can be no strategy implications among independent or noninteractive entities. For strategy to exist one must be confronted or interact with the conflicting or cooperating movements and behavior of persons, groups, firms, institutions, or "nature" herself.

Throughout our discussion we have emphasized the interactive nature of firm-customer behavior. Naturally there are other forms of interaction such as that between firm and competition, between firm and governmental regulatory agency, or between firm and the social-political environment. However, our central focus has been on the manner in which firm and customer interact; our inquiry has been further directed toward the manner in which the firm might better understand the consumer behavior of given market segments so that the firm might, in turn, adjust or adapt its market offerings in an effort to better serve and capture these given market opportunities.

230

From our early focus on marketing strategy we have ended up with communication strategy. It is expected that this intellectual voyage, like travel generally, would have served to broaden our perspective and to give us new insight and understanding of the world around us, especially the world of commerce and marketing, but more directly, the role of consumer behavior in shaping and influencing marketing activity and behavior.

Our study has led us to a fuller appreciation of communication in relationship to the total marketing effort. A firm utilizes the techniques, concepts, and insights of communication theory to build an effective marketing strategy. Communication, with its concern for establishing a "commonness" or agreement between the sender and receiver of messages, necessarily constitutes the very "heart and soul" of the marketing strategy. And it may very well be that marketers ought to rethink their strategy developments along the lines of "communication" rather than just "marketing." Marketing behavior in its various forms from product development to promotion "speaks" to its target audience. But the real question of concern to marketers is, "Is anybody listening?"

The increasing emphasis on consumer orientation stemming from the wider appreciation and implementation of the marketing concept must be credited for the increasing interest in both the techniques and theory of communication. The role and importance of communication must be incorporated into the overall corporate or management philosophy. And as firms increasingly tend to implement the findings of communication theory and research into their marketing programs and strategies, they must not repeat some notable errors of the past, namely, the tendency to firm orientation instead of consumer orientation, selfish interest instead of self-interest, greater interest in what is said and how often than in how something is said and what the effect is likely to be on the listener. *The complete and total activity of a firm's marketing strategy might very well be summarized as that of developing and maintaining useful communication between the firm and its market.*

The objective of this, the final chapter of our treatment of the psychology of consumer behavior, is not to produce a definitive statement regarding the construction of a communication strategy or comprehensive plan of action. Such an undertaking is well beyond the scope of this book. Our purpose instead is to once more underline the necessity of incorporating the findings of behavioral science research concerning learning and communication theory into the firm's marketing planning; to reconsider some of the key concepts around which strategy and marketing planning hinge; and finally, to produce a series of generalizations, or what might be called operational theorems, stemming from our overall discussion, upon which marketing planners might predicate their own marketing and communication strategy.

SOME CONSIDERATIONS FOR STRATEGISTS

The purpose of marketing management is to design a series of activities and then coordinate them in such a manner that the company as a whole behaves in a reasonably goal-directed way in adapting to changes in environment. The manner in which a given manager appraises a situation and proceeds to design a series of activities, the purpose of which is to accomplish certain results, will be conditioned among other things by his own decision-making style, past experience, frame of reference, and other constraints. The primary role of the executive, according to Oswald Knauth, is to create a system of action and then make it work.[1] He may very well have been talking about the marketing executive. Knauth distinguished between competitive enterprise and what he called "managerial enterprise." Managerial enterprise, he argued, was a relatively new thing. The essence of managerial enterprise is that it does not respond to competition by day-to-day adjustment of price and quantity sold, but by rounding out and perfecting plans for moving vast quantities of goods. The central core of managerial enterprise is that it starts with consumer orientation, the preconceived idea of service to the market, and works regressively backward toward a plan of action or strategy with every link in the sequence making its proper contribution. Another marketing theorist has observed that to build a marketing system means looking both forward and backward—backward toward suppliers of goods and raw materials and forward toward customers and potential customers.[2] Only then does the marketing firm become a link in the behavior system and sequence. If there are sequences and combinations of sequences whose total activity or output is greater for the same or smaller inputs, then suppliers may discover that system efficiency is increased by substituting another firm for ours or customers may discover that alternative combinations or sequences offer them increased amounts of satisfaction in relation to those offered by our firm. *The inevitable result is firm substitution.*

It is somewhat apparent that the marketing manager's task is that of organizing, coordinating, and controlling one organized behavior system, the firm, in response to other organized behavior systems—customers,

[1] *Managerial Enterprise* (New York: W. W. Norton & Company, Inc., 1948).

[2] Wroe Alderson and Paul Green, *Planning and Problem Solving in Marketing* (Homewood, Ill.: Richard D. Irwin, Inc., 1964), p. 8.

groups, institutions. It is not, however, necessarily so apparent that changes in various dimensions or major factors relating to the organized behavior of the external systems will bring about modifications and adaptations in the behavior of the internal system, the firm.

Baranoff argues that changes in the following major factors relating to group behavior will affect the structure and, more specifically, the function of marketing and marketing executives.[3]

1. *Perception.* The firm is a sensory and data gathering organism but its reaction to stimuli is affected by how it *perceives* the market opportunity, i.e., the customer segments, competition, and other environmental aspects.

2. *Goals.* Goals result from perceived opportunities. Two firms competing in the same market may quite well have different goals. Goals change with time and they also change as a result of other internal company changes.

3. *Power.* Power is ability to act. A market opportunity may exist only for a firm with considerable resources capable of releasing a given market opportunity. Much of the adaptive behavior of the firm is designed to either preserve or enhance the firm's power to act.

4. *Knowledge and Education.* The firm's power to act may result from command of economic resources or assets. Another asset of the organization, however, is information. The firm's "knowledge" is related to its ability to collect or command information. Quantity of information is important but, more importantly, it is the quality of a firm's information relative to its competitors which enhances its power to act.

5. *Flexibility.* Organisms survive only if they are sufficiently flexible in their operation and behavior to allow them to adapt to changing environmental conditions. A large part of any firm's behavior is "positional" as opposed to "operational," i.e., the firm strives to improve its competitive strength and survival for the long run. Planning is the principal means of injecting flexibility into a firm's operation.

6. *Organization and Control.* These are the concepts which inject unity and cohesion into what otherwise can be a series of loose jointed, jerky and spasmodic behavior relationships. Through the interconnected decision centers of the firm, the manager or peak coordinator balances behavior via organization and control.

The impetus to action of any organized behavior system consists of a series of inputs and outputs. The inputs and outputs vary from system to system or from firm to target market or customer groups. The inputs and outputs will almost always vary according to the factors just listed and discussed above. Alderson argues that every organized behavior system is discriminating and selective in terms of what it takes

---

[3] Seymour Baranoff, "Retailing as an Operating System," in *Theory in Marketing,* ed. Cox, Alderson and Shapiro (Homewood, Ill.: Richard D. Irwin, Inc., 1964), pp. 157-158. The factors are Baranoff's; however, the explanations are the author's.

from the environment and, as we shall explore further, the behavior system is careful to discriminate in terms of what it produces by way of output in relation to the inputs which it consumes or utilizes via its production processes.[4]

> Progressive differentiation of products and services is the key to defining the values created by marketing. This is based on the assumption that each individual's needs are different from every other individual's needs in one or more respects. Thus the basic economic process is the gradual differentiation of goods up to the point at which they pass into the hands of consumers.[5]

The principal output of a marketing system is usually listed as the creation of time, place, and possession utilities. The often overlooked output of marketing is that it is an information system and creates an information utility. The ability of a thing to satisfy a want or a need as a result of having it available to a customer segment at a given *time,* and a given *place,* and facilitating ownership or *possession* of it, is certainly important enough. But to a considerable extent, the real value of marketing, and therefore its most important output, is the information it creates via its communication function in terms of aiding the consumer in the whole spectrum of his purchase behavior from the design of his purchase problem, the structuring of search guidelines, and finally, in aiding him in his actual choice or decision.

Communication of information is therefore a means of enhancing the total output of the marketing system. While the system does create time, place, and possession utilities, the central task is to inform potential customers of the time, place, and possession implications of the firm's behavior in relation to customer needs and wants. In effect, the firm's output is a stream or bundle of satisfactions designed to satisfy customer inputs of needs and wants. The results amount to what one writer has called "matched parallelism." [6] The function of the marketing system is therefore to produce "matched parallelism"—to coordinate and match the many wants of consumers with those available goods and services which will satisfy those wants.

Developing system balance between inputs and outputs, or what we called "matched parallelism," is the principal task of marketing transactions. "Transactions are sets of behavior by means of which markets

---

[4] Wroe Alderson, *Marketing Behavior and Executive Action* (Homewood, Ill.: Richard D. Irwin, Inc., 1957), pp. 65-97.

[5] *Ibid.,* p. 69.

[6] Baranoff, *op. cit.,* p. 162.

coordinate the demands of buyers with the supplies offered by sellers." [7] The performance of transactions, needless to say, is costly and complicated; but once again it must be repeated that the essence of all transactions is communication flow.

Communication is primarily responsible for binding the United States together into one great national market. It will be communication which will ultimately bind the nations of the world together into one gigantic international market. The flow of information between organized behavior systems is as much, if not more, important than the flow of goods and services. So we repeat, the most important and essential function of marketing is that of processing: receiving and sending information, and acting as a great information center or data bank connecting the consumer who has a specialized need with the specialized product which offers the promise of satisfying this need.

THE SEARCH FOR DIFFERENTIAL ADVANTAGE

Most companies have as a central core in their operating philosophy or strategy the desire "to do best that which they are best suited to do." In effect this means that the company is seeking to find its differential advantage. Differential advantage is a concept which underlines the importance of developing and competing in the market place on the basis of the company's uniqueness.

As heterogeneous market targets have emerged, it has been necessary for equally heterogeneous marketing firms to emerge to fulfill the needs of the different target markets. The ability of a firm to survive the competitive rigors of the market place is to a considerable extent a function of how successfully the firm utilizes its competitive or differential advantage. An organization's style or its cultivated and projected image is indicative to some consumers of the firm's differential advantage. For example, a firm might attempt to find its competitive niche by appealing to that market segment which is most sensitive to low prices, or it may attempt to appeal to that market segment which is more interested in quality or style, and less interested in price. There are innumerable ways in which a firm might attempt to find its market niche; the process is inevitably one which seeks out the best course of action for the firm, given alternative market opportunities.

Kotler describes the company's search for differential advantage

---

[7] George Fisk, *Marketing Systems: An Introductory Analysis* (New York: Harper & Row, Publishers, 1967), p. 5.

when he states that "the company's share of total market demand will depend upon the quality of its product and marketing effort relative to competitors." [8] Marketing effort relative to competition would be directed along the lines of what the company saw as its unique marketing opportunity aligned with those things which the company felt it could do better than its competition. The total market demand for a good or service is largely a function of the total marketing effort of all sellers competing in that market. But a given company's demand is largely a function of the amount and effectiveness of its marketing expenditure in relation to the other competing marketing firms. These two propositions can be shown a bit more tidily and precisely by using mathematical notation. [9]

(A) $$S = f(K_1M_1, K_2M_2, \ldots K_iM_i, \ldots K_nM_n, a,b,c)$$

(B) $$S_i = f \frac{(K_iM_i, a,b,c)}{K_1M_1 + K_2M_2 + \ldots K_iM_i + \ldots K_nM_n}$$

where: S = market demand
K_i = company i's marketing effectiveness per unit expenditure
M_i = company i's total marketing expenditure
K_iM_i = company i's demand
$a,b,c,$ = other factors
S_i = subscripts referring to different sellers
$1,2, \ldots i \ldots n$ = company i's marketing expenditure (the first seller is 1, the last is n)

Generalization (A) states that the total market demand for a good or service is a function of the total marketing effort of all sellers competing in that market, plus other factors. Generalization (B) states that any given company's demand is a function of the amount and effectiveness of its marketing effort in relationship with, or relative to, the marketing efforts of competing firms, plus other factors. Several important conclusions can be drawn from these generalizations.

The most important conclusion for our purposes, however, is one related to market effectiveness and the concept of differential advantage. If all firms were capable of spending a marketing dollar with equal effectiveness, then a company's marketing share would be directly proportional to the amount of its expenditures. The fact that companies do not spend their marketing dollar with equal effectiveness points up the existence of

---

[8] Philip Kotler, *Marketing Management: Analysis, Planning and Control* (Englewood Cliffs, N.J.: Prentice-Hall, Inc., 1967), p. 103.
[9] *Ibid.*

market opportunity via the discovery and exploitation of one's differential advantage. Products can be differentiated; prices can be adjusted in some instances in consideration of different prevailing elasticities of demand; unique customer or market segments can be located and defined; appeals can be changed, altered, or modified on the basis of the different characteristics manifested among different groups or market segments. These are all obvious ways of viewing a marketing opportunity via differential advantage. Most importantly then, the search for effective marketing strategies is a search for the firm's differential advantage, which of necessity must incorporate an appraisal of market opportunity in light of the countermoves of competition, possible changes in internal company policies, a search for new or overlooked opportunities, and other anticipated or forecasted changes in the external operating environment of the firm.

But what of communication? Communication lies at the very heart of the strategy formation and offers to a firm the possibility of greatly extending the range of its behavior in terms of furthering its differential advantage.

The impetus to market and consumer behavior is communication. The exchange process is triggered on the basis of information flows which bring buyer and seller together. Staudt and Taylor assert that "the marketer seeks to close the gap between the information potential buyers have, and what they should have if impact requirements that trigger the desired purchase decisions are to be met. Market impact is, of course, a much broader complex of forces than merely information flow." [10]

The full range of what must be accomplished in terms of marketing impact by way of communication might be viewed in the following way:

I = interest
M = motivation
P = persuasion
A = attention
C = contact
T = transmission

These factors reflect the result of a firm's total market posture or its differential advantage. The communications task then becomes one of achieving the proper level of market impact—the sum total of a firm's product, price, place, and promotion policies all effectively communi-

---

[10] T. A. Staudt and D. A. Taylor, *A Managerial Introduction to Marketing* (Englewood Cliffs, N.J.: Prentice-Hall, Inc., 1965), p. 371.

cated so that they strike the consumer-buyer as a unified bundle of utilities and expectations.

The increasing concern of the marketing manager, as well as the organization as a whole, is that management decision processes depend more and more upon an understanding of the communication process as it exists within the firm [11] and equally, if not more importantly, an understanding of the communication process as it pertains to the firm and its markets. Howard states that a firm requires four kinds of communication: [12]

1. Communication to develop new programs, such as the transmittal of information about competitors' prices, etc.
2. Communication to evoke programs, such as the transmittal of information about competitors' prices, etc.
3. Communication to provide data for application of strategies.
4. Communication to provide feedback information on the results of activities.

COMMUNICATION STRATEGY

One could hardly develop here a complete and useful communication strategy which would have meaning or operational validity for a particular firm. The idea of strategy, i.e., "movement and countermovement in pursuit of goals," negates both the thought and the undertaking. Communication strategies for particular firms must be developed within the heat and light of real world market competition. However, our analysis and discussion thus far should enable us to lay down a few normative considerations for communication and marketing strategy considerations. We might begin by outlining the basic dimensions of communication strategy and then posit a series of generalizations or operational theorems which strategists might incorporate into their marketing planning or use as premises or assumptions upon which to build specific communication programs or campaigns. Our basic proposition concerning communication ought to be fairly well understood by now. *It is, in essence, that a well-developed set of systems and procedures for sending and receiving information is vital and necessary to the welfare of the firm and that the firm speaks or communicates with its markets via a mix of media and messages.*

---

[11] For an illustration of the communication process within the firm, see R. Clifton Anderson and Edward W. Cundiff, "Patterns of Communications in Marketing Organizations," *The Journal of Marketing,* July, 1965, pp. 30-34.

[12] John A. Howard, *Marketing Theory* (Boston, Mass.: Allyn & Bacon, Inc., 1965), pp. 35-36.

Given this central proposition, it follows that communication strategy development ought to center around at least the following factors: communication analysis, communication planning, communication organization, and communication control.

Communications analysis is concerned with two important considerations: Who is communicating, and what is or what needs to be said. Firms lacking this information or only guessing at the answers are not likely to be communicating effectively. Communications analysis centers around such issues as the flow of information, i.e., the origin and destination of communications, as well as their subject or content matter.

Communication planning is the natural follow-up of communication analysis. Planning is almost always normative, that is, it states what needs to be done when confronted with certain kinds of situations or environments. Communication analysis is a means of finding out "what is" and proceeds to "what ought we to do." Communication planning is also responsible for the establishment of communication goals and objectives.

Communication organization is responsible for establishing some relationships within the organization between communication tasks and the people who are responsible for performing the communication tasks. Communication organization is responsible in a functional sense for the establishment of decision centers in the organization for the purpose of coordinating and controlling communication activities.

Communications control is responsible for the setting of communication standards, for measuring and comparing communication activities and results with planned activities and results, and finally for taking corrective actions.

The communication task viewed more macroscopically consists of determining to whom one wishes to communicate, determining what one wishes to say and how, and finally evaluating the effectiveness of what has been communicated, if anything. Stemming from this statement of the communication problem there arise what, from a management point of view, are two of the central dimensions of the communication function: (1) the determination of the optimum communication mix, and (2) the evaluation of communication effectiveness.[13]

The discussion thus leads us to this important conclusion. The development of communication strategy is another exercise in applied problem solving. A problem exists when there is something in need of being

---

[13] Neither of these problems have easy or practical solutions even though both have been subjected to rigorous theoretical analysis. For an interesting discussion of (1) see Staudt and Taylor, *op. cit.*, Chap. 21; and for a lengthy discussion of (2), see Darrell Blaine Lucas and Steuart Henderson Britt, *Measuring Advertising Effectiveness* (New York: McGraw-Hill Book Company, 1963).

done and there is uncertainty specifically either about what it is that should be done or what course of action to pursue to enable us to attain our goal, once it is well defined.

Problem solvers most often begin by proceeding from what is known and attempting to project these facts to the area or realm of the unknown. In short, problem solvers generally begin with some core or common elements and attempt by way of generalization to apply these to the new problem situation. This approach really amounts to a search for the significant structure of a problem. Once significant structure is formulated, problem solving often proceeds by way of insight, which means seeing into or through a subject. Our ability to solve problems is related closely to our possession of knowledge or our command and understanding of certain fundamental relationships which may be only indirectly related to new problem areas. Imagine how difficult even the simpler problems would be if we were incapable of storing up acquired experiences, of attaining knowledge or understanding, and if we had to proceed from a point of complete or near ignorance to a point of understanding for every decision process. However, inasmuch as man possesses the wonderful and marvelous capacity not only to store up information or experiences, but to relate them in a meaningful pattern of understanding and structure, his decision making and problem solving can be greatly accelerated by applying what he considers to be relevant insight, a common core of understanding, or significant structure, to the new problem situations which he must face. These factors are often called theory. Theories are generalizations or general propositions used as principles or explanations for a class of phenomena. Philosophers as well as marketers utilize theory for the purpose of problem solving. It can now be stated that the total effort of this text has been to discuss and to establish the theoretical relationship among a number of phenomena such as consumer behavior, learning, communication, and the firm. Our goal has been to develop a body of theory or what preferably might be called a set of operational *theorems* upon which market planning and communication strategy might be predicated. *An operational theorem is a proposition which can be deduced from the premises, assumptions, or findings of a system and used for the purpose of operational decision making.*

The operational theorems which follow and around which decision makers might develop certain strategy considerations are based on these qualifications:

1. Communications findings stemming from research in fields other than marketing can be broadly generalized to the field of marketing.[14]

---

[14] This conclusion and others herein listed differ somewhat from other findings. See Allan Ginsberg, "Is Communication Research Really Worthwhile?" *Journal of Marketing,* January, 1967, pp. 48-50.

2. When applicable, operational theorems should never be treated as laws of behavior or absolute truths.
3. Until actually tried and verified under specific marketing conditions, operational theorems should be viewed as testable hypotheses only.
4. Decision makers in marketing and communications should not only rely on others to develop operational theorems concerning aspects of marketing planning, but should exercise their ingenuity and creativity for the purpose of developing their own operational theorems and testable hypotheses.

The analysis and findings of the systems and phenomena which we have investigated lead us to offer for practice and further research the following operational theorems. This is by no means an exhaustive listing but rather a listing of those hypotheses which appear to offer the greatest possibility both for immediate application and for those persons who in the longer run are searching for new dimensions and new directions in their marketing planning.

1. Marketing management has significance only *if* the concept of customer orientation is invoked.
2. Customer orientation can only be invoked if channels of communication are developed to specific market targets.
3. Marketing management, which embraces the concept of customer orientation, must make certain underlying determinations concerning customer behavior.
4. The fundamental issue of customer behavior is centered around customer motivation.
5. The basic approach to understanding customer motivation in the past has been oriented around Freudian psychology.
6. Freudian psychology is based upon a series of sweeping generalities which Freud discovered in the subconscious and upon which he predicated a theory of behavior oriented around repressed sexual urges.
7. Consumer motivation stemming from Freud's theories has stressed the hidden nature of the motivation mechanism.
8. Consumer motivation, because of the influence of Freud's theories, has placed an over-emphasis on sexual implications.
9. Existential psychology, because of its argument against generalizing about the "nature" of man, offers greater promise for deducing considerations pertaining to both consumer motivation and behavior.
10. Existential psychology has as its basic premise regarding personality, motivation, and behavior that man acts not so much from primordial drives but rather as a result of individual characteristics developed and occurring over a lifetime and arising out of the conditions of the environment or existence of the individual.
11. Consumers have a needs-wants hierarchy which they strive to fulfill as a result of their purchase behavior.
12. Manifested consumer behavior has relevance only when examined in relationship to the consumer's needs-wants hierarchy.
13. The life style of the individual affects his needs-wants hierarchy.

14. Life style is an existential phenomena, i.e., life style stems from personality characteristics but more importantly from such existent phenomena as learning and communication in a given social context.
15. A satisfied need-want is no longer an important source of motivation.
16. Consumer behavior is purposeful. It possesses both meaning and direction from the point of view of the actor but not necessarily the observer.
17. Most consumers have an idealized conception of themselves. This is the consumer's self-image.
18. The consumer's self-image stems from his personality characteristics plus existential social forces such as social learning and communication.
19. Consumers' purchase behavior is a form of problem-solving behavior.
20. Consumer problem solving is concerned with the search and attainment of goods which will bolster or maintain his self-image.
21. The problem-solving behavior of consumers is largely of a heuristic nature, i.e., trial and error produces "improved" decision processes.
22. Purchase decisions of goods or services which the consumer perceives as highly important to his needs-wants hierarchy become ego-involved purchases.
23. Where uncertainty exists as to the ability of a purchase decision to satisfy the demands of the ego involvement, anxiety arises.
24. Anxiety manifests itself in the purchase behavior in the form of confusion or accelerated search activity, or more deliberate behavior on the part of the purchaser.
25. Consumer behavior can be viewed in terms of risk characteristics. Where resources are limited or the consequences of the behavior are serious in terms of jeopardizing further behavior, consumer behavior is likely to be modified.
26. Purchase decisions that the purchaser perceives as not being consistent with the self-image cause guilt feelings, which produce a state of post-decision dissonance.
27. Post-decision dissonance can be reduced or eliminated by a search for additional information or rationalization.
28. Broadly conceived, consumer decision processes can be divided into two categories: programmed and non-programmed. Programmed decisions are generally well structured and decision procedures fairly well formulated. Non-programmed decisions are not well structured and therefore behavior is likely to be more concerned with generating information, i.e., more concerned with developing search procedures.
29. The marketing firm is an organized behavior system.
30. Convenience goods purchases are characteristic of programmed purchase decisions. Shopping and specialty goods are more characteristic of non-programmed purchase decision processes.
31. The marketing firm as an organized behavior system is a sensory and data gathering and dissemination system.
32. The marketing firm must adapt its offerings to the changing needs of the market place.
33. Organized behavior systems are motivated to act via the inducement of gain or survival.
34. Consumer behavior is a form of adaptive behavior as is that of the firm.

35. Adaptive behavior of the firm and the consumer is facilitated by the use of information flows or communication.
36. Adaptive behavior necessarily involves learning.
37. Learning is involved with the process of acquiring the ability to respond adequately to a situation which may or may not have been previously encountered.
38. Learning is important to marketers inasmuch as learning results in both behavior and attitude change.
39. The two principal theories that apply to learning are stimulus-response and cognitive.
40. Stimulus-response learning models are *not* necessarily the models or generalizations around which marketing programs should be built.
41. Cognitive learning is concerned with changes in the structure of the life space or in cognitive patterns. It involves the development of insights or a reorganization of perceptions.
42. Marketing programs ought to incorporate the principles and generalizations which emerge from the cognitive learning theories.
43. Communication is the firm's way of linking itself to the learning process of consumers.
44. Consumer needs-wants are discovered via communication. This is a form of communication that feeds information to the firm.
45. Consumer needs-wants are satisfied via communication. This is a form of communication that feeds information to customers or market targets.
46. The most obvious form of communication that feeds information to the firm is its sales volume. A less obvious form is that of market research.
47. The most obvious forms of communication that feed information to the customer or market target are advertising and personal selling, collectively known as promotion.
48. The entire organization, however, with its resultant behavior is in one sense at least a form of communication. The firm is both a sign and a significate.
49. Communication, from a managerial point of view, is designed to place the firm in a better adaptive and competitive posture.
50. Marketers must of necessity give increasing attention to the structure and function of communication as an adjunct to their marketing strategy.
51. Personal selling offers greater communication flexibility but generally entails higher costs per receiver.
52. Advertising offers less communication flexibility but generally entails lower costs per receiver.
53. Communication of all kinds is an adhesive which can effectively bind firm and customer together.
54. Mass communication is seldom direct in its effects nor can its effects be judged effectively.
55. Communication of a mass nature is often subject to a two-step flow, with the messages first being received by key influentials or opinion leaders and then being channeled on to followers.
56. The effects of communication are likely to be twofold: those which are intended and those which are accidental and arise as a result of message distortion or misinterpretation.

57. Market imbalance or discrepancies can be overcome through innovation in communication methods and processes.
58. Communication is affected by social learning.
59. Social learning results from man's tendency to acquire something of the ideals, opinions, and attitudes of the groups to which he belongs, or aspires to belong, and from his culture.
60. The proper framework for understanding consumer behavior is that of social psychology.
61. The interaction between firm and customer can be analyzed as a basic interpersonal behavior event.
62. Such interpersonal behavior events are called dyads. The principal parties of the dyad for our purposes and their interaction can be shown as:

$$\text{Firm} \rightleftharpoons \text{Customer}$$

63. Marketers must understand attitudes and attitude formation inasmuch as attitudes that purchasers hold are predispositions to behavior.
64. The group may well be the relevant unit of analysis for marketers because it is groups that constitute relatively homogeneous market segments.
65. Consumers are members of many groups and aspire to membership in others. Consumers seek realization by their membership in other behavior systems.
66. Consumer behavior is bounded by cultural considerations. Inculturation is a most important existential determinant of behavior.
67. There exists a broad-gauged core culture which influences and affects the behavior of the U.S. consumer.
68. The firm and consumer are both input-output systems, and their respective behavior is designed to bring about matched parallelism.
69. Strategy design from the standpoint of the firm is an exercise in the search for differential advantage.
70. Product differentiation and market segmentation are both efforts to capitalize on differential advantage.
71. Products are seldom ever perceived by consumers as homogeneous, because a product is a bundle of expectations, and expectations are likely to vary from individual to individual.
72. The better understanding, development, and management of information systems will affect marketing planning and strategy in many ways.
73. The seasoned and sophisticated decision maker or problem solver has a reservoir of models, theories, or operational theorems in mind, from which he selects one that appears to fit the current problem.
74. The increasing complexity of modern business and modern decision theory requires the *involvement, commitment,* and *participation* of the marketing executive in problem solutions.
75. The operational theorems listed above ought to be discussed, used for the purpose of communication and marketing strategy design where better information or premises are nonexistent, further researched and analyzed, and where evidence warrants, abandoned in favor of more valid and reliable operational theorems.

INDEX